W9-DDH-202

MORE THAN TALK

Communication Studies and the Christian Faith

Bill Strom
Trinity Western University

KENDALL/HUNT PUBLISHING COMPANY
4050 Westmark Drive   Dubuque, Iowa 52002

Contents

Acknowledgments

The completion of a book, like the running of a long distance race, represents the goal of one person, the runner, with the assistance of a team, most of whom are volunteers.

I am pleased to have run this race with my students at Trinity Western University for whom *More Than Talk* was first intended. Their reviews of early versions and their participation in focus groups made feedback full and future directions clear. They deserve thanks for plowing through the working manuscript.

Other students helped more directly. I would like to thank Jeff Dewsbury, Louise Rousseau, Jacky Naayer, and Steve Leyenhorst for their assistance in proofreading, suggesting changes, finding sources and performing the focus group research. At the time all four were students; now they are graduates who show much promise for God's kingdom. In addition, Amber Stankievech, Alistair Young, Jaime Toews, and Kris Krug deserve warm thanks for their help at crunch time.

Several colleagues at Trinity Western University deserve recognition for their interest and support in this project. I would like to thank Geri Forsberg and Lynn Szabo for comments on early drafts, and Harold Faw, Harro Van Brummelen, and Philip Wiebe for their insights into the publishing process. My department secretary, Lilli Kehler, a published author in her own right, listened to my queries and reports with an empathetic ear. Craig Montgomery, friend since day one, learned more about communication at *Spill the Beans* than he may have liked, but always graciously.

Distant colleagues who reviewed chapters or the entirety of *More Than Talk* included Em Griffin at Wheaton College, Scott Turcott at Indiana Wesleyan University, Michael Dreher at Bethel College (MN), and Shirley Shedd at Evangel College. Thank you for your investment in communication education.

Kendall/Hunt's Seattle District representative served as my enthusiastic and encouraging editor. Her professional skills and patience with my questions encouraged me each time we talked. Their developmental and production editors in Dubuque deserve thanks for crafting a quality text. A big thank you goes to my friend John Greaves who translated cartoon ideas into memorable artwork. I hope readers enjoy John's illustrations as much as he enjoyed drawing them.

Many others chose to cheer from the sidelines, including Rick Thiessen and Dan Guggenheimer (the breakfast guys in chapter six), and commuter colleagues Dave Stinson and Kurt Lundberg. Paul and Alisa Burkey know their commitment to this project, and for that I thank them warmly as well.

Two of my favorite fans have been my parents, Neale and Jean Strom, who have contributed in various ways to this book's completion. I especially want to thank my father for reading the manuscript cover to cover for readability, misspellings, typos, and word choice. He's a fine wordsmith.

To my young boys, Taylor, Clark, and Eric, I want to say thank you for respecting my space in the home office. Your visits brought me breaks, and your departure helped me concentrate. Some day you will be able to read this book and understand why it took dad so long to write.

Finally, I am grateful for my wife, Shelaine, who was the first to read and make comment on each chapter. Her humor and wisdom coached me through valleys and up steep hills as I researched, wrote, and revised this work over the years. She shares any congratulations on a race well run.

Above all, I give praise and glory to God, by whom the mysteries of communication were given us, and to my Savior, Jesus Christ, through whom all things hold together, and to his Spirit who encouraged me with truth and hope. May this book be a sweet smelling sacrifice to the Lord God Almighty.

Introduction
From Rhetoric to Microchip

Whatever you do, do it all for the glory of God.
1 Corinthians 10:31b

When David Allen boarded a plane in Thailand in March of 1997, he probably didn't imagine that his world would change so dramatically before touchdown in Los Angeles. When the jet departed, David was experiencing flu-like symptoms, but by mid-flight, the pain became so great, he wondered if he would make it to California. This was not the flu; David was dreadfully ill.

Doctors at a Los Angeles emergency room couldn't figure out the source of David's pain or relentless diarrhea. Several days later he flew to Dallas, only to find doctors perplexed again. For two months David suffered from severe intestinal pain, juggled a battery of drugs, and dashed to the local ER more than once. David's weight dropped from 172 to 139 pounds as a result of his body's acceptance of little more than Gatorade, crackers, and vegetable broth.

Then hope poked through. As David writes, "A few tests found the existence of two different microscopic intestinal parasites. Yet, despite 5-6 doctors examining the parasites, positive identification could not be made. Finally, I was admitted into the hospital in early May and started on IV feeding in an attempt to stop the weight loss. It was at this point that an amazing thing happened."[1]

The seed for that amazing thing began a week before his hospitalization when David emailed a heart-felt message to the team of missionaries with whom he worked in Thailand. The memo detailed his physical deterioration and resulting spiritual famine. David felt God's peace for salvation, but he struggled over what his death would mean for his wife, new baby, and a budding Thai church.

"When my teammates read the email, they responded in immediate prayer, and called on close friends to join them. And then God began to move among His people in an amazing way. I cannot exactly explain how it happened, but somehow that email spread to Christians in every corner of the globe. Within days, hundreds of people began to write, call, and pray. Different groups of believers decided to fast, dedicating the period to lift me up before the Lord. Altogether more than 7,000 emails of encouragement and prayer were sent to me from 70-80 different countries. From what I gather, this was only the tip of the iceberg. About half of these emails represented whole congregations or Christian organizations which were corporately in prayer for God's intervention. My family received phone calls of encouragement and prayer from morning to evening for months. The family of Christ ministered to us with such love and concern that I was simply overwhelmed."[2]

Can you envision it? One message from one hurting believer coursed the Internet and human channels to be received by responsive, responsible members of God's church. David's colleagues told Thai believers, pastors told congregations, managers passed it on at staff meetings, friends told friends, family members mentioned it to siblings and parents, and a ton of them emailed on what they had heard and read.

But perhaps most remarkable was what Dallas doctors failed to discover that first week of David's hospitalization. "From the time the prayer blanket began to cover the world, every test taken to find parasites came back negative."[3] Within a week of his notifying his colleagues of his dire straits, David Allen's body was free from the parasites that doctors had spotted weeks before.

David's story could serve as a springboard to discuss God's response to prayer, but you can probably see that the other thread is *communication*. The message that took root in David's soul spread out by email, between friends, in public speeches, within small groups, through organizations and across cultural boundaries. Communication did not heal David; God did. Communication cannot save us; only God can. In God's design, however, he seemed fit to adorn us with this gift that allows us not only to convey information, but also connect as kindred spirits. In this sense we can say that communication is redemptive in that words and actions help us heal, bond, learn, and grow. From rhetoric (the art of public speaking) to microchip technology, the *means* of communicating among us represent but a thin slice of all there is to the communication process. Its diversity alone makes for an intriguing study.

Twenty-some years ago I enrolled in an introductory communication course like the one you are probably in today. For the past ten years I have taught a similar course. As a professor, I have found Christian books about small group, interpersonal, and media communication, but to date I have not found one that takes a look at the whole gamut. This fact, in part, motivated me to write this book.

The primary motivation, however, was my curiosity to know how a biblical perspective informs our study of communication. Can a Christian world view enhance our understanding of public speaking and computer mediated communication (CMC)? What about language and nonverbal cues? What biblical themes inform our understanding of words and gestures?

Does God's picture of interpersonal and intercultural relating look different from a standard model? How should we go about searching for truth in communication studies anyway? Do social scientific studies about television bear any more weight than well-written critiques? How do biblical truths play into our response to virtual reality headset games or bloody slasher movies? These kinds of questions intrigued me enough to attempt answering them.

I chose the title *More Than Talk* for several reasons. For starters, it indicates that the study of communication includes more than the study of everyday conversation. As you might suspect, our journals are full of articles ranging from why people lie (definitely a "talk" issue) to how computer compulsives think differently than non-hackers (a humans-and-technology issue). Some scholars might examine David Allen's story as a case study in God-human communication, while others might frame it as a testimony to the efficiency of email technology.

The phrase "more than talk" also indicates that this book is not just about communication. It's also about theology, research methods, and what it means to be a Christian. I hope you find these "extras" enlightening, not distracting.

Finally, "more than talk" can also mean "more than mere lip service." Writing and reading about communication is one thing; making redemptive communication happen is another. My hope is that this book will discourage duplicity — when our words and our walk are out of synch — and encourage a life of unity and integrity.

To these ends, Part 1 looks at the spoken word and nonverbal cues. What choices can we make to use language and actions redemptively? Chapters 1 and 2 address verbal and nonverbal communication.

Part 2 looks at seven places where communication issues hit us closest to home: our self-talk, our relationships, in families, in small groups, behind podiums, with culturally different others, and in the media.

How our view of our self leaks out in interaction with others is our starting point in Chapter 3, and a look at redemptive interpersonal communication in Chapter 4 is the logical follow through. For some people, connecting with family members remains a bittersweet obligation and even threatening chore; Chapter 5 considers family communication gone awry and extends hope to those in the thick of it. For others the frustration is with your work colleagues or other small group members. Chapter 6 investigates the role of community within group interaction.

Other readers may value wisdom about how to nudge others closer to God. Chapter 7 suggests that we fear public speaking, in part, because we recognize that persuading others entails moral obligations. Chapter 8 considers Jesus' life as a model for incarnational connection with culturally different others. Finally, Chapters 9 and 10 examine the bleak and blessed outlook believers often express toward media technologies and media content, and what believers might do about it.

Finally, Part 3 addresses questions related to communication inquiry. How do communication scholars define truth these days? How do social scientists differ from humanities professors in their approach to research? You'll find both types in departments of communication, so these chapters help you understand their differing assumptions and methods. The last chapter is a call to excellence as practitioners, whether we produce videos or minister abroad.

As you get into the busyness of a new semester, I hope you take the time to highlight sections of this book that you might turn back to in less hectic times. Perhaps you might return to these ideas after the term for a more casual read, and reflect on what's relevant for you.

Notes

1. Email update received from David Allen, January 2, 1998.
2. Allen, January 2, 1998.
3. Allen, January 2, 1998.

To Shelaine

PART 1

Talk About Words and Actions

1

High Fidelity Speech
Putting Faith in the Spoken Word

*In the beginning was the Word, and the Word was
with God and the Word was God.*

John 1:1

Pick up any newspaper and you're bound to see headlines and advertisements such as "Merger Leads to Downsizing," "Leaders Suggest Revenue Enhancement," "Save $1200 on the all new Altima," and "V.O. is V.O." You don't have to be an economist to figure out that "downsizing" means "layoffs" or even "firings," and "revenue enhancement" means "taxes." Of course to "save" $1200 on the Altima, someone would have to spend (that is, lose) $15,000, and that the vodka company uses circular logic to sell V.O. is not surprising—booze commercials rarely describe the actual product.

You may recognize these examples as representative of doublespeak, a term coined by George Orwell in his famous novel *Nineteen-eighty-four* (his grim prophecy written in 1948). There the government used doublespeak and "newspeak" to confuse the citizenry with absurd claims such as "War is Peace" and "Freedom is Slavery" and "Ignorance is Strength." The purpose of such convoluted language was to obscure the truth and avoid responsibility.[1]

Although Orwell's doomsday predictions weren't realized in full-blown form by 1984, many scholars note that doublespeak is still rampant in our culture today. For example, when Oliver North was asked about his role in constructing a false chronology of events for Congress regarding the Iran-Contra affair, he answered, "I was provided with additional input that was radically different from the truth. I assisted in furthering that version."[2] He didn't say, "Yes, I lied." When NASA officials asked engineer Roger Boisjoly of Morton Thiokol to quantify his concerns regarding the Challenger's fateful mission, he said he couldn't quantify it with data, but "I knew that it was away from goodness in the current data base."[3] He did not say, "The O-rings could break—don't launch." You and I are probably equally guilty of using doublespeak. I've used "righteous indignation" to avoid saying I *hate* someone, and I've said, "Let's discuss the needs of others" to avoid being called a *gossip*. We don't have to be public leaders to hide behind words; we do so habitually.[4]

While doublespeak is an ongoing concern about the ways in which we use and misuse language, I think it is safe to say that it is but one symptom of a larger issue. That issue is that many North Americans lack faith in the ability of words to communicate truth in the first place. Put more strongly, many Americans and Canadians believe you can use words to create any truth you like. Without the basic starting point that truth is knowable and reasonably objective, surface words then have little foundation. Words become a commodity to be twisted and inflated, packaged and sold toward some utilitarian end (for example, "buy the all new Altima"). It is no wonder that we do not trust the words of advertisers and, worse yet, our leaders.

This distrust began as early as the 17th century when philosophers and scientists made a division between that which was material (such as atoms, earth and technology) and that which was immaterial (such as faith, reason, and language). They considered the material real and the immaterial, well, not *really* real. You can see the implication of this duality. If words are not real, so goes the logic, then words probably do a lousy job of referring to or creating anything real. Practically speaking, one can say almost anything and get away with it, because, after all, "it's only words."

Despite the popularity of this view, it runs contrary to other philosophical and theological positions. It must also pain God who seems committed to the idea that, in language, he has given us a tool for not only referring to truth and reality, but also creating important truths and realities. What needs to be pointed out though is that there's a difference between physical, social, and mental reality. Understanding how language works will help us understand its relationship to these entities.

WORDS AND THE PHYSICAL WORLD

A pastor of mine once asked our congregation, "Why did Adam name the elephant an elephant?" His answer? "Because it looked so much like one!" The sad thing was, the pastor was serious.

There is a temptation to think that objects around us cry out their word label. (And, for the record, some sounds like a car's *squeal* and a candy wrapper's *crinkle* are imitated in the words we attach to them.) But if this held true of all God's creation, then the world would speak one language— "universese." Rather, the number of languages on earth is about 6,200 and few have the same word for even the most common objects. For example,

English-speakers refer to shaggy canines with "dog, while the French use "chien" and Germans utter "hund."

A more accurate model of how words relate to the physical world is depicted in Figure 1.1.[5] The dotted line between *symbols* (that is, words) and *referents* (the things to which symbols refer) indicates that this relationship is largely arbitrary. By arbitrary we mean words usually do not look, smell, taste, feel, or sound like the things to which they refer. Rocks don't cry out "call me granite" or "call me quartz." Rather, ever since Adam was given the job to name the animals, people have had the responsibility and privilege of labeling the cosmos and their experience in it. Humans name their reality. Languages develop well when a large community of people agree to call mutts by the same term, whether "dog" or "hund."

The human factor in meaning making (or call it the Adam factor if you wish) is represented by the solid lines in Figure 1.1. By an act of our will and by agreement from our language community, we make associations between words and the world and attempt to store these meanings in our mind and spirit. Once we make these associations though, we often prefer using some words (for example, "restroom") rather than other words (for example, "toilet") and often build on existing words to create symbols for new objects or ideas. Even the word "communication" is a derivative of "commune" which means "to share in common." "Communication" is the process by which we come to share meaning with others.

Thought or reference (found in people who link symbols with referents)

Symbols	Referents
"dog"	(the particular
"hund"	dogs referred to
"chien"	in the real world)

Figure 1.1.   The Meaning Triangle. From The Meaning of Meaning, eighth edition, C.K. Ogden and I.A. Richards, Harcourt Brace & World, Inc., 1946.

Just because the *labels* we attach to God's world may be arbitrary, please don't think that the *claims* we make about it are fickle. For example, the words "dog," "sleeping," and "mat" may not imitate the things to which they refer, but my claim that "The dog is sleeping on the mat" is by no means arbitrary. That claim can be judged true or false depending on where Rex is and what he's doing. The same is true if you make an abstract claim such as "God is sovereign." Just because a French speaker may say "Dieu est souverain" does not render this claim meaningless, irrational, or hidden from investigation.[6]

WORDS AND THE SOCIAL WORLD

The drawback of the model in Figure 1.1 is that it fails to capture how people bond through language. Take this book for example. Although it refers to dogs and George Orwell and Altimas (that is, material objects), it is also establishing a relationship between you and me. I trust that that relationship is a respectful, trusting, and instructive one, but how it shapes up exactly is dependent in part on how you take my words. It doesn't help that you can't give me feedback as quickly as you could in conversation. (If you want to comment about something, check out my email address under footnote #7 at the end of this chapter and drop me a line.[7]) Our language is so meat-and-potatoes to life that we sometimes forget that everything from our greetings, phone calls, coffee chats, and emails depend on words to create trust, love, instruction and the like among us. Of course words can also break trust ("Oops, I forgot I promised"), show hate ("She's nothing but a #%&*!!"), and deceive ("Officer, I was going only 57 m.p.h."). In extreme cases, words contribute to mental disorders such as schizophrenia and add pain in abusive relationships.[8] We will look more at the destructive social potential of language in the chapters on interpersonal and family communication.

WORDS AND OUR MENTAL WORLD

Another drawback of Figure 1.1 is that it doesn't recognize the amoeba-like nature of meaning in our heads. Even if we all agreed on the *denotative* (that is, dictionary) definition of "Altima" as "one type of mid-sized sedan," we would likely differ in the *connotative* (that is, personal) meanings we attach to it. Osgood and his associates examined *affective meaning* (another term for connotative meaning) and discovered that we tend to favor three emotional dimensions when attaching meaning to terms: evaluation, potency, and activity.[9] If we did the same, I might ask you to check what "Altima" means to you on three seven-point scales anchored by "good" and "bad" (for evaluation), "powerful" and "weak" (for potency), and "fast" and "slow" (for activity). An example of the kind of scale Osgood used looks like this: Good ___ ___ ___ ___ ___ ___ ___ Bad. Muscle-car enthusiasts would likely rate the family sedan as okay, weak, and slow whereas someone who drives a tiny Austin mini might rate the Altima good, powerful, and fast. Like the ever-fluxing perimeter of an amoeba, the personalized meaning both people attach to the word "Altima" may change with time.

Figure 1.1 also hides the fact that words can blind us to alternative ways of thinking. This is the hypothesis of Edward Sapir and Benjamin Whorf.[10] Rather than say our thoughts precede our language, they propose that our language precedes and molds our thinking. Their strong version claims that the language we speak *determines* our higher level thought processes. They call this *linguistic determinism*. Their soft version suggests that the language we speak helps or hinders our ability to understand the world. They call this *linguistic relativism*. It's not that our brains and five senses can't perceive the world in different terms; it's that our language discourages us from doing so. So, in our car-crazed culture we find it easy to picture and discuss cars because of words such as *sedan, Ford, compact, Toyota, sports coupe, Suzuki, convertible, four-wheel drive, prairie cruiser, Audi, commuter car, Chevrolet,* and *two-door*. People who immigrate here from cultures where bicycles or rickshaws prevail, probably hold long mental lists of terms to think about those modes — lists we don't hold.

The point here is that without a word for a concept, it's mighty hard to think about that concept. For this reason my wife and I try to expand our children's vocabulary so they can knit together a tightly woven word-net with which to "catch" their experience. We also keep some ugly words from entering their vocabulary in hopes that their response to life's challenges will be lexically biased toward grace, not garbage.

GREAT SYSTEM, BUT STILL FLAWED

The rich potential for language to point to the physical world, create edifying relationships, and nurture right thinking should compel us to study its intricacies. God made his entire creation good, including our gift of speech. But after creation came the fall of the human race and ever since Genesis the whole creation, language included, carries the burden of sin one way or another. Language, for all its potential, still has pitfalls. We might regard some flaws as inherent to the software (that is, the grammar and vocabulary), while other shortcomings are due to fallen programmers (that is, sinful and limited people). What are some of those pitfalls?

Abstract language. Linguist S. I. Hayakawa shed light on this problem with his abstraction ladder.[11] Imagine a ladder, grounded in dirt, that reaches into the sky. At the bottom imagine a word like "Brindle" which refers to a dog we once owned. "Brindle" refers to one such dog with her own unique eyes, hair, yip, and manner.

Up one rung is the word "dog" that refers to all shaggy canines (the Brindles, Rexes, and Scuppers), and up another rung is the word "pet" that refers to all domesticated animals owned for human pleasure (such as cats, fish and gerbils). Each new word refers to a more abstract referent as in "animal" and "organism." Brindle *is* a dog, pet, animal, and organism, but I would never say "I'm going to walk the organism."

But in other conversations we have—and do—speak so abstractly. We say "I'll be home early" and mean midnight but our partner reads it as 10:00 p.m. We say "I want to commit my life to God more fully" and mean "attend worship regularly," but our friends think "she's going to become a nun." A simple verbal check often avoids the misunderstanding. "What do you mean by *early*?" "What do you mean by *more fully*?"

"A good while back, our male progenitors put their best foot forward on this socio-political conglomerate…"

Euphemism. "Through euphemism we substitute mild, vague, or less emotionally charged terms for more blunt ones."[12] When I refer to my hate for someone as "righteous indignation," I'm window dressing my emotion. I may be kind, but I'm not honest. Some Christians suggest that Ephesians 4:15 is a good standard for guarding against euphemism. If we "speak the truth in love" we will choose words that are kind and accurate. In good conscience I can call a friend "rotund" even though he's "overweight" because "rotund" extends mercy while still admitting he's fat.

Our conscience should revolt when euphemism distances us from mistakes and horrors that we could have avoided. When American pilots accidentally shot down a British fighter plane during Operation Desert Storm, the military brass attributed it to "friendly fire," not "our flub." Whether you supported that military endeavor or not, you can see how even the label "Operation Desert Storm" attempts to cast the destruction of Hussein's army as a natural and uncontrollable event. Hitler recast his horrors as "the final solution;" the rest of us have since called it "holocaust."

Equivocal language. A word is said to be equivocal when it has two or more legitimate interpretations. The more abstract a word, the more equivocal its potential. When George Bush was running for re-election on a "family values" platform, Barbara Bush was reported to have said, "However *you* define family, that's what we mean by family values."[13] Mrs. Bush banked on the equivocal nature of this political buzz word to win voter support.

Equivocation can lead to humorous clash between the meanings. Consider the headlines that read "Red Tape Holds Up New Bridge," "Man Struck by Lightning Faces Battery Charge," and "Farmer Bill Dies in House." More strategic use of equivocation is Nike's successful "Just Do It" slogan. Nike advertisers are content to let the audience decide what "it" is.

Equivocal terms come in all too handy if you want to fake someone out. "How was your day?" can be answered with "I had a terrific day." Whoever asked the question will probably assume you studied hard or got a desired grade on an assignment; only you know it was swell because you skipped class and drank lattés all afternoon.

Dichotomies. Dichotomies, or polar words, are terms that color a person or object entirely one way or another. Polar terms stem from the verb *is* as in "John *is* lazy. He doesn't like to get up in the morning." But John might be energetic between noon and two a.m. All of John isn't lazy, but "John *is* lazy" makes it seem so.

Suppose the student government president at your school is a math whiz, average public speaker, and terrible cook. If we call that president "successful" we're bound to lose some of the truth about him or her. Suppose a fellow believer gives $1000 to the church per month, attends thirty of fifty-two Sunday worship services, and has never spoken of her relationship with God to another human being. If we call her "uncommitted" we're masking her complexity. Few of us are all one way or all another way, but our language tends to draw boxes into which we can cage others.

Two ways to avoid false dichotomies are to ask "to what degree is someone like X?" (the degree question) and "What specific behavior appears to indicate quality Y?" (the specificity question). To what degree is someone lazy or successful or uncommitted? What specific behavior makes us think this? Both help us avoid sweeping generalities.

Abstract language, euphemism, equivocal terms, and dichotomies represent a handful of problems with language. Interestingly though, these problems rarely render our talk completely meaningless. Through feedback, body language, and context we understand what others say with uncanny accuracy. These successes and joys convince many Christians that language is more than mere talk; it's a gift from God that we use for his pleasure and our own. God seems to have faith in language to accomplish his ends, whether divine or human.

On God's Faith in Words

The Bible testifies to the fact that God puts a high value on communication. From God's creation of light from his declaration of "Let there be light" (Genesis 1:3) to the apostle John's warning to anyone who "takes words away from this book of prophecy" (Revelation 22:19), we understand that God communicates with us, his creation, and has high value on communication. More specifically it can be shown that God has a high value on words in particular. We know this from several bases, but mainly from the accounts that God spoke the universe into existence, relies on words to instruct us in his moral way, and will one day defeat Satan by the words of his mouth. God's words lack no ontological (real) force.

As Christians we believe God created the world *ex nihilo* (from nothing). Indeed, he spoke it into existence. Sometimes we forget this fact or we fail to appreciate its relationship to our study of language. "Said" is such a non-exotic verb, but its use in Genesis 1 takes on monumental meaning.

And God *said*, "Let there be light."

And God *said*, "Let there be an expanse between the waters…"

And God *said*, "Let the water under the sky be gathered to one place…

and on it goes in verses 11, 14, 20, 24, and 26. Moreover, what God spoke into existence was very good. The scriptures also record that this "speaking forth" the world into existence was done through Christ. The Gospel of John, chapter one begins

> In the beginning was the Word, and the Word was with God, and the Word was God. He was with God in the beginning. Through him all things were made; without him nothing was made that has been made.

In one sense God is saying here is my Word — my message — to you in the person of Christ. If you want to understand me better, take a look at Jesus. He's God in the flesh.

In another sense though John's use of "word" (Greek *logos*) means something more generative, more explosive. As the psalmist writes, "By the *word* of the Lord the heavens were made, and all their host by the breath of his mouth" (Psalm 36:6). Jesus was co-creator of the universe.

Finally, lest we be deists and believe that God through Christ got the cosmos going and then stepped back from it, we should also acknowledge that *logos* can also mean *the sustaining force in the universe*. Greek writers such as Heraclitis had already used "logos" to mean the cosmic principle of order, or the eternal, impersonal reason that pervaded and directed the universe. Now God instructs the apostle to call his son the personal *logos* — the one by whom, for whom, and through whom all things consist.[14]

We also have evidence that God relies on language to communicate to us his nature and purposes. In Exodus 3:14 he calls himself "I AM" and thereby defines himself as timeless. Other times he calls himself Creator, Sustainer, Provider, and Judge. We realize that these are merely the English terms which represent God's nature; nevertheless, the fact that God used words to convey his nature and purpose to us (originally in Greek, Hebrew, and Aramaic) shows his faith in language.

God also relies on words to instruct us. To Moses and Aaron he promised "I will help both of you speak and will teach you what to do. He [Aaron] will speak to the people for you [Moses] and it will be as if he were your mouth and as if you were God to him" (Exodus 4:15b-16). Furthermore, of Jesus Christ the temple guards said "No one ever spoke the way this man does" (John 7:46). As Huston Smith writes of Jesus' language: "If simplicity, concentration, and the sense of what is vital are marks of great religious literature, these qualities alone would make Jesus' words immortal. But this is just the beginning. They carry an extravagance of which wise men…are incapable. The language is part of the man himself, stemming from the urgency and passions of his driving conviction."[15]

People as Word-Users

Our language ability is part of what qualifies us as "made in God's image." Even the Gentile rhetoricians who lived before Christ viewed speaking as what makes us supremely different from the animal kingdom. A Greek orator named Isocrates (350 B.C.) noted that while some animals are stronger and swifter than us, language still sets us apart.

> ...[B]ecause there has been implanted in us the power to persuade each other and to make clear to each other whatever we desire, not only have we escaped the life of the wild beasts, but we have come together and founded cities and made laws and invented arts; and, generally speaking, there is no institution devised by man which the power of speech has not helped to establish.[16]

Scholars through the ages have affirmed this view.

King Solomon played a similar song for the gift of speech when he wrote "A word aptly spoken is like apples of gold in settings of silver" (Proverbs 25:11) and "From the fruit of his lips a man enjoys good things" (Proverbs 13:2).

Out of context, it would appear that Isocrates and King Solomon believed that speech and language are inherently good. But neither was so naive. For Isocrates, eloquence was the outward sign of being a university-educated individual—one who knew philosophy, mathematics, history, and other subjects. Solomon had a different idea. To him, what one said was the sign of what was in one's heart, whether it be folly or wisdom, evil or good. He wrote: "The tongue of the wise commends knowledge, but the mouth of the fool gushes folly" (Proverbs 15:2) and "The lips of the wise spread knowledge; not so the hearts of fools" (Proverbs 15:7). This theme is repeated throughout the proverbs.

Jesus' teachings about the tongue follow the same way of thinking when he addresses the issue of blaspheming the Holy Spirit (what some Christians consider the one unpardonable sin). His strong words indict the Pharisees: "Make a tree good and its fruit will be good, or make a tree bad and its fruit will be bad, for a tree is recognizable by its fruit. You brood of vipers, how can you who are evil say anything good? For out of the overflow of the heart the mouth speaks" (Matthew 12:33-34).

Although it is not said outright, the principle here seems to be that it is not the tongue which is good or evil, but the heart; the tongue only "spills" the contents of our heart for others to see and hear.

Aren't we fortunate though that this heart-tongue connection isn't automatic? If so, we would often speak like inconsiderate idiots, spewing every minor thought and fleeting emotion. We would be a lot like the Jim Carrey

Our speech spills from our heart, and is therefore a sign of our heart's condition.

character in *Liar Liar* who spoke his mind but had no social grace. For good or for bad, we can override our heart condition with a choice of the will.

James affirms this view when he observes that the same tongue can praise God or curse people.

> All kinds of animals, birds, reptiles and creatures of the sea are being tamed and have been tamed by man, but no man can tame the tongue. It is a restless evil, full of deadly poison. With the tongue we praise our Lord and Father, and with it we curse men, who have been made in God's likeness. My brothers, this should not be. Can both fresh water and salt water flow from the same spring? Can a fig tree bear olives, or a grapevine bear figs? Neither can a salt spring produce fresh water. (James 3:7-12)

George Campbell, an 18th century Presbyterian pastor and speech scholar, suggested that human nature consists of the intellect, the emotions, the imagination, and the will.[17] I think his views help us piece together how we use words. Sometimes our emotions rule and we blurt profanities or cries of joy (depending on the emotion). Other times we carefully reason what we should say first and then speak. Still other times our language reflects our imagination and creative side (as in poetry and drama). But governing each, most the time, is our will and moral sense of what is right. As Proverbs 10:32a reads, "The lips of the righteous know what is fitting." Whether we follow through on what we know to be right is a matter of choice.

Because God has made us responsible creatures, it's worth asking "How would God *choose* that we speak?" Put another way, "How might we use words in a manner pleasing to God?"

Five Biblical Guidelines for How We Might Use Words

1. Speak intelligibly. In his letter to the Corinthians, Paul encouraged the believers to prefer intelligible (that is, understandable) words over unintelligible ones. The issue he was wrestling with was *glossolalia* or speaking in tongues in the worship service. Though he spoke in tongues himself, he writes "But in the church I would rather speak five intelligible words to instruct others than ten thousand words in a tongue" (1 Corinthians 14:19).

Paul seemed to know what communication theorists claim: symbols do not contain meaning, rather people do. You can stare at "mi atta war camalla jato' all you like, but it is as good as gibberish or glossolalia unless you know Marathi or have an interpreter. (The translation is, "I am going to work now.") If we want our speech to be intelligible, we need to link it to people's experience.

Recently I had a conversation with my Brazilian neighbor, Geraldo Gubiotti. Geraldo and I shared the frustration that we had no street lamp in our section of the road. On this particular day, though, I had learned that the city crew was installing the light in two months, and I told Geraldo. Geraldo's English is superior to my Portuguese (his first language), but still pretty rough. Despite this handicap he paused a moment, considered the good news about the street light, and then beamed, "Hope is better than disillusionment." In five words my Christian neighbor conveyed significant truth that linked to my experience.

"I've heard she's very bright. The only problem is, you can't understand a thing she says."

Christian words (and ideals) such as "peace," "love," "justice," and "hope" are likely to make intelligible sense wherever we use them. Other terms such as "redemption," "justification," "Eucharist," "predestination," "apostolic procession," and "KJV" may only obscure our message. *Codeswitching* is the habit of changing our vocabulary or style of talk for different audiences so each can understand us and identify with us. We would be wise to switch from "Christianese" to a more fitting vocabulary if we want our message to be intelligible.

2. Speak Culturally. One of my colleagues, Mike Walrod, is the director of the Canadian Institute of Linguistics. Each year he gives a presentation to first year students that shows a technique translators use to write down sounds of languages unknown to them. The presentation requires a volunteer from the audience.

On one occasion the volunteer was a chap from a remote African area who had been at our school for over a year. Dr. Walrod asked him to use his native language to describe his experience at Trinity Western University. As the student spoke, my colleague converted the sounds into the International Phonetic Alphabet, wrote them on the blackboard, and, when finished, repeated them aloud to the student. He then did some mental analysis and created a new sentence from the sounds on the board. The student's response was first shock and then tears! He had not heard anyone speak his language in over twelve months, and the sounds and meanings tumbling fresh on his ears and mind triggered a mix of emotions.

One communication scholar has suggested that the goal of communication generally and of persuasion specifically is not to share meaning but to show *identification*.[18] If you can say of my words "Yep, that's me; that's my experience too," then I've succeeded in identifying with you. We've connected. This is what Dr. Walrod had done. His effort to speak a relatively little-known language communicated respect and kindness to a culturally stressed student. His effort conveyed an appreciation for the student's primary symbol system for thinking and connecting to the world.

Even if we aren't in the position of needing to learn another language, the guideline to speak culturally still applies. P. K. McCary took this to heart after she saw how some of the Old English words of the King James Version Bible didn't wash with young black kids in her church. Her vision was to retell the greatest story using inner city black slang. The result is *Black Bible Chronicles* (African American Family Press), a paraphrase of the Pentateuch (Genesis through Deuteronomy). When God confronts Adam after the Fall, he says "What's up, brother? Who hipped you to the fact you don't have on any clothes?" And, similarly, when Moses receives the Ten Commandments we hear, "You shouldn't diss the Almighty's name, using it in cuss words or rapping with one another. It ain't cool and payback's a monster."

While some may criticize the book, calling it irreverent or an endorsement of substandard English, the fact is that God's word is more alive to some readers than ever before. Keep in mind though that what is "hip" today may be "lame" in five years. Language evolves as people add, subtract and revise it to meet their needs. Astute communicators pay attention to these changes for the benefit of their audience.

3. Speak graphically. As we noted earlier, the problem with abstract and euphemistic language is that they dodge clear meaning. "Revenue enhancement" is not only six times longer than "tax" but vague too. Who's supplying this revenue? "Tax" tells us we are. Saying "air support" instead of "bombing" makes us wonder if the sky needs buttressing of some kind. "Bombing" clarifies what is really falling. When we shy from using the more graphic term we may be exhibiting an unwillingness to deal with their realities.

Besides dodging responsibility, abstract talk turns us into poor communicators. One of my favorite examples of how many-syllable words can kill ideas is found in George Orwell's essay, "Politics and the English Language." Watch what happens when he takes a graphically rich passage from Ecclesiastes and then "modernizes" it with academic language. From Ecclesiastes 9:11:

> I have seen something else under the sun: The race is not to the swift or the battle to the strong, nor does food come to the wise or wealth to the brilliant or favor to the learned; but time and chance happen to them all.

In academic English:

> Objective consideration of contemporary phenomena compels the conclusion that success or failure in competitive activities exhibits no tendency to be commensurate with innate capacity, but that a considerable element of the unpredictable must invariably be taken into account. [19]

One remedy for abstract talk is Jesus' example of using the parable and metaphor. We remember ideas better in story form and can see their life application more easily. I bet most of you can finish these stories and indicate their moral teaching:

> Who is your neighbor? Consider a man who was beaten and robbed on his way to Jericho....

For the word of God is like a seed planted along the way. Some of it fell on the path, some on the rock, some among weeds....

Then the son took his inheritance and traveled to a far away land where he lived a life of merriment until....

Jesus' metaphors were equally graphic. He called himself the Way, the Truth, the Life, the Door, the Water, the Bread, the Vine, and the Good Shepherd. He called Christians light, salt, and harvest workers. He compared the Kingdom of God to a mustard seed, yeast, a treasure hidden in a field, a pearl and a net.

We need to be observant. Does our neighbor garden? We might talk about zucchinis and vines and some day talk about Christ the Vine. Does our neighbor build homes? We could talk architecture and design, and eventually talk about Christ the door who gave ultimate design to the universe. Does our neighbor have a wayward son or daughter? We might acknowledge how much love is required to welcome that child home and parallel this love to God's unconditional love for us.

4. Speak actions. The first three guidelines — to speak intelligibly, culturally, and graphically — concern the *referential* function of language. As we noted in Figure 1.1, we use language to refer to (name, point to, conjure up) the world around us.

But we also noted that we use language to create social realities. This concerns the *performative* function of language, meaning we use words to perform actions such as making promises, blessing others, and expressing love.[20] Think about it. Can you promise a friend that you'll meet her for lunch without using words? Can you make a bet that the New York Yankees will win the pennant this year without language? Consider too how these acts are like little contracts we make with each other. *I* promise *you. I* make a bet with *you.* These are *speech* acts (that is, acts made possible through speech). They also show how speech *acts* (that is, how speech is an active agent in social relationships).

Jesus seemed to appreciate the referential and performative ways language works. He used its referential function to claim profound truths such as "I and the Father are one" and "I am the Way, the Truth, and the Life." He used its speech acts function to author new relationships. Consider how Jesus

Blessed children.
Warned evil doers.
Comforted the sick.
Expressed love.

Forgave people their sins.
Commanded the dead to rise.

Perhaps the two most important speech acts we perform as believers are confession and forgiveness. Whether we admit our sin to a priest or a friend, we wind up different because of it. Our burden is made lighter and accountability with our confidant often kicks in. Receiving someone's forgiveness doubles the blessing.

Expressing to God how we've messed up may seem to some an unnecessary act because, they say, God knows our hearts already. I think, however, that putting our vice into words is good for us. God knows that language is one more tool that can help us become more like him.

5. Speak worthily. A couple of nights ago four of our communication graduates threw a party for a fifth one, and for a couple of hours my wife and I were nose to nose with them over ice cream at Dairy Queen. One of the guys, Derek, could hardly contain himself. Earlier this year he had been asked to be the graduation speaker at his old high school. "I have never been so nervous in my life," he said, "but with ample preparation, it went okay."

How would you feel if your former principal invited you to speak at a grad? Derek's nerves got rattled. But why? I could be wrong, but I think it was because Derek fathomed the implications of the invite: the grads and the principal thought he was worth listening to.

Being worth listening to is not easy, and saying something of worth is a heavy responsibility. How many of us have slipped away from a sermon or switched channels because "it just isn't worth it"? To meet the expectation of worthiness, Derek logged 20-30 hours to construct a 20-30 minute speech. He meant business and his investment seemed to pay off.

In the book of Jeremiah, God lays out his criteria for the prophet to be his ambassador. Among other things God says "If you repent, I will restore you that you may serve me; if you utter worthy, not worthless, words, you will be my spokesman" (Jeremiah 15:19). First comes the speech act of repentance which leads to reconciliation with God. Second comes the words that God deems worthy that we might be ambassadors.

I would bet a year's wage that Derek did not fill his time with crack-me-up one-liners, sexual innuendoes, and descriptions of his own accomplishments. (I know he started off by referring to what a big night graduation meant to his audience and that he quoted Winston Churchill.) Rather he probably followed the guideline in Ephesians 4:29 to "not let any unwholesome talk come out of your mouths, but only what is helpful for building others up according to their needs, that it may benefit those who listen" and Colossians 4:6 to "let your conversation be always full of grace, seasoned with salt, so that you may know how to answer everyone."

My struggle is with what I call gray talk. It isn't pernicious or venomous, but it isn't seasoned with salt and grace either. A lot of it qualifies as godless chatter, foolish talk, and even coarse joking (see 2 Timothy 2:16 and Ephesians 5:4). I struggle with what's between obvious trash talk and what's truly edifying.

Worthy words communicate truth, correct wrong thinking, show a thankful heart, encourage the downtrodden, plead the case of the less fortunate, and most of all express love. The words of Christians should also be delightful, winsome, informed, and gentle. This type of talk develops disciples who love God with their heart, mind, soul — and even their language.

Summary

People have a suspicion about language today, a suspicion that language is "mere talk" with no real force and a weak link to reality. This chapter has been an attempt to dispute that way of thinking.

Language is God's gift to us which distinguishes us from animals. Language drives the bulk of our communication with others whether that be to describe God's creation, form human bonds, or pattern how we think. Language is by no means a perfect system, and we noted several problems such as abstract terms, euphemisms, equivocal terms and dichotomies.

God's value for language is shown in his speaking the universe into existence and Christ's sustaining the universe as the personal *logos*. God also relies on language to reveal himself to us in the scriptures and through godly people. Our language indicates our heart's condition as well as our choices. Because we can mask the condition of our heart by what we choose to say, I described five ways we might choose to speak. These are: to speak intelligibly, culturally, graphically, in speech acts, and worthily.

Worth the Talk

1. In what ways has the material in this chapter influenced your views of language use in everyday life? In particular, what do you think of someone who remarks "He's only saying that"? What view of language does this phrase depict? What might one's response be to someone with such a view?
2. Which of the five biblical guidelines for using words speaks most to your own use or misuse of words? Why has this area become a weakness or strength in your life? How might you make an effort to improve in this area?

Consider the Walk

1. Make a list of terms or phrases which are well known and often used by Christians. Call this a "Christianese" list. Beside each term write down how other religious groups might interpret the term. For example, the term "born again" might be interpreted by a Hindu person as meaning "reincarnation." After that, write down a definition which you think that a person from this other religious group might understand.

2. Do an analysis of a magazine or television advertisement for its use and abuse of language. Use the five criteria provided in this chapter to ask whether the ad uses language intelligibly, graphically, culturally, worthily, or in a speech acts manner. You may use other criteria for language use and abuse found in other textbooks as well. The goal of your analysis should be to determine what truth claims the ad is making and what linguistic strategies the advertisers have used to persuade people of those claims.

Notes

1. Orwell, G., *Nineteen-eighty-four: A novel*. Harcourt, Brace & World, New York, NY, 1949.

2. Quoted from footage of the Iran-Contra inquiry as found on the educational video *Doublespeak*, Films for the Humanities & Sciences, 1988.

3. Quoted from footage of the *Challenger* inquiry as found on the educational video *Doublespeak*, Films for the Humanities & Sciences, 1988.

4. For a full discussion about doublespeak, see William Lutz, *Doublespeak*, Harper & Row, New York, NY, 1990.

5. See C. K. Ogden and I. A. Richards, *The meaning of meaning*, Harcourt, Brace & World, New York, NY, 1946, pp. 1-23.

6. For an advanced look at this idea, see John R. Searle, *The construction of social reality*, The Free Press, New York, NY, 1995.

7. My email address is **strom@twu.ca** . The **twu** stands for my school, Trinity Western University, and the **ca** is the suffix for email addresses in Canada.

8. See P. Watzlawick, J. H. Beavin, and D. D. Jackson, *Pragmatics of human communication: A study of interaction patterns, pathologies, and paradoxes*, Norton, New York, NY, 1967 and P. Evans, *The verbally abusive relationship: How to recognize it and how to respond*, Adams Media Corporation, Holbrook, MA, 1996.

9. Charles Osgood, George Suci, and Percy Tannenbaum, *The measurement of meaning*. University of Illinois Press, Urbana, IL, 1957.

10. Edward Sapir, *Culture, language, and personality*, University of California Press, Berkeley, CA, 1970, and Benjamin L. Whorf, *Language, thought, and reality*, MIT Press, Cambridge, MA, 1964.

11. S. I. Hayakawa, *Language in thought and action*, 4th ed., Harcourt Brace Jovanovich, Orlando, FL, 1978.

12. Stewart L. Tubbs and Sylvia Moss, *Human communication*. (7th ed.), McGraw-Hill, Inc., New York, NY, 1994, p. 84.

13. As quoted in Chuck Colson, *A dance with deception: Revealing the truth behind the headlines*, Word Publishers, Milton Keynes, England, 1993, p. 167.

14. The centrality of Christ as the *logos* of the world and the basis for intelligible use of language is not shared by eastern religions. In *The religions of man* (Harper & Row, Publishers, New York, 1965, p. 71), Huston Smith writes of the Hindu religion and notes that in its view "Man is forever trying to lay hold of Reality with words, only in the end to find mystery rebuking his speech and his syllables swallowed by silence." Similarly, Buddha's followers gave him the name Sakymuni or "silent sage." This name denotes the idea that, in Buddha, there existed a mystery and depth beyond what could be said or thought with words. Finally, those who are Taoist (pronounced Dowist) strive for the goal of "creative quietude" as they live in the force which has no name but which they simply call the Tao (the Way).

15. Smith, p. 305

16. "Antidosis," *Isocrates*, trans. by George Norlin, Cambridge: Harvard University Press, 1929, reprinted 1956, II, p. 327

17. See James L. Golden Goodwin F. Berquist, and William E. Coleman, *The rhetoric of western thought*, (5th ed.), Kendall/Hunt Publishing Company, Dubuque, IA, 1993, pp. 129-138.

18. Kenneth Burke, *A rhetoric of motives*, University of California Press, Berkeley, CA, 1950.

19. George Orwell, "Politics and the English language," *New republic*, June 17, 1946.

20. For a full treatment of how we use words to perform actions see John Austin, *How to do things with words*, Harvard University Press, Cambridge, MA, 1962, and John R. Searle, *Speech acts: An essay in the philosophy of language*, Cambridge University Press, New York, NY, 1969.

CHAPTER 2

Edifying Behavior
Gracious Interpretations and Congruent Expression in Nonverbal Communication

Do not merely listen to the word, and so deceive yourselves. Do what it says.

James 1:22

My spirit still twinges when I recall the incident. Shelaine and I were attempting to exit a parking lot onto a busy divided thoroughfare. I kept looking to my left for a break in traffic, and then came my chance. Without looking back to my right, I gave the van some gas. FLASH! BRAKE! What was that?

A twenty-something male on a mountain bike skidded abruptly to a stop to my left. He had just ridden in front of us on the sidewalk from our right, and I had almost mowed him over with my van. He was furious. I was shocked.

"What the ____ do you think you're doing?" he shouted, straddle-walking his bike back to my open window. "Don't you know how to drive!" he raged, his eyebrows slanted down and inward like a Japanese warlord's. "You almost killed me!" His nose was eighteen inches from mine, his eyes ablaze as they seared my own. I expected that he would punch me any moment. "Look both ways you idiot!" His shirtless chest and neck-length black hair made him an intense image as he squeezed the bike's handle-grips and bumped the wheel against the van. Yep, I thought, I'm going to lose at least two teeth. What to do?

"I'm sorry," I intoned softly. "You're right," I managed with some humility. "I'll be more careful next time," I offered slowly, my hands still on the steering wheel and the rest of my body frozen with fear. Shelaine sat motionless as well, her heart racing as fast as my own. The biker huffed one more look of disgust and pulled back, and in another second was gone.

Any distant passerby didn't need to know a single word of our exchange to figure that trouble brewed deeply. Raised voices, squared-off posturing, rapid speech, and gnarly faces usually mean an easy read for anger. But seldom are nonverbal behaviors linked to such intense emotion, and rarely are they interpreted so easily. How did the biker make sense of my short hair and wire-rimmed glasses? My "night out" dress and teal van? How should I have understood his helmet-less head or scratched-up CCM bicycle? And what of his black backpack?

Pick up a book on nonverbal communication and you'll get two distinct but not incompatible claims. One is that nonverbal behaviors are less controllable than our tongues. This fact makes it sound as if we're like the *Far Side* cartoon guy whose leg thumps wildly on the floor as a dog scratches his stomach. This view is pretty depressing, but it applies to some auto-response cues such as sweaty palms (when we are nervous) and dilated pupils (when we are interested).

The other claim is that despite our lesser ability to control them, we can improve our sending and receiving of nonverbal signals through awareness and practice. Some authors even provide tips for sending and receiving cues.[1] Of course this implies that there's a standard for competent nonverbal communicating and hints that we're responsible for improving our baseline ability. So there's hope—hope that with God's strength we may choose to act redemptively towards others whether with micro actions such as eye winks and body angle or with macro statements such as lives of service and earthly sacrifice. On the receiving end, the hope is that we exercise caution and alertness as we decipher other people's mosaic of nonverbal signals.

THE LAY OF NONVERBAL LAND COMPARED TO THE WORLD OF WORDS

"Nonverbal" means "not of words" and it's just a little strange that we define this field by what it is *not*. Nonverbal communication "includes all the *non*linguistic things a person does to which others ascribe meaning" whether we intend so or not.[2]

A positive definition leads to a lengthy but helpful list. Nonverbal communication is the process by which people create or send messages with their *appearance* (such as body type and attractiveness), *artifacts* (of clothing, jewelry, eye wear, etc.) and *body movement* (such as body angle and posture; also called body language or kinesics). It also includes our *facial expressions*, *eye behavior*, *personal space* and *territory* (also called proxemics), *touch* (also called haptics or tactile communication), *voice* (also called paralinguistics or vocalics), *smell* (also called olfaction), *use of time* (also called chronemics), and *physical environment* (as in rooms, buildings and cities). Let's consider how these means of communication, as a group, differ from our use of words.

First, verbal messages tend to be *single-channeled* and *received one at a time* whereas nonverbal messages are *multi-channeled* and *received in mosaic simultaneously*. The words and concepts that the biker-guy hurled at me crashed one by one on my ears like cars of a train spilling from a bridge. However, his appearance, voice, spacing, and van-bumping touch arrived as a package to my ears, eyes, and skin. These cues — or clues if you wish — are like tiled bits of an intricately crafted mosaic. Researchers encourage us to read these clusters of cues in relation to each other[3] and to guard against channel overload. I've described the biker's mosaic above, but due to stress I've surely missed something. As much as we can though, we need to consider the whole mural others paint for us.

Second, nonverbal messages differ from verbal ones in the degree that we can turn them on and off. Because we are either speaking or not, writing or not, word processing or not, we call verbal messages *discrete*. In contrast, we are not very able to turn off nonverbal cues like a spigot does to water — they are *continuous*. I couldn't stop using *some* kind of eye behavior with the cyclist as well as *some* kind of posture and *some* tone of voice. Since others interpret these continuous cues at any time, we acknowledge what is now a communication truism: We cannot *not* communicate.[4] All behavior carries communicative potential.

Third, verbal messages tend to be deliberate whereas nonverbal messages are often unconscious. I assumed this when I encouraged you in chap-

Like tiles on a mosaic, a person's nonverbal cues come at us all at once.

ter one to speak intelligibly, culturally, graphically, and worthily. That same wisdom goes for how we should act around others, except with the understanding that it's more difficult to know what our left hand, right foot, palms, and voice are doing at any one time. I bet a ghostly white face and dilated pupils accompanied my calm voice and resting hands. Biker-man probably knew that I was scared silly.

Fourth, verbal messages tend to be clear while nonverbal messages tend to be ambiguous. I knew the meaning of every word the cyclist shouted in my face (you, idiot, watch, drive, killed...), but I still don't know how to read his riding on the sidewalk at 15 m.p.h. Aren't sidewalks for people? Or what of his riding helmet-less? Since the city of Surrey has a helmet bylaw, my ungracious read is that he was an insolent rebel or a forgetful oaf. But maybe he was rushing to help someone in an emergency. Maybe he couldn't afford a helmet. Some research indicates that we tend to be more confident about our cue-reading than we ought to be. Both women and men tend to report higher levels of confidence in their decoding accuracy than their actual performance merits.[4] The rule of thumb appears to be that we should be cautious and gracious when reading ambiguous cues.

Fifth, verbal codes are especially adept for conveying raw data whereas nonverbal systems are best at conveying relational messages. We play on this bias to show love to pre-language infants by the way we hold, cuddle and coo them. We return to this bias when we want to show strong emotion towards adult friends. One researcher estimates that as much as ninety-three percent of the *social meaning* we derive from others stems from facial expressions and tone of voice, and only seven percent from what they say.[6] We might fuss over these specific percentages, but I think you'll agree that nonverbal signals tell us much about how others feel and the nature of our relationship. If we want to encode an abstract idea such as "Look both ways before you proceed," words are still preferred.

Finally, nonverbal messages tend to win out when our words and actions don't jive. Suppose the cyclist had shouted, "You drive better than Michael Andretti—I sure wish everyone drove like you." Would I believe him? Probably not. When what we say conflicts with what we do, people normally pay attention to our actions to determine our true sentiments. The biker is being sarcastic, I'd infer.

The weighing of nonverbals more heavily than words reflects a value God seems to put on this code as well, at least as an indication of our heart. As Eugene Peterson renders Paul's words, "Merely hearing God's law is a waste of your time if you don't do what he commands. Doing, not hearing, is what makes the difference with God." And later, "You can get by with almost anything if you front it with eloquent talk about God and his law."[7] Almost anything. Consider the messages we send when we claim to love fellow sinners but give them looks that could kill or shoulders that freeze them out. I think our greatest challenge is to show the balance between justice and love—the first so often delivered through what we say; the latter through how we say it.

Worthy Goals: Edification, Grace and Congruence

Then how should we act? And to what standard should we aspire? The answers may come to light with an illustration. In *The Jesus I Never Knew*, Philip Yancey writes:

> I know of one AIDS patient who traveled eleven hundred miles to be with his family in Michigan for Thanksgiving dinner. He had not seen them in seven years. The parents welcomed him warily, and when dinner was served everyone got a heaping portion of turkey and all the trimmings on the best Wedgewood china plates—except their son the AIDS patient, who was served on Chinette, with plastic utensils.[8]

The parents' wariness is at least explainable—AIDS can kill. Their choice of place setting, however, makes us wonder if they own an ounce of sensitivity. What impact do you suppose their actions had on their son's sense of belonging? On trust? On hope? Because nonverbal behavior is an index to relational health, it seems that the standard to which we aspire may be edification and grace. *Edification* simply means "building up," as in supporting a person's sense of worth and progress toward Christ-likeness. Consider the difference had mom and dad served up the full meal deal to their son on a china plate they stacked later with other plates in the dishwasher. *Grace* is the slack we cut others—the unmerited favor we grant them as we make sense of their confusing or seemingly nasty behavior. Just like the grace God grants to us. My guess is that tension ran deep as the son made arrangements for returning to Michigan. Perhaps he had lost his parents' trust; perhaps they had already lost his. Consider the rekindled hope the parents could have engendered had they treated him graciously, even royally.

But here's the snag. What if our feelings really are detrimental to others? What if we loathe the other person or wish to end the relationship? A rule of thumb for every situation is tough to find, but I like the idea by noted psychologist Carl Rogers who suggested that people should try to show congruence.[9] Congruence is being real with our emotions: knowing them, feeling them, and showing them genuinely to others around us. This doesn't mean blurting out or bodily expressing every flitting evaluation. It does mean avoiding long-term facades. We rarely trust people who seem to be faking their feelings. By this standard the parents were at least being honest, but still not sensitive. Unlike the Jim Carrey character in *Liar Liar*, being honest about our feelings does not mean we are tactless kooks.

Understanding how the nonverbal channel differs from the verbal one is a move toward edification, grace and congruence. The next step is to recognize the range of cues at our disposal and their primary messages.

Voice

During my college years I met a woman with Elizabethan features. Karen's light skin, shoulder length dark hair, and 5' 8" frame would cast her well on an *A&E* production of *Hamlet*. When she spoke though, something didn't seem right. Rather than hear a full, mellow voice, one heard a tinny, high-strung, nasal twang. One had to fight the stereotype, but it was easy to believe that Karen was immature, insecure, indecisive or weak.[10] From what I knew about Karen, this stereotype didn't fit, but strangers wouldn't know better. Sometimes life's not fair.

Vocalics include the pitch, volume, rate and quality of voice as well as disfluencies such as "um" and "ya' know." Our bias is to favor people who speak with lower pitches (consider any anchorperson, male or female), average to above average volume, moderate to quick rate, and rich quality. Extremes usually turn us off. Too high pitch equates with youthful inexperience; too low with mental dullness. Too quick a rate speaks of nervousness or wanna-buy-a-watch sales tactics; too slow a rate may indicate incompetence. Too aspirate a voice can be interpreted as spinelessness; too orotund as pompous.[11]

Our voice is as unique as our fingerprint, and, along with our face, a key source by which others infer our credibility and how likable we are. Maybe you tend toward a voice like Karen's or more raspy or throaty. If we want others to take us and our ideas seriously, it's worth asking "How do I sound?" Tape recording our conversations and trying exercises that vocalists use might improve our vocal habits and sensitize us to others less blessed like Karen.

Eye Behavior

If the eye is the window to the soul, I know very little about Sid's soul. I bumped into Sid on the sands of Cannon Beach, Oregon this summer and liked him immediately. Within minutes we learned that we shared the faith, loved vacationing in the sun, and struggled as parents of young children. Only one thing bugged me—Sid wore his shades during the entire conversation. Try as I did, I never met Sid "eye to eye."

In western cultures we use our eyes to communicate liking, attention, respect, and control.[12] And we do so through two modalities: location (where we look) and duration (how long we look there). If I had known that Sid was really checking out the beach during our conversation, I might figure him to be rude or distracted. Whoever is listening in a conversation usually makes direct eye contact with the speaker about sixty percent of the time; looking away the other forty percent provides important psychological space for the speaker. Whether sending or receiving, people who stare ninety-nine percent of the time are usually considered oddballs.

The bicyclist's searing glare defined the power dimension in our relationship. He was (and perhaps deserved to be) one-up; I was one-down. My task was to give him enough eye contact to convince him I was listening, but not so much that he thought I was challenging him. Our job as a teacher or pastor may require us to use our eyes to show others that we are appropriately in control of a relationship or situation. In friendships the eyes usually reflect parity of power.

Pictures of Christ usually depict him with warm, welcoming brown eyes, but I doubt that love gushed from them every waking second. Remember when Peter rebuked Jesus for predicting his death by saying "This shall never happen to you!"? How do you suppose Jesus looked at Peter when he responded, "Get behind me, Satan! You are a stumbling block to me; you do not have in mind the things of God, but the things of men" (see

"Of course you can trust me."

Matthew 16:21-28). Or how did Jesus eye the money-changers as he flipped their temple tables in righteous anger? If we hold to a flannel graph view of Jesus, we limit his human ability to use his eyes to speak with authority as well as love.

FACIAL EXPRESSION

One reason I took a liking to Sid was because even without eye contact his smile told me he was a congenial guy. We rely on the face more than any other source to read how others are feeling. There's even evidence that people interpret basic emotional states similarly from culture to culture in the smiles, grimaces, and furrowed brows we muster. "Japanese, Americans, English, Spanish, French, German, Swiss, Greek, and South Pacific Islanders recognized happiness, surprise, fear, anger, sadness, disgust, contempt, interest, bewilderment and determination in the photographed faces of people from other cultures."[13] Be careful though. Just because someone is smiling isn't a guarantee they're whistling Dixie. In cultures where creating and saving face are especially important, people become adept at obeying *display rules*. Whereas employees in the United States and Canada might be allowed to show mock shock at a bosses' mistake, Japanese subordinates are encouraged to play a poker face or polite smile.

We know that women are better than men at expressing their emotions with their faces and at interpreting other people's faces as well.[14] One reason why is because it seems that women have a biological edge in that the corpus callosum that connects their right and left brain hemispheres is more developed than men's. This enables them to recognize facial expressions with their motor-dominant right hemisphere *and* attach a word label to an expression with their language-dominate left hemisphere. Men recognize emotions well, but have a harder time calling one "contempt" and the other "disgust."

A second reason is termed accommodation — the tendency women have of paying attention to channels considered polite and controllable by others and ignoring impolite and less controllable channels. The control hierarchy is face (first), body, then voice (last). On a first date, for example, where nerves run high, the gal might attune to her date's face more than his tapping foot because it eases tension and is kind.[16] We can all learn from this practice of favoring the more controllable channels when we want to respect others.

Judith Hall's primary explanation for why women read faces better than men is sociological: Women's role in society prescribes it.[17] If a stay-home mom can't figure out why infant Emma is crying, it's going to be a long day. The same goes for women who help clients in the health and social work fields. When my counselor friend Kurt heard this explanation he suspected he might be as adept as most women because his role as a counselor requires reading clients' faces daily. I take Kurt's hope as hope for all guys — practice makes perfect.

GESTURES

In the movie *Shine*, David's sisters lean out of the window to watch their pianist brother and their father return from a music talent competition. "Did he win?" one sister asks. The second one studied the gait of the father and her brother. "No..." her voice trailed off, "he lost." And she was right. What gave it away was not David's playful hopscotch on imaginary chalked lines, but the father's stiffened walk and business-like pace. His body read bitterness.

Gestures are body movements made from the neck down. Deciphering what gestures mean may be a cinch at times and bedeviling at others. Lest we claim that we can read others like books, it's better to admit that, like a good novel, some behaviors are open to multiple interpretations. Asking friends to verbalize their ideas is probably the best check for understanding their gestures.

Emblems are behaviors that serve as substitutes for words. The raised finger in a restaurant means "service, please." The shrug of the shoulders when asked a question means "I don't know." The hook and wiggle of the finger in front of us usually indicates "Come here." Keep in mind though that emblems are culturally bound. Like their vocabulary counterparts, emblems are virtually meaningless cross-culturally.

While in India doing mission work I found this poignantly true when walking the streets of local Chandur Bazaar. A merchant saw me coming and held out his hand in a downward, limp fashion, and "scratched" the air while saying "Ee-ka-ray, ee-ka-ray." My Minnesota roots were of no use figuring out his gesture nor his Marahti. He seemed to be "shooing" me away, as if I were a dog, and I recall wondering what I had done wrong. Later I learned that his "shooing" gesture was our "come here" gesture — the exact meaning of "Ee-ka-ray."[18]

Illustrators help us visualize what someone is saying. Suppose I made my hands in the shape of an over-sized football. Without accompanying words this gesture means little to North Americans. But when I say "A rugby ball is about 30% larger than a football and shaped the same way," the light goes on. Good public speakers are especially adept at picturing ideas and objects with their hands, arms and bodies.

Affect displays are bodily expressions of emotion. Some are automatic like our hopping about on one foot after stubbing our toe. Others are more intentional and symbolic. A study in worship styles will tell you that believers follow God's desire that we worship him in spirit and in truth through an array of emotional display. The Kenyan believer dances; the mystic monk sits in quiet. Another believer raises her hands; another feels compelled to kneel. My own resolve is that discussions about worship style create more division than multiplication of God's kingdom in part because affect displays are more about preference and tradition than biblical edict.

Regulators are gestures that guide the flow of conversation. A head nod "yes" and an open palm invite others to chime in; a head nod "no" and a palm turned down announce you want to keep the floor. Picking up on regulators and reading them well takes mindful skill. They make the most sense when viewed with the rest of the mosaic—including what is being said.

Adaptors are gestures left over from past associations that give release to present tension. As I write these ideas I pause occasionally and find myself chewing on a nail. It's a bad habit I picked up in my youth when under stress and it still provides some kind of comfort today. You might bounce a leg or twirl a pen or finger your long locks when under duress. We don't intend to use adaptors around others, but due to their deep roots they creep in anyway. Fortunately we use fewer adaptors as we get to know people well, by which time they care less about our nervous fidgeting anyway.

ARTIFACTS AND APPEARANCE

Artifacts are the changes we make to our bodies, including our clothing, hairstyle, jewelry, and the like. *Appearance* refers to the look we present to others based on our physical attributes. While we can control what we wear and how we style our hair, we have less control over our body type and facial contours. But people still read both.

Writing about appearance this week is a bitter-sweet activity. Today is the Tuesday after Princess Diana's death in a Paris car crash. News anchors still hold back tears of remorse as they comment on the role of the papparrazi photographers and the drunken Ritz Hotel driver in the death of the world's most public woman. When asked why she was so popular with the masses, one British commentator put it bluntly: because she was so beautiful, so photogenic.

It is harsh irony that Princess Di's physical beauty would contribute to her death at an early age. Most attractive people only benefit from the long list of advantages we extend to them. So significant and influential are these advantages that some authors have called them a prejudice.[19] Prejudice is to pre-judge people's unobservable qualities based on too little information, in this case, their looks. Calling it prejudice may be appropriate given the lop-sided favoritism we play with handsome individuals.

This bias begins with perceptions from a distance. Subjects who observe photographs of attractive people perceive them as more sexually warm and responsive, sensitive, strong, and sociable than less attractive people.[20] It also applies to how we think body type links to personality. We tend to perceive skinny people as more suspicious, tense, nervous, pessimistic, and reticent but plump people as more lazy, warm-hearted, sympathetic, good-natured, and dependent. Muscular people get the edge as we assume them to be more strong, adventurous, mature, self-assertive and sexually warm than the other two types.[21]

The beauty bias extends to how we treat and talk with attractive and unattractive people. Consider Table 2.1. It reports how we are more likely to self-disclose to, reward, help, pay attention to, give in to, and date attractive people more than unattractive people. While there's nothing wrong with being beautiful, it seems that our response to beautiful people is putting value on the wrong thing.

Remember when Samuel was searching for King Saul's replacement? He thought he had a winner with tall, good-looking Eliab (or today his name would be Scott or Michael!). But God said no — "Do not consider his appearance or his height...The LORD does not look at the things man looks at. Man looks at the outward appearance, but the LORD looks at the heart" (1 Sam. 16:7). Being tall was nothing against Eliab. What God judged unworthy was the condition of his heart. Eliab lacked the heart of a king for God's people. Later Samuel selected David, a man who was good-looking *and* a person after God's own heart.

Moreover, consider Peter's challenge to women of faith to seek inner beauty. He writes: "Your beauty should not come from outward adornment, such as braided hair and the wearing of gold jewelry and fine clothes. Instead, it should be that of your inner self, the unfading beauty of a gentle and quiet spirit, which is of great worth in God's sight" (1 Peter 3:3-4). Peter was not saying one should not dress stylishly, but that one's charac-

---

1. We are more willing to self-disclose to a physically attractive person.
2. We are more willing to reward physically attractive people monetarily.
3. We are more willing to extend help to physically attractive people.
4. We are more likely to be persuaded by a physically attractive person.
5. If we are an elementary school teacher, we are more likely to interact with good-looking students more often and more positively than unattractive students.
6. We are more likely to date and marry someone we consider physically attractive.

Table 2.1.   How Beauty Affects Communication Behavior[22]

ter should be based on inner qualities. By extension it seems reasonable that we should get to know people through dialogue rather than judge them from their looks.

The tabloid editors who published Princess Diana's picture month after month acted on a cultural assumption that beauty is good. Even the scriptures acknowledge the worth of that which is noble, right, pure, admirable, and *lovely* (see Philippians 8:4-9). But beauty, like life, is here for a season.

SPACE AND TERRITORY

Sid and I stood just out of arm's reach as we chatted on the beach. Doing so communicated attention and respect. *Proxemics* is the study of how we use mobile space around us and *territoriality* is our penchant for calling a patch of immobile space our own and defending it. If either is intruded upon, we usually get antsy. We don't like others butting in too close.

Space indicates status and intimacy in relationships. In my intercultural communication course my students play a game called *Overpower*. Like its name implies, the goal is to get a leg up on players in other groups by amassing more points. Group members are identified either with a blue square, yellow triangle, or green circle pinned to their clothing, and they are required to exchange point cards on the trading floor. At the outset the tone and activity is lively and sincere — blues trade with greens, greens chat with yellows, and yellows approach blues with equal privilege. Then scores are announced and students see where their group lies relative to others. We repeat this play-and-report sequence four times. By round four the wealthiest group hardly comes out of its huddle and members who do fold their arms announcing, "I'm not trading." (Not trading insures that they won't lose money in a trade; their status is secure.) I've seen the two poorer groups continue to intermingle closely as they discuss ways to approach the elite well-to-do's. Later in the debriefing, the "rich" students realize how their use of space shouted rejection to friends with whom they had just enjoyed lunch. The parallel to social and racial class interaction is obvious to everyone.

Space communicates more than degree of affinity and power. It's also a register for where your relationship is with others. Jesus loved to break the spacing rules of Palestine to show his extravagant love for sinners and outcasts. As F. F. Bruce writes, "He accepted sinners, and they were glad to accept him. He was glad to share their meals...He gave the impression, indeed, that he really enjoyed the company of such people — that he preferred it, in fact, to the company of those who had a good opinion of themselves."[23]

The rules he broke resemble the expectations many cultural groups have as expressed by Edward Hall. *Intimate distance* (0-1.5 feet apart) is generally reserved for best friends and lovers, not weeping prostitutes with vials of perfume. *Personal distance* (1.5-4 feet) is accessible to friends and disciples, not low-life tax collectors. *Social distance* (4-12 feet) is where we do our daily work with colleagues and strangers, but usually not outcast beggars and lepers. And *public distance* (12 feet and beyond) is habitually used to wall us from our audience. Jesus spoke from a boat to separate himself from the mass; other times he encouraged children to sit with him. It would be too simple to say that Jesus always welcomed others closer than the norm. We know he went far away to pray undisturbed and returned refreshed to serve.

Touch

Four months after Shelaine and I married we traveled to my sister's home in San Francisco for Christmas. One evening after supper my sister Jane began the task of washing five stacks of dishes in her little kitchen sink. As she did I gave her a shoulder rub, which she appreciated thoroughly.

Later that evening Shelaine asked, "What was *that* all about?

"What was *what* all about?" I answered.

"That shoulder rub for Jane."

"Well...she was working hard for all of our good; I thought she could use some encouragement."

"But I thought you only gave *me* shoulder rubs," Shelaine replied.

I could sense that my wife felt hurt. She thought, with good reason, that back rubs were just between us.

This scenario illustrates how our use of touch is a whole new ball game from our use of space. (Had I just stood close to Jane, I think it would not have been an issue.) Touch is governed by unspoken rules massaged into place by our culture (as in the bumper sticker that reads, "You toucha my car, I breaka your face!") and laid down by our parents and sibs (for example, "No, you can't wrestle with your sister. It's not appropriate."). Who may touch whom, where, when, and for what reasons vary widely, but here are some rules of thumb.[24]

Touch is usually status linked. Bosses, doctors, teachers, and ministers are more likely to touch employees, patients, students, and parishioners than the other way around. Appropriate status-linked has many benefits to the recipient as the next point shows.

Appropriate touch increases health and good will. We know that body massage stimulates vitality in premature babies and boosts the immune function in cancer and HIV patients. Appropriate touch by a counselor encourages clients' self-disclosure, self-acceptance, and a positive client-counselor relationship. A simple touch on the hand by a cashier improves

shoppers' impressions of the store.[25] Jesus often touched those he wanted
to heal or encourage.

Touch can be easily misunderstood in relationships. More specifically,
we guys have a harder time distinguishing between friendly touch and
sexual touch. Authors of a book chapter titled "Friendly? Flirting? Wrong?"
write that "the publication of Antonia Abbey's work (1982) raised the awareness that males generally construe the world in more sexual terms than do
females, and indicated that, as a group, men were much more likely than
females to judge 'friendly' behavior as 'seductive' or 'promiscuous' behavior."[26] These results may help explain why William Kennedy Smith misin-
terpreted "bumping" behavior from a woman in a party atmosphere. It
does not excuse him or any other man for not verbally asking—and believing—what a woman's true intentions are. A verbal check may be costly,
but the payoff is worth it in the long run.

SMELL

Get close enough to others and their odor tells us something or reminds
us of something. A friend of mine in college gave off the same odor as my
grandfather. As we talked, my mind would flit from present Illinois to past
Iowa, from that conversation to images of Grandpa Ammer's soft face and
over-stuffed chair.

A billion-dollar personal hygiene industry indicates that we are not comfortable with our natural breath, body, and clothing odor. There's even
evidence that we need to artificially mask (or perhaps "musk") our work

environment. A Japanese company, Shimizu, engineered a device that releases aromas into a building's air-circulating system. With a mix of peppermint, lemon, eucalyptus, rosemary and pine they can induce alertness. Lavender and clove calm the nerves. Citrus, pine and eucalyptus refresh.[27]

Greek Orthodox believers take seriously the potential of smell to enhance their worship experience. The priest burns incense in an ornately decorated canister as a symbol of God's Spirit. Both odor and Spirit are invisible yet surround and influence the worshippers.

USE OF TIME

Early in my visit to India the director of the orphanage told me that we would be traveling to nearby Amravati the next morning. I asked him when we would leave and he said ten 'o clock. The next day I paced my preparations and was ready to go with lunch bag in hand at 9:55. But there was no car. And no people. I waited for fifteen minutes and then half an hour. Then others began to arrive, one by one. We left the orphanage at 11:15 a.m.

Many of the world's cultures, like India's, hold a *polychronic* view of time—they place people and events ahead of schedules and clocks. You leave when everyone gets there, not when the clock says so. You preach until you're finished with the message God gave you, not until four minutes past noon. Interruptions and delays are the norm, not the exception. Our North American culture holds a *monochronic* view of time. We see time like a segmented film, and we expect people to conform to its frames for the sake of efficiency. We pride ourselves in punctuality and marvel at computer technology that can measure the nanosecond (one billionth of a second).

Jeremy Rifkin describes the shift from polychronic time to monochronic time in western culture in *Time Wars*. As the title suggests, Rifkin is not encouraged by changes brought on by our reverence for harnessing time. One spin-off is impatience. He cites studies showing how computer whizzes suffer especially.

> ...psychologists have observed that computer compulsives are much more intolerant of behavior that is at all ambiguous, digressive, or tangential. In their interaction with spouses, family, and acquaintances, they are often terse, preferring simple yes-no responses. They are impatient with open-ended conversations and are uncomfortable with individuals who are reflective or meditative. Computer compulsives demand brevity and view social discourse in instrumental terms, interacting with others as a means of collecting and exchanging useful information. Above all, they put a high premium on efficient communication.[28]

An email memo I received from one of the computer technicians at my school bears this out. The subject line read: "Computer system down from 1-2 today," and the message read "see subject"!

A lineal view of time does seem to mirror the Christian view that God is working purposefully through history. Taken to its extreme, however, we can easily spiritualize punctuality and exhausting schedules beyond reason. I think this is what is going on in the case of the Florida pastor who asked his deacons to write down the number of hours they thought he should spend with various duties *per week*.[29] The results were:

sermon preparation, 18 hours
administration, 18 hours
visitation to people's homes, 15 hours
prayer, 14 hours
worship, 10 hours
outreach, 10 hours
counseling, 10 hours
community activities, 5 hours
denominational tasks, 5 hours
church meetings, 5 hours
miscellaneous, 4 hours

The total came to 114 hours; there are 168 hours in a week.

ENVIRONMENT

Recently a friend of ours took us to a new condo development in town. The furnished visitors' suite demonstrated some classic environmental research. For starters, the visual effect was most pleasing: warm taupe walls with white trim matched the drapes and woodwork in the vaulted living room and breezy kitchen. A well-worn book laid face down on a padded chair and we saw two pair of fuzzy slippers and a robe in the walk-in closet. Instrumental music played from a distant bedroom. These props were not accidental, of course, but strategic efforts by the realtor to pique our interest.

In a classic study on the ways in which our environment affects our mood, researchers placed subjects in an ugly, an average-looking, or a beautiful room and had them evaluate photographic negatives of faces. People in the ugly room rated the faces more negatively than those in the beautiful room. They also said that the room created a sense of monotony, fatigue, headache, discontent, sleepiness, irritability, and hostility. On the contrary, subjects in the decorated room "reported feelings of pleasure, importance, comfort, enjoyment, energy, and the desire to continue the activity."[30]

Our environment can also affect our performance level. In another study, students who received lectures in a pleasantly decorated room scored significantly higher on exams and rated the teacher's performance more competent than did students in a sterile classroom.[31] Who of us has not entered a room to experience either a gut-level "aaah" or "ugh" depending on its look?

What's the lesson for believers? It is at least to recognize that how we keep our homes and build our churches may not only reflect our values, but nurture them as well. Or as Winston Churchill once put it: "We shape our buildings, thereafter they shape us."

Summary

Nonverbal communication is the process by which we create meaning from nonlinguistic cues others send us. Nonverbal behavior differs from language in important ways, most notably that they are continuous, less controllable, more ambiguous, and packaged in clusters that hit us all at once. We convey much to others about our feelings toward them and our relationships by way of nonverbal cues.

Due to the relational nature of nonverbal communication, I suggested that Christians be gracious interpreters, edifying senders, and genuine expressers of their feelings. Faking emotions can take its toll on us and friends.

People often infer our credibility and how likable we are from our voice alone, so it's worth asking, "How do I sound?" Similarly, the placement and duration of our eye contact can communicate liking, attention, respect, and control. Where do you look? And for how long?

Gestures range from quirky twitches to intentional embraces. We would do well to master the language of the body. How we dress and our God-given looks can bring us blessings and trials, but investing in character qualities rather than cosmetics will return a valuable premium. Our use of dialogue with others will help us get past masks and guard against the beauty bias.

Space often communicates degrees of liking and power as well as the tone of the relationship. It seems that Jesus broke space rules to demonstrate his welcoming of anyone into God's kingdom. Touch is often status linked, but when used fittingly can affirm others in spirit and body. Mistaking friendly touch for sexual touch is a tendency men should guard against.

Smell can draw up deep connections to our past and aid worship in the right context. How we use time will reflect our value on people (polychronism) or schedules (monochronism). A balance between these styles is no doubt achievable. Finally, how we keep our rooms, homes, and churches will ultimately influence our moods and even our performance. Cleanliness and aesthetics nurture a positive spirit.

Worth the Talk

1. What other criteria besides grace, edification, and congruence can you think of that might guide our use of nonverbals?
2. When are you least likely to give eye contact with someone else? Can you determine why? What might you do to improve your use of eye contact with others?
3. As a student you will likely be giving oral presentations. How might you use facial expressions, gestures and vocalics to your advantage? What kinds of faces, body movement, and voice qualities turn you off to other speakers?
4. Do you think it's in our best interest to dress well every day? What do you think of people who are "dressed to the max" daily?
5. Try to think of the instances where the Bible notes that Jesus touched others. Can you surmise a general truth or pattern from his actions?
6. What do you think about using aromas to artificially induce certain moods in office buildings? In churches?
7. What does your arrival time to class communicate to your professor? What does your professor's arrival time communicate to you?
8. Personal bedrooms often depict a person's style and views. What does your room say about you? How does your room influence you or your roommate?

Consider the Walk

1. Do a full analysis of Jesus' nonverbal communication. What do the scriptures say about his clothing and personal artifacts, his body movement and gesturing, his facial expressions and eye behavior, his use of personal space, and his voice characteristics? You will likely have to consult scholars who have pieced together such insights because often the scriptures make little comment. Can you determine any rules of thumb we ought to follow in our nonverbal interaction?
2. Try any of the following nonverbal experiments and observe how people respond to you. Report back to your class if possible.
   A. Sit in the front row of class and give unyielding eye contact to the professor.
   B. Enter an elevator but don't turn around to face the door; face the people.
   C. Put on some cologne you wouldn't normally wear. Extra strong.
   D. The next time you shake hands with a new acquaintance, don't let go for five seconds.
   E. Wear the most uncharacteristic shirt or blouse you can find for a day.

NOTES

1. For example, Dale Leathers offers lists of guidelines for every sort of nonverbal behavior in *Successful nonverbal communication: Principles and applications,* Macmillan Publishing Company, New York, NY, 1986.
2. E. Griffin, *Making friends (& making them count,.* InterVarsity Press, Downers Grove, IL, 1987, pp. 114-115, italics added. See Griffin's entire chapter 6 "Nonverbal communication" for a discussion of nonverbal communication in relationships particularly.
3. Roy M. Berko, Andrew D. Wolvin, Darlyn R. Wolvin, *Communicating: A social and career focus,* 6th ed., Houghton Mifflin Company, Boston, MA, 1995, p. 154.
4. Paul Watzlawick, Janet H. Beavin, and Don D. Jackson, *Pragmatics of human communication,* W. W. Norton & Company, New York, 1967, p. 49.
5. Reported on in Judith A Hall, *Nonverbal sex differences: Accuracy of communication & expressive style,* John Hopkins Press, Baltimore, MD, 1984, p. 24.
6. Albert Mehrabian, *Silent messages: Implicit communication of emotions and attitudes,* 2nd ed., Wadsworth Publishing Company, Belmont, CA, 1981, p. 77.
7. See Eugene Peterson, *The Message: The New Testament in contemporary English,* NavPress, Colorado Springs, CO, 1993, p. 306 & 307. These passages are renditions of Romans 2:13 & 23.
8. Philip Yancey, *The Jesus I never knew,* Zondervan Publishing House, Grand Rapids, MI, 1995, p. 172.
9. See Carl Rogers, "The Interpersonal Relationship: The Core of Guidance," pp. 352-358 in John Stewart, *Bridges, not walls: A book about interpersonal communication,* 4th ed., Random House, New York, 1986.
10. See J. D. Burgoon, D. B. Buller and W. G. Woodall, *Nonverbal communication: The unspoken dialogue,* Harper & Row, New York, 1989, p. 70.
11. These findings reported in Gay Lumsden and Donald Lumsden, *Communicating with credibility and confidence,* Wadsworth Publishing Company, Belmont, CA: 1996, pp. 148-150.
12. Ronald Adler and Neil Towne, *Looking out/Looking in,* (8th ed.), Harcourt Brace College Publishers, Forth Worth, TX, 1996, pp. 249-250 and Lumsden and Lumsden, p. 153.
13. Lumsden and Lumsden, p. 154.
14. Hall, p. 19 & p. 53.
15. Hall, Chapter 3: Explaining Judgment Accuracy.
16. Hall, Chapter 3.
17. Hall, Chapter 3.
18. The East Indian "scoop" gesture for "come here" is common in southern and southeast Asia. I've been told that it's U.S. and Canadian equivalent, the "hook," is appropriate only for calling young children and animals (as if to hook by the nose).
19. Berko, and others, p. 178.
20. E. Dion, E. Berscheid, and E. Walster, "What is Beautiful is Good," *Journal of Personality and Social Psychology,* Vol. 24, 1972, pp. 285-290 as quoted in Dale Leathers, *Successful nonverbal communication: Principles and applications,* Macmillan Publishing Company, New York, NY, 1986, p. 104.

21. See, for example, W. Wells and B. Siegel, "Stereotyped Somatotypes," *Psychological Reports*, Vol. 8, 1961, pp. 77-88, and David Lester, "Ectomorphy and Personality," *Psychological Reports*, Vol. 51, 1982, p. 1182.

22. These findings are reported in L. A. Malandro, L. Barker, and D. A. Barker, *Nonverbal communication* (2nd ed.), Random House, New York, NY, 1986, and in Leathers.

23. F. F. Bruce, *Jesus: Lord & Savior*, InterVarsity Press, Downers Grove, IL, 1986, p. 46.

24. See Leathers, p. 119.

25. See Adler and Towne, pp. 255-257.

26. Lumsden and Lumsden, p. 154

27. Quoted in L. B. Koeppel, Y. Montagne-Miller, D. O'Hair, and M. Cody, "Friendly, Flirting, Wrong?," p. 13 in Pamela J Kalbfleisch (Ed.), *Interpersonal communication: Evolving interpersonal relationships*, Lawrence Erlbaum Associates, Publishers, Hillsdale, NJ, 1993, pp. 13-32 (Chapter 2). The Abbey article is located at A. Abbey, "Sex Differences in Attributions for Friendly Behavior: Do Males Misperceive Female's Friendliness?," *Journal of Personality and Social Psychology*, Vol. 42, 1982, pp. 830-838.

28. See T. Hall, *The New York Times*, November 27, 1991, pp. C1, C6 as reported on in Lumsden and Lumsden, p. 168.

29. Jeremy Rifkin, *Time wars: The primary conflict in human history*, Henry Holt and Company, New York, NY, 1987, p. 17. The Brod quote he cites comes from Craig Brod, *Technostress*, Addison-Wesley, Reading, MA, 1984, p. 94.

30. Reported in *The Mennonite Brethren Herald*, November 24, 1995, p. 26.

31. L. Malandro, and others, p. 156 describe the Maslow and Mintz study which may be found at: A. M. Maslow & N. L. Mintz, "Effects of Esthetic Surroundings: I. Initial Effects of Three Esthetic Conditions Upon Perceiving "Energy" and "Well Being" in Faces," *Journal of Psychology*, Vol. 41, 1956, pp. 247-254. See also N. L. Mintz, "Effects of Esthetic Surroundings: II. Prolonged and Repeated Experience in a "Beautiful" and "Ugly" Room," *Journal of Psychology*, Vol. 41, 1956, pp. 459-466.

32. D. D. Wollin and M. Montagne, "College Classroom Environment: Effects of Sterility Versus Amiability On Student and Teacher Performance," *Environment and Behavior*, Vol. 13 , 1981, pp. 707-716.

PART 2

Talk About Communication Contexts

CHAPTER 3

The Anchored Self
Our Identity and Communication

*For we are God's workmanship, created in Christ
Jesus to do good works, which God prepared in
advance for us to do.*

Ephesians 2:10

Her outward appearance painted a picture of an attractive, communicative college sophomore. Allyssa was slim and pretty and could flash an endearing smile. But down deep loomed a view of herself which was unattractive and which froze her relationally and communicationally. On up days she was confident and talkative and interpersonally savvy. On down days she was confused, withdrawn and interpersonally inept.

Allyssa's roller-coaster emotions were due, in part, to some non-traditional ideas about her standing before God. She felt that God considered her in right standing (that is, justified) only if she had confessed all her known sins. If a recent sin was still not confessed, Allyssa believed she would drop from grace and go to hell if she died that moment. This explained her emotional — and communicational — ups and down. Some days she was confidently sure of her salvation; other days she felt she was on the brink of damnation. Allyssa bounced from feeling justified to feeling condemned, and back, day after day. She was a spiritual and psychological wreck.

As her spiritual mentor, my wife had the joy of describing to Allyssa a more traditional view of salvation. Once we come to Christ and repent the first time, he welcomes us into the safe fold of salvation. Sins we commit thereafter grieve the Lord, but they do not jeopardize our standing before him as recipients of his gracious salvation. Like the traveler in the parable, we don't need to wash our entire body after a walk on a dusty trail. We need only wash our feet.

Upon understanding this view of God and her sure place in him, Allyssa's inward view of herself and her outward demeanor changed dramatically. My wife watched Allyssa develop into a confident woman of God who spoke easily about her faith. A year later Allyssa led her own discipleship group and after graduation took on the role of a missions worker in Asia.

The Self Concept

The idea of self-concept helps us understand Allyssa's communication and thousands like her. *Self concept* is the relatively stable set of impressions I have about myself as a spiritual, social, personal, and physical being. This definition differs from most textbook definitions because it assumes that we see ourselves as more than social, personal, and physical beings; we see ourselves as spiritual too. Even the atheist and agnostic who believe that God does not exist, or are unsure if he exists, may define themselves as "non-spiritual." It's difficult to define ourselves without the continuum of spirituality. In some circles today—Christian and otherwise—it's even fashionable to do so.

Our self concept affects how we talk to ourselves (what we call intrapersonal communication) and our talk with others. How do you see your self? You can get a handle on your self-impressions by doing an exercise with me. Doing so will help you gain self-awareness that goes way beyond just reading about it. Here's how it's done. Take a blank sheet of paper and number it 1-20 on the left-hand side. Now answer the question "Who am I?" Begin each line with "I am . . ." and write down words and short phrases that describe you. Write what comes to mind, and don't worry about what others might think. Only you will see this list. Take five to seven minutes to do this now.[1]

If you're like me, you found it increasingly difficult to think of descriptors near the end of the list. This is because some images and feelings are less defining, more buried. My easy first five answers were father, husband, professor, Christian, and disciplined. I call these my workhorse images because I'm enacting them daily at home and school. My last five responses were positive, energetic, conservative, funny at times, and joker. As a group they look more like Jerry Seinfeld than Bill Strom, but in some respects I see myself like Seinfeld.

The types of descriptors you chose probably fell into two categories: nouns and adjectives.[2] Nouns represent the roles, groups, and positions you call your own. They are how you see yourself in relation to others. One can't be a dad without kids or be a student without a school. Adjectives represent personality traits that describe your character. They are how you see yourself despite your relation to others. Even hermits can be disciplined. Being the father of three young children taxes my time and spirit. Minutes ago my three boys visited me beside the computer on which I type and asked if I could play with them, *now*. While my father role wanted to respond "yes," my "disciplined" trait led me to say "No, but I will play with you at five o'clock when I'm finished with my work." (Just for the record, I did.)

The descriptors you chose also hint at three other dimensions of our self-concept: self-image, self-esteem, and importance level.[3] *Self-images* are the pictures I have of myself whether clear or fuzzy, accurate or inaccurate. *Self-esteem* is my generalized sense of personal worth — whether I like or dislike my self-images. *Importance level* is the weight I attach to any one image and related esteem. For example, I have a clear picture of myself as a rotten golfer, and my scores will prove it. I don't particularly like being a poor golfer, but because I have low value on golf generally, my global sense of self-worth remains buoyant. What you should keep in mind is that while we usually treat self-images as separate frames (such as "student" + "daughter" + "runner") we are more likely to speak of our esteem in general terms. The frames may change, but the mood or music of our esteem plays on. We are more likely to say "Jen has low esteem" than "Jen dislikes the part of her that golfs poorly."

FORMATION OF THE SELF CONCEPT

Christopher Columbus believed that if God made us in his image, then people raised outside the influence of the known world would automatically speak God's language — Hebrew. Columbus therefore brought a Hebrew scholar with him on his trip to the New World as an interpreter. As we know, he was wrong. God may have stamped on us his imprimatur, but he left our cultural and personal identities largely in the hands of our social community. We may even have some genetic tendencies as in body type and temperament, but what we do with these givens and what friends and parents add in our communication environment complete the picture.

Others communicate to us who we are. Every semester the students at my school (and probably yours too) are required to evaluate their courses and professors, and each semester the instructors grin and bear it as they read student comments. What students say can influence a dean's decision to promote a professor, and more than one instructor has hung up the profession based on poor evaluations. "I must not be a good instructor" they lament, "the evaluations tell me so."

Paying attention to what others say about us is called *reflected appraisal*, and it is the key idea in works such as George Herbert Mead's *Mind, Self, and Society*.[4] He defined the self as the picture others mirror back to us. As I interact with you, you tell me who I am in direct and indirect ways. Eventually I begin to believe that what you say about me is true. This is why

Mead dubbed it "the looking-glass self," because I come to know myself through the mirror of you.

The major mirrors we face each day include other people and the media. High school girls and college women in particular suffer stress in the shadows of gorgeous, slim super models who set impossible standards of beauty and sexual appeal. Although media scholars have been unable to prove a direct link between the "thin is in" message and eating disorders in young women,[5] others suggest that it may contribute to anorexia nervosa (self-imposed starvation) and bulimia (binge eating with self-induced vomiting) when combined with achievement messages.[6] Of course we can find healthy messages in magazines and on television if we look hard enough, but most college students still prefer real people as role models. When Harvard sociologist Arthur Levine asked young adults to note who they considered their "heroes," they listed their parents, close friends and relatives three-to-one over musicians, entertainers, and clergy.[7] In a similar study by the Children Defense Fund, "the youths [ages 13-15 years old] said they consider their parents and other adult family members to be the most powerful influence on them—more important than friends, television, and other media."[8]

As believers the question worth considering is whether our heroes reflect God's view of us. I realize that no one has a direct hook-up to God's

"I've always told little Teddy he was a mixed up kid."

mind on every matter, but we can at least test what others say about us by seeing how it squares with scripture. Perhaps it was some well-intentioned but theologically off-base person who told Allyssa that she needed to confess sin daily to be in right standing before God.

We compare ourselves to others. My brother Brad was my yardstick for personal development while growing up. Only fifteen months older than me, he seemed to be five years ahead in athletic prowess, leadership skills, and dating. Even though he genuinely encouraged me in these areas, I still felt about two feet short of his maturity. Fortunately for me, Brad was less able than I was in cracking jokes and carrying a tune. He made a great point guard but a clumsy wrestler. My parents could see the difference and were wise enough to encourage my interest in ventriloquism, choir, band, and wrestling. Later my brother's interests in business were cantilevered by my desire to teach, and today we are diverse in identity but appreciate respect from each other.

Social comparison is this habit of comparing ourselves to others around us—whether brothers or bullies—and judging ourselves accordingly. In our better moments we probably compare ourselves to godly, humble people whom we emulate and wish to imitate. Doing so may lead to short-term low esteem ("Gee, I sure don't serve others as well as she does") but long term maturity ("Thank you, God, for this new opportunity to serve. It makes me feel worthwhile.") In our worse moments it's easy to compare ourselves to down-and-outers and take short-lived pride in our superiority. The question seems to be whether or not those with whom we compare ourselves ultimately build us up in the likeness of Christ.

We watch how we behave and communicate. Another way our self concept develops is through self observation. Perhaps after a heated debate with a friend about some issue you have thought, "I must really feel deeply about this issue. My avid debating here proves so." You may have had a weak sense of your attitude about the issue before your debate, but your behavior affirmed and heightened it. Daryl Bem would say you engaged in *self-attribution*, because you attributed (linked) your behavior to a presumed, driving identity.[9]

This idea reverses conventional wisdom. Most of us think that attitudes and identities precede behaviors. I bike because I like biking. Bem suggests that I like biking because I bike, especially if I believe I choose to bike on my own free will. One summer I attended a conference where the speaker claimed "You only believe that which motivates you to action." He asked us to make a list of where we invested our energies and then asked "What do these things tell you about you?" He encouraged us to make self-attributions for the sake of self-awareness.

We organize all these impressions into a sensible whole. Three of the ten words in the middle of my list of personal descriptors include "proud," "competitive," and "old athlete." On first blush these seem at odds with my concept as believer, husband and conservative. Does our self concept make sense, or is it a mixed bag of conflicting images and esteems? Morris Rosenberg suggests the former. Our self concept is "an *organization* of parts, pieces, and components...that...are hierarchically organized and interrelated in complex ways."[10] Remember how your first five descriptors came easiest? They probably govern how the others fall into line. As a father I don't think of myself as competing with my children, but as a father I teach my children that healthy competition can be fun and rewarding. I see myself as a dad (first) who enjoys competing. An Olympic athlete may see herself as a competitor (first) who enjoys mothering.

As believers we are encouraged to have the mind of Christ which in turn informs other images. For just as Jesus saw himself as son/savior/compassionate/carpenter/rabbi/friend *seeking to do the will of God the father*, so we can see ourselves as students/friends/struggling/proud/athletes *under the Lordship of Christ*. Having the mind of Christ informs my image as athlete, friend, and the like. With this said though, let's not forget the struggle we all experience similar to Paul's. Despite his new identity in Christ he still struggled with sin. "What I want to do I do not do. . . ." and "I have the desire to do what is good, but I cannot carry it out." Our identity in Christ does not change our humanness. We may be justified in God's eyes, but we are still justified sinners.[11]

To summarize, our self concept is molded by what others say to us, by our comparing ourselves to others, by observing our own communication habits or behavior, and by organizing these perceptions. Left at that, these truths smell like a postmodern view of identity formation. Postmodernists believe that we are largely (if not entirely) the product of our social environment. Humans are mere cogs in a social machine.[12] This type of recent thinking has birthed *victimology* (the idea that we are not responsible for evil acts because our environment nurtured our response) and *anti-speciesism* (the idea that we ought not assume that humans are any more superior than animals).[13] Perhaps you've seen the Joop Jean advertisement that shows a fashionably dressed model walking a "flying" baby on a leash. The title: "A Child is the Ultimate Pet." The creators of the ad don't want us to take this message literally, but their values appear loud and clear.

While we can't ignore the fact that our social environment molds our sense of self, we reject the notion that it is the sole definer. Believers begin with a different premise: because God exists and cares deeply for his creation, we find identity and purpose in him, not in Joop Jean ads or the opinions of others. Our identity is not subject to every symbolic wave that crashes against the helm of our person. Rather, our identities are anchored by God's design and we steer through storms with the keel of his Spirit. We are foremost his workmanship (Ephesians 2:10). While God may choose other people and circumstances to nurture our identity, he also seems fit to knit together our identity through several other channels.

The scriptures form and inform our identity.[14] The word of God is not merely ink on onion-skin paper. Like a two-edged sword, it cuts to our conscience with the reminder that every person, from serial killer to missionary child, is made in God's image and deserving of respect. What does it mean to be made in the image of God? Traditional interpretations of this image refer to our original perfection (in the Garden of Eden), our ability to use knowledge, our moral awareness and our immortality.[15] Others have added that we are rational, historical, valuing, social, and symbol-users.Furthermore, God's word is able to judge our thoughts and intentions (Hebrews 4:12) and teach, reprove, correct and train us (2 Timothy 3:16, 17). God's word also renews our minds so we can inwardly decide God's will (Romans 12:2).

Prayer reminds us of what and whose we are. Prayer is a speech act that puts our identity in perspective. Even the physical act of kneeling and bowing one's head reminds us of our creature status before God.

In Matthew 6 Jesus teaches his disciples how (not what) to pray. His method helps us understand whose we are. Calling God holy reminds us that we are his creation, placed on earth to worship and enjoy him forever. Asking that his kingdom come and will be done reminds us of our part as instruments of his redemption on earth. Requesting daily bread and the forgiveness of sins points to our need for physical and spiritual food. Asking for freedom from temptation and Satan reminds us that without God we are the devil's quarry.

Our conscience molds our identity. Finally, God seems fit to use our conscience to mold us morally. Our local newspaper published a story about a man who was accused of wife abuse. He didn't understand why. His father's behavior towards his mother and his friends' treatment of their spouses led him to believe that verbal attacks and slaps to the face were widely accepted in marriage. Long ago his small voice of conscience became callous by ugly models.

In several of his letters the apostle Paul speaks of the conscience which God has given us to defend and accuse our thought life and behavior (see Romans 2:14 & 15, 1 Corinthians 8:9-13, and 1 Timothy 4:2). Unfortunately, sin often tilts our conscience off center. For the abuser it fell to the side of leniency. Abuse seemed okay to him. For others it may lean toward legalism. Consider how some believers interpret Christ's call to be in the world but not of it to mean that they don't speak with unbelievers. Others extend this rule and don't speak with believers who speak with unbelievers! I suggest that their consciences are too sensitive.

A turning point in my own identity formation came on a day when I mentioned to my father that I was contemplating a teaching career. He responded with a broad smile and an energetic comment: "Yes Bill, I think teaching fits you." Neither of us looked up chapter and verse on what I should become, but both of us knew that God would be honored in a life of instructing others. And so goes the interplay of forming and discovering who we are: by paying attention to God's voice, our own observations, and the reflected appraisals of others.

Self Concept's Influence on Communication

Knowing who we are has great benefits. Feeling worthwhile has even more. One author suggests that when we have a clear identity we feel unique in a good way.[16] I get a measure of satisfaction knowing that I may be the only teacher/ventriloquist/old athlete/conservative/joker on this earth.

Another asset of a clear identity is that we know what to expect of ourselves.[17] Should we say yes to the principal who asks us to speak at the high school graduation? Should we agree to lead a small discussion group? A clear sense of self can direct our decision and give us peace at heart. We can also predict fairly well how the speech or small group discussion will go if we know ourselves.

Appropriate esteeming of our identity also has its benefits. In fact, a variety of research projects suggest an impressive yet sobering list of behaviors that show up routinely with low or high esteem. Figure 3.1 summarizes some of these findings.

A fear I have in noting this research is that you fall prey to the belief that self-esteem is a scapegoat for all of life's problems — communication problems included. If you experienced ugly or horrible things as a child, and today your esteem suffers because of it, you might think you have the right to be mad at the world. The issue is whether you will view your level of esteem as an "invaluable key or an irresponsible excuse."[19] It is a key when we use these findings to help us understand who we are and why we act as we do. It is an irresponsible excuse when we believe our esteem is directly wired to our behavior with no allowance for choice. Given this word of caution, let's look at each tendency in turn.

Our self-evaluation leaks out in what we say about ourselves. Remember Jesus' words? "Out of the overflow of the heart the mouth speaks" (Matt. 12:34).

Growing up in the shadow of a competent, respectful brother made me wonder when I would arrive. You would most likely hear me say "No, I can't — at least not as well as Brad" than "Sure, I can." When others picked up on my self-doubt, they played into it whether consciously or uncon-

Persons with High Self-Esteem	Persons with Low Self-Esteem
Are likely to think well of themselves and voice this opinion.	Are likely to think poorly of themselves and express this view.
Are likely to make statements that show an expectation of acceptance by others.	Are likely to make statements that show an expectation of rejection by others.
Are better able to defend their ideas publicly.	Are less able to defend their ideas publicly.
Are less easily persuaded from their original beliefs.	Are more easily persuaded from their original beliefs.
Perform well when being watched (e.g. giving speeches, playing sports); not afraid of others' reactions.	Perform poorly when being watched; sensitive to possible negative reaction.
Talk more freely in groups.	Talk less frequently in groups.
Find it easy to initiate conversations with strangers.	Find it difficult to initiate conversations with strangers.

Figure 3.1.   Esteem and Communication[18]

sciously. Who should be on the church youth executive? Nominate Brad, not Bill. Who should be captain of the cross-country team? Strom, not Little Strom. (Even this nickname, given to me by my brother's friends, made positive self-talk tough to muster!) Maybe the church youth and the cross-country coach were just using the logic that "older is wiser," but it was hard to receive these self-fulfilling messages year after year. It took effort to carve out my image as a wrestler and musician so others could evaluate me on different terms.

Perhaps the wisest thing I ever did was to attend college ten hours from home and eight hours from Brad's college. It was there that I was able to say "Yes, I can," and I did. Oddly enough, it felt like heaven when Brad transferred to my school a year later and people began to ask, "Who's that?"

The answer was sweetness to my ears. "He's Bill Strom's brother — but he's not a ventriloquist or a singer." Speaking more optimistically about myself never came more easily after that.

Liking ourselves usually leads to expressing that we expect to be liked by others; not liking ourselves forecasts rejection from others. We've all made those nervous first phone calls to people we'd like to get to know better. "Hi, Leanne? *You won't remember me*, but I'm in your French 101 class. *I suppose you're too busy*, but I was wondering if you'd like to see the movie at the bijou tonight. I know you do a lot with Erica, so *I won't be surprised if you want to go with her instead.* So, what do you say?" The poor guy doesn't have a chance. His every line begs Leanne to say "no." Using more neutral language is more likely to lead to a "yes." It's probably more true too. "Hi, Leanne? This is Ted from your French 101 class — the guy who said he visited Paris last summer. I don't know how busy you are, but I was wondering if you'd like to see the movie at the bijou tonight. My friend Mike could join us too if you are already planning to go with Erica." I realize that this is a hypothetical example, but I hope the spirit of the idea is worth making. We can work at expressing anticipated approval.

People with poor self-esteem are less able to defend their ideas than people with high esteem. Preparing and delivering a public debate gives people with low esteem the willies. Somewhere along the way they learned to hush up and not ask questions. Somewhere they were instructed to do what they were told without discussing options or asking for reasons. And now they have a tough time thinking critically and defending their ideas. Although ten to fifteen percent of the population may be born shy, it seems that most folks with low esteem have been conditioned to shut up, not speak up.[20] These folks experience a double whammy. Not only do they doubt their perceptions and ideas, they also have fewer strategies to voice them.

Women in verbally abusive relationships are a primary example. George Bach and Ronald Deutsch observe these people's plight.[21] They often feel thrown off balance (by the abuser) and unable to right themselves. They feel lost and in search of direction. They discover they are "mistaken" in their evaluation or grasp of a situation. They feel pushed around and not in control of their lives. They are unable to get off the merry-go-round of redundant thought patterns. Given this list, it's little wonder recipients of verbal abuse feel poorly about themselves and shy from expressing their views. It's also compelling evidence to the role others play in molding our sense of self.

People with low esteem are more easily swayed to new opinions. Perhaps you've seen the *Far Side* cartoon that shows a shadowy door-to-door salesman presenting a book titled *Double Your IQ Or No Money Back* to a would-be customer. The goofy-looking homeowner is scratching his head and remarking "Well, I dunno…OK, sounds good to me." Giving in to peer pressure and sales tactics help low image folks gain acceptance from others. It also makes life easier for them if someone else is calling the shots.

Lest we think that God's ideal is that we become high-esteeming shot-callers, consider the type of believers that made up the first century church. As one author observes, "Paul notes that the early church wasn't peopled with many winners. Few of Christ's followers were wise as the world judges wisdom; not many were powerful, and only a smattering were of noble birth. Most were weak, low and despised (1 Cor 1:26-29)."[22] The reason why God chooses to work through down-and-outers is to convince us of his love and righteousness and to help us guard against our own proud efforts to please him. Giving in to God, even due to a suffering self-esteem, appears to be more favored than playing solo on our own accomplishments.

People who think well of themselves tend to perform better publicly than those who think poorly of themselves. Students on the debate team come to mind again. And the musicians. And the best athletes. These individuals seem to glory in the spotlight, earning acclaim and envy. I recall a movie that illustrates this. In *Hoosiers*, the little basketball team that could, makes it to the finals of the Indiana State Boys Championships only to face a Goliath city squad. The game is a tight one and comes down to the predictable last-second shot. The coach figures he'll fake out the opposing team by calling a play that shovels the ball to a lesser able guard. The huddled players respond anxiously. Then their star, Jimmy, speaks up, "No coach. Give me the ball. I won't miss." The coach agrees, and seconds later, *swoosh*, Jimmy nets the game. People like Jimmy usually think well of themselves.

What's encouraging is that we all get better with practice (as long as we're receiving quality instruction. Poor instruction perfects mistakes!) I can list scores of students who enter my public speaking course with little confidence but who leave with a surer sense of self and their ability. Esteem doesn't drive everything. How we choose to prepare will influence our delivery, and the feedback we receive when we give a sound speech builds our sense of worth. Speaking clubs such as Toastmasters and assertiveness training seminars are based on this optimistic premise.

People with less esteem tend to keep quiet during group discussion; those with more esteem voice their views. Put together these tendencies mean that high esteemers carry the conversation while low esteemers suffer from missed opportunity to speak. My contribution in small groups followed this pattern during my adolescent years. Someone else would offer an opinion or make a suggestion and I would think "Yeah, I agree with that," but not wanting to risk face, I'd wait to see what others said. After one or two others commented, I felt more prepared to state my opinion, but it was too late. The topic would shift and I often found myself saying "Rats, I missed my opportunity." Other times a joke was made and group members would laugh, but it seemed someone else got a witty retort in before I did. Any contribution after the first retort fell flat. My self-doubt made me hesitant, and my hesitance jeopardized the timeliness of my contribution. The job of a group leader is to draw out the quiet individual. "We know what Elaine and Chris think. What have you got to say, Bill?" Such an invitation usually got me talking.

Of course exceptions abound. You probably know of someone who thinks little of him- or herself but who chatters away even still. Their constant comment probably signals a need for acceptance. As long as they have the floor, they may reason, we at least owe them attention.

One's level of esteem affects his or her willingness to interact with strangers. Speaking with someone we don't know induces more stress than chatting with a friend, but folks with a low self-image find novel interactions particularly stressful. What's at stake is their bank account called "face." Low esteem people work very hard to gather strokes and rewards to fill that account so they may present a positive public image. Interactions with strangers potentially debit that account. They might think, What if I say something stupid? or What if she doesn't like me?

At the start of each semester in my cross-cultural communication course we play "The Name Game." After forming a circle with our chairs, I ask everyone to write a note that asks a stranger to lunch. This alone puts many on edge. After sending and reading these notes, we proceed to announce our names in turn. Before someone introduces him- or herself, however, he or she must introduce everyone else who has spoken so far. The student next to the leader has it easy. "As you heard, this is Karbinder and I'm Anne." Six introductions later someone has to recall eight names. "This is Karbinder, Anne, Ted, Elaine, Soo-Young, Jen, Kwon, and I'm Mike." Sometimes the course attracts over thirty students. You can imagine the anxiety of students 33 and 34! We play the game to prove a point: interaction with strangers produces anxiety and uncertainty,[23] especially when one's concerned about face.

But there's more to the game. After the introductions, I ask students to write a second note to the same person, asking him or her to lunch again. During the debriefing we discuss how they felt while writing the second note. "Much more relaxed," many say. "Like we were all in this together." "Like I knew her a little." "Not so hokey." These comments underscore the second point of the game: initial interaction with strangers, even if forced and stressful, increases the ease with which we interact again. Choosing against the grain of low esteem can get a relationship started.

As I said earlier, I fear that some readers may take their bruised esteem as reason to lash out at others. I hope that's not the case. Rather, my desire is that you understand how certain communication behaviors tend to accompany a wounded esteem, and then I hope to encourage you to choose against the grain. That's a theme that runs throughout this book—that we have choice in how we respond to others and how we talk to ourselves.

So How Should We Talk to Ourselves?[24]

This is an important question. For Allyssa the answer was to berate herself for every little mistake and convince herself that she, like Paul, was chief among sinners. Theologians call this worm theology and a good number of Christians subscribe to it. They point out that Adam and Eve's *pride of self* (not their hate or lust or envy) brought sin into the world, and that pride continues to be a root of much sin. Therefore, they reason, any kind of self-pride is wrong. They also note that when people come to grips with God's holiness and grace they should respond like Jacob who resolved, "I am but dust and ashes" (Genesis 40:4).

At the other end of the continuum are believers who contend that Christians are perhaps the only group of people who have reason for a clear self-image and high self-esteem. They reason that through Christ we have taken off the old self and put on the new self—a self that is Christ centered, but still our own identity (Ephesians 4:24). Also through Christ we are freed from the incapacitating effects of guilt—we are new creatures in him. Believers who subscribe to this good-news view suggest that thinking and speaking positively about ourselves signals hallmark Christianity.

Somewhere in between are believers who suggest that both are true. "If we claim to be without sin, we deceive ourselves and the truth is not in us" (1 John 1:8) is tough to ignore. We *are* sinners. However, that God called us *very good* when he created us (see Genesis 1:31), made us right before him through Christ's death, and empowered us by his Spirit to do good works, are bases for a sense of worth. The key seems to be balance. I love the way Paul says it in Romans 12:3. "I say to every one of you: Do not think of yourself more highly than you ought, but rather think of yourself with sober judgment, in accordance with the measure of faith God has given you." A sober analysis helps us appreciate our made-in-God's-image likeness, skills and gifts without getting pigheaded.

This makes good theology but how does it translate into self-talk? While these suggestions are not meant to be a sure-fire, money-back guarantee for increasing your sense of self-worth, they are intended to help you guard against unfounded negative self-talk.

Guard against the fallacy of perfection.[25] If you give in to this myth it will be too easy to berate yourself for not giving a "perfect" speech or not saying the "perfect" thing to a friend. We should strive for our best but not tongue-lash ourselves for falling short. We're all human, and that means we're limited in our knowledge and still working out our salvation.

Don't think you have to please everyone.[26] An old wag once said, "You can please some of the people all of the time, and please all of the people some of the time, but you can't please everyone all of the time." There's wisdom here. While it's desirable to say what is appropriate and effective, we can't anticipate every response others may make toward us. Honest mistakes happen, and when they do we need to cut ourselves some slack.

Avoid overgeneralizing your faults.[27] Have you ever caught yourself saying "I *always* do that!" or "I *never* say the right thing!"? Are these statements true? Probably not. What happens is that we remember our flubs more than our successes because the flubs draw more attention. If you consider all the evidence though, you can probably say with proper humility "I messed up this time, but that's not characteristic of me." Of course we don't want to be blind to ongoing patterns that need work; we just don't need more work than such patterns warrant.

Then it happened. After seven years of first-place orations, it all ended when Irene uttered her first "um."

Play to your strengths. After Paul instructed believers to view themselves soberly, he goes on to explain how God's people differ in giftedness. Some are gifted to serve; *let them serve*, he says. Others are wired to encourage; *let them encourage*, he writes. It's as if he's saying "don't try to be what you aren't, rather glory in what you are, for God has made you that way" (see Romans 12:6-8). I can thank God for his gifts to me—that I am an old athlete/teacher/joke teller—and not compare myself to others who are gifted differently. I'm free to be me.

Make humility your goal. This may sound like a call to sackcloth and ashes, but hear me out. Being consumed with our self-concept and making a mantra out of the phrase "be humble" is self-defeating. The more consumed you are with your self-esteem, the lower it will go.[28] True humility kicks in when we stop looking inwardly and start looking outwardly. True humility frees us from self-absorption so we can see the needs of others. As one author put it, "True humility is neither thinking too much of oneself or two little of oneself; it is not thinking of oneself at all."[29] This is the spirit of Paul's writing when he says, "Do nothing out of selfish ambition or vain conceit, but in humility consider others better than yourselves. Each of you should look not only to your own interests, but also to the interests of others" (Philippians 2:3-4). Humble self-talk says, "How can I help? How can I encourage? How can I show hospitality? How can I love?" Just when we're feeling the dumpiest about ourselves is when looking to others returns a truckload of blessing.

Recognize that your self is in community with others. For decades our culture has promoted an opposing view—we are *individuals* much like the rugged Marlboro man and you've-come-a-long-way-baby Virginia Slims woman. But the philosophic tide is now turning to what has been a biblical model all along: we are social creatures who shape and nurture each other from infancy to old age. No one flies solo, nor is flying solo possible or desirable. We need others.

The next two chapters are built on the idea of self-in-community. Chapter 4 addresses interpersonal communication and Chapter 5 looks at family communication. Both underscore the theme that our talk and walk with others does more than convey meaning. They define us and our relationships as well.

Summary

Who we become is not a willy-nilly affair. God has impressed upon us his divine image and with that status comes the responsibility that we build up others into his likeness. This is not to ignore the fact that we define and discover ourselves through other means as well. Other people impress on us who they think we are (or should be), sometimes with soiled images and roles. We can also get wrapped up in comparing ourselves with others for good or for bad, depending on who that standard is and how we respond to measuring up or not. We can also figure out who we are by being a student of our own communication. We figure out how we tick by how we speak and act toward others. We make sense of all these impressions by organizing them and treating some more dominant than others. It's also helpful to recognize that our self-images (the pictures we have of ourselves) are not the same as our self-esteem (the degree of self-worth we attach to those images). How important an image or feeling is will often govern our global esteem.

Left at this it would seem that the formation of our self is an entirely human affair. Believers assume that God's program anchors our image in his larger design and that we clue in to that truth from scripture, prayer, and our conscience. Realizing that we are God's workmanship helps us weather the cultural and social storms that attempt to define us otherwise.

Our level of self-esteem can have a significant effect on our self-talk and communication with others. We observed how people with low esteem are likely to verbally express this view, often expect rejection from others, struggle to defend their ideas in public, often give in to persuasive ploys, do not perform as well when being watched, speak less frequently in groups, and find it tough to initiate conversations with strangers. While these are not moral deficiencies, most people desire to improve in these areas for the sake of personal development and communicative competence.

We concluded by suggesting that we not think too much of ourselves but not too little either. We need to practice healthy self-talk and look outwardly to others rather than always inwardly. True humility frees us to meet other people's needs.

Worth the Talk

1. What sources of influence do you think have shaped your self-concept? What sources influenced you when you were young? What sources influence you today?

2. Why do you think self-esteem has become a prevalent concern in today's society? Some thinkers attribute it to the rise of humanistic psychology in universities and counseling practices. Others say it is due to technology (such as telephones, computers, and television) that depersonalize our environment. Are these explanations sufficient or are there other reasons too?

3. What do you think of the comment that "True humility is neither thinking too much of oneself, nor too little of oneself; it is not thinking of

oneself at all"? Do you agree with the idea that our goal should not be to strive for high esteem but rather preoccupation with serving others?

Consider the Walk

1. Doing a full self concept analysis can lead to self awareness. You may have done the twenty statements exercise at the outset of this chapter. Here is a more full version to complement that exercise.
   a. What twenty words or phrases best define who I am? Start each answer with the phrase "I am..."
   b. What types of descriptors are these? You may use one of several category schemes to do so: the nouns/adjectives ideas discussed in this chapter, the images/esteem/importance level discussed as well, or the terms used in the definition of "self-concept," namely, the impressions we have of ourselves as spiritual, social, personal, and physical creatures. These categories are defined as:
      Spiritual: terms that indicate your religious beliefs and type of relationship with God.
      Social: terms that describe any relationship you have with other people as in roles ("student"), friendship ("girlfriend"), etc.
      Personal: terms that describe personality traits, likes and dislikes, etc. (e.g., "fun-loving," "studious," "athletic")
      Physical: terms that describe your height, weight, color, looks, etc.
   c. Evaluate each term. Do you like this picture of yourself? Are there other pictures you have of your self that you like or dislike which are not in the list of twenty?
   d. Name the top five people or experiences that have had the most impact on your self-concept.
   e. Analyze whether this view of your self is aligned with the Christian views of self described in this chapter.
2. Do a self concept and communication analysis. Re-read the list of researched findings in Figure 3.1. Note which ones seem to be true of your behavior. Discuss whether esteem seems to be causing this behavior or is a result of this behavior. Also discuss how you think you might choose to communicate or behave in ways which are not consistent with these general patterns.

NOTES

1. I got the idea of including this exercise from Em Griffin in his book *Making friends (And making them count)*, InterVarsity Press, Downers Grove, IL, 1987, p. 28. Many standard textbooks suggest a similar exercise.
2. Griffin, p. 28.

3. The self-image and self-esteem distinction is a common one made in communication textbooks. For example, see Rudolph Verderber's *Communicate!* (8th ed.), Wadsworth Publishing Company, Belmont, CA, 1996, pp. 34-39. The idea of importance level is my contribution.

4. George Herbert Mead, *Mind, self, and society*, University of Chicago, Chicago, IL, 1934.

5. See Jane D. Brown and Kim Walsh –Childers, "Effects of Media on Personal and Public Health," in Jennings Bryant and Dolf Zillmann, *Media effects: Advances in theory and research*, Lawrence Erlbaum Associates, Publishers, Hillsdale, NJ, 1994, pp. 389-415, especially page 397.

6. See P. E. Garfinkel and D. M. Garner, *Anorexia nervosa: A multidimensional perspective*, Burner/Mazel, New York, NY, 1982, p. 10

7. A. Levine, in an article published in *Change*, September/October 1993, p. 14.

8. *The state of America's children yearbook 1994*, Children's Defense Fund, Washington, D.C., 1994, p. 56 as quoted by Steffen T. Kraehmer, *Heroes: Shaping lives through family and culture*, Fairview Press, Minneapolis, MN, 1995, p. 16.

9. See D. Bem, "Self-Perception Theory," in *Advances in Experimental Social Psychology*, Vol. 10, Leonard Berkowitz (ed.), Academic Press, New York, NY, 1977, pp. 173-220.

10. Morris Rosenberg, *Conceiving the self*, Basic Books, New York, NY, 1979. p. 73.

11. This was a central tenet of the Protestant Reformation and the teaching of Martin Luther, namely, that we are simultaneously justified and sinful, this side of heaven. See Michael Horton, *Putting amazing back into grace: Who does what in salvation?* Baker Books, Grand Rapids, MI, 1994, Chapter 9 (pp. 165-204).

12. For a critique of the postmodern view of self from a Christian perspective see Dennis McCallum (ed.), *The death of truth*, Bethany House Publishers, Minneapolis, MN, 1996.

13. For another critique of the postmodern view of self, including anti-speciesism, see Gene Edward Veith, Jr., *Postmodern times: A Christian guide to contemporary thought and culture*, Crossway Books, Wheaton, IL, 1994.

14. This and the following two observations are made by Grant Howard in *The trauma of transparency*, Multnomah Press, Portland, OR, 1979.

15. This list comes from Bruce Milne's *Know the truth*, InterVarsity Press, Downers Grove, IL, 1983, p. 96.

16. Griffin, p. 31.

17. Griffin, p. 32.

18. Item 1 is reported on in Verderber's *Communicate!*, p. 38 where he cites J. D. Campbell, "Self-Esteem and Clarity of the Self Concept," *Journal of Personality and Social Psychology*, Vol. 59, 1990, p. 538. Items 2, 3, and 5 are reported in D. E. Hamachek, *Encounters with others: Interpersonal relationships and you*, Holt, Rinehart and Winston, New York, NY, 1982, pp. 3-5. Items 4 and 6 are reported on in Griffin's *Making Friends*, pp. 41 and 43 where he cites D. Hayes and L Meltzer, "Interpersonal Judgments Based on Talkativeness," *Sociometry*, Vol. 35, 1972, pp. 538-61and G. Lesser and R. Ableson, "Correlates of Persuasibility In Children," *Personality and Persuasibility*, ed. C. Hovland and I Janis, Yale University Press, New Haven, CT, 1959, pp. 187-206. Item 7 is reported on in M. Rosenberg, *Conceiving the Self*.

19. Harold Faw, "Self-Esteem: Invaluable Key or Irresponsible Excuse?" Unpublished paper. Summer 1994, Trinity Western University, Langley, British Columbia, Canada.

20. See "Extreme Shyness Linked to Biology, Researchers Say," *Cleveland Plain Dealer*, June 28, 1987, p. A-15, reporting the work of psychologists Jerome Kagon, Robert Pomin, David Rowe, and Stephen Suomi, as cited in Roy Berko, Andrew Wolvin, and Darlyn Wolvin, *Communicating* (6th ed.), Houghton Mifflin Company, Boston, MA, 1995, p. 65.

21. See George R. Bach and Ronald M. Deutsch, *Stop! You're driving me crazy*, Putnam Publishing Group, New York, NY, 1980, pp. 272-273. I was directed to their work by Patricia Evans in, *The verbally abusive relationship: How to recognize it and how to respond* (2nd ed.), Adams Media Corporation, Holbrook, MA, 1996, p. 25-26.

22. Griffin, p. 43.

23. William Gudykunst builds an intercultural communication theory around these two concepts. See W. B. Gudykunst, "Toward a Theory of Effective Interpersonal and Intergroup Communication: An Anxiety/Uncertainty Management (AUM) Perspective," in *Intercultural communication competence*, R. L. Wiseman and J. Koester (eds.), Sage Publications, Newbury Park, CA, 1993, pp. 33-71.

24. This section is based on Wayne Joosse's booklet, *The Christians' self-image: Issues and implications, Occasional papers from Calvin College*, Second Printing, 1990.

25. See Ronald Adler and Neil Towne, *Looking out/Looking in*, (8th ed.), Harcourt Brace College Publishers, Fort Worth, TX, 1996, p. 152.

26. Adler and Towne, p. 154.

27. Adler and Towne, p. 156.

28. S. Duvall and R. Wicklund, *A theory of objective self-awareness*, Academic Press, New York, NY, 1972, p. 4, as cited in Griffin, *Making friends*, p. 52.

29. David Clark, "Philosophical Reflections on Self-worth and Self-love," *Journal of Psychology and Theology*, Vol. 13, 1985, pp. 3-11.

CHAPTER 4

Redeeming Our Dialogue
Looking at Interpersonal Communication

*By speaking the truth in a spirit of love, we must
grow up in every way to Christ, who is the head.*
                                        Eph. 4:15

Several years ago my wife surprised me with a question out of the blue.
"Guess who's having an affair?"

I shrugged my shoulders, and asked, "Who?"

"Robert—and it's been going on for over four years, but it didn't get
sexual until two years ago. Vicky has only known about it for a year."

This was the first case of infidelity close to home for me and my wife.
We had known Robert and Vicky for nearly ten years. They were raised as
"good Christians," made personal commitments to God early in their lives,
attended Bible college, faithfully attended church, supported missionaries,
served on committees and taught Bible studies.

But after 33 years of marriage, Robert felt controlled by his wife and
reported to have no feelings for her. After knowledge of the affair became
public, they saw a counselor for a short time, but it became evident that
Robert did not intend to break off his adulterous relationship. His tears
were not over the loss of their relationship, but having to choose between
his wife and his mistress. What went wrong?

Without doubt, Robert and Vicky suffered from numerous strains in their
relationship—debate about money, fatigue from a double-income lifestyle,
the challenge of three children, and negotiation for affection. However one
strain which seemed most telling was their basic way of interacting. When
problems arose, Vicky was likely to discuss them avidly, suggest solutions,
and make moves to solve them. Robert usually went along with her analysis but rarely voiced his own needs or perspective. Unknown to Vicky,
Robert quietly shoved his resentments toward her assertiveness down deep.
During one counseling session, Robert explained how Vicky had barged in

on a business deal he was cutting with a salesperson that resulted in him losing the deal. Thirty-one years later she was now hearing about it for the first time.

While we should be careful of making communication *the* defining variable of relationships, we know that it plays a *central role* in constructing them; (this seemed true for Robert and Vicky). The tough part is visualizing how communication and relationships merge. For starters, let's begin with three pictures of interpersonal communication. They should help us grasp the mystery of between-person communion whether among married couples, friends, or workplace comrades.

What Is Interpersonal Communication?

In *Making Friends (& Making Them Count)*, Em Griffin depicts in visual metaphor three common models of human communication.[1] Some people picture communication like bowling, others like Ping-Pong, and still others like charades.

What happens when we bowl imitates what some scholars call the *linear model* of communication.[2] Success is dependent on the bowler/sender's efforts to select the right ball/message and cruise it down the alley/channel so that it strikes/affects passive pins/receivers with predictability. The wrong ball/message results in a gutter ball or split/misunderstanding, but the right ball/message scores a strike/understanding. "Understanding" is cast as knocking preferred meaning into pins/receivers who don't or can't respond uniquely with feedback. Perhaps some of the lectures that Vicky sent Robert were intended to bowl him over. In this respect, the sender-message-channel-receiver-effect model may depict how some people relate. Down deep though we hope for more redemptive communication and a more complete model.

Unlike bowling, Ping-Pong requires two people to play—a better model already. Ping-Pong seems to typify what scholars call the *interactive model* of human communication.[3] In Ping-Pong someone serves/sends and someone returns/responds, and then they reverse roles. A skilled server can put the ball/message where she wants and a seasoned opponent/responder knows how to handle what's coming. The more each player knows the other's history, the more readily he or she can predict and respond to the immediate shot. The plusses of this model are that it begins with two people, acknowledges our use of feedback, and recognizes our history with our partner. Its minuses include the assumption that our human environment is predictable, and that there's only one message/ball in play at a time. It also assumes that communication is chiefly a power game rather than a cooperative dialogue. This model typifies some people's pattern of interaction, but falls short for others.

Enter the idea that communication is like charades, or what some scholars call the *transactional model* of communication.[4] As Griffin puts it, "A
charade is neither an action, like a strike in bowling, nor an interaction, like
a point in Ping-Pong. It's a transaction."[5]

People playing charades might be competing against another team, but
as a unit they're working together to share the same meaning or image.
They are also actively reading each other for every clue to solve the puzzle.
The actor thinks hard about his partner's experience and their shared experience. He might use symbols or sounds unique to their relationship that
strike a responsive chord. All the while he uses every channel imaginable,
from facial expressions to gestures, and tries to hide frustration. Together
the partners hammer out enough words of the clue until its denotation
(explicit meaning) clicks and the friend shouts, "Oh I know what you mean,
'Two Heads Are Better Than One.'" If they happen to share the same connotative meaning (personal evaluation) of the "Two Heads..." adage, their
common experience overlaps even more. In playing the game they've done
more than just conjured up the same quotation; they are more linked in
spirit than before the game began. That linkage, while usually positive, can
be damaging though if the game was played in an unredemptive style.

Each model attempts to capture how interpersonal communication *is*,
but we are tempted to say that the charades model is *how interpersonal communication ought to be*. We should be careful though. Can you imagine a
sergeant using a mutual-regard model in the heat of battle when what the

private wants is a top-down, bowl-over command? Or consider a bank teller attempting to bond with every client at the mutual-regard level rather than relying on role expectations. Every model captures some of the truth of how certain people interact, but I'd like to assume that we're attempting to relate in a transactional manner with our closest friends. Let's look at two definitions of interpersonal communication in the transactional vein.

In *Interpersonal Communication: Pragmatics of Human Relationships,* Aubrey Fisher and Katherine Adams write, "interpersonal communication is the process of creating social relationships between at least two people by acting in concert with one another."[6] Sounds a lot like charades. Along the same lines, in *Bridges, Not Walls,* John Stewart writes "For me interpersonal communication is the type or quality or kind of contact that occurs when each person involved talks and listens in ways that highlights the individual's and the other person's humanness."[7] Note his emphasis on quality, not structure. A structural definition would outline interpersonal communication as face-to-face talk between two or three people. But it's more than a Ping-Pong word exchange—or it should be. Let's look more deeply at these definitions to understand why. We'll start with John Stewart's.

INTERPERSONAL COMMUNICATION HIGHLIGHTS OTHER PEOPLE'S HUMANNESS, NOT THEIR OBJECTNESS

If you feel quirky when leaving a message on a telephone answering machine, then you can relate to his first distinctive of interpersonal communication. An answering machine is an object, not a person. It might "talk," but it's not human. Stewart defines "human" by contrasting it with "object," based on the work of Jewish philosopher Martin Buber.[8] What distinguishes humans from objects? Stewart interprets Buber as standing for these distinctives:

Humans are	Objects are
1. Unique	1. Standardized
2. Unmeasurable	2. Measurable
3. Choice-makers	3. Not choice-makers
4. Addressable	4. Non-addressable

People are unique, not standardized. We talked about our uniqueness in the self-concept chapter. That I'm a father/professor/believer/old athlete/joke teller means I'm probably a one-of-a-kind. Objects aren't so blessed; they're standardized with component parts. When we talk to people without consideration for their unique make-up, we treat them as objects.

Computerized calling services treat us like objects. The other day I picked up the phone to hear "Hello. Please hold to hear an important pre-recorded message. The product you ordered from _____ has arrived. You may pick up your package between the hours of...." This technology is in place for the sake of efficiency, but it made me feel like bowling pin #32851 rather than the guy who ordered the medium taupe sport shirt.

People are unmeasurable, not measurable. Social scientists have made valiant attempts to measure people, but in the final tally their questionnaires and experiments fall short, at least in the eyes of Stewart and Buber. Stewart writes "'Pulse 110, respiration 72, Likert rating 5.39, palmar conductivity .036 ohms' might be accurate, but it doesn't quite capture all what's going on in me when I greet somebody I love."[9] Some people call the unmeasurable part of being human the "psyche" or "personality." Christians call it the "soul" or "spirit." Whatever the label, this feature of being human makes us unpredictable in a good way. No one can define and measure all the variables in my spirit accurately enough to predict how I'll choose to act.

People are choice-makers. We've already noted that to be made in God's image is to have a will to choose (see Chapter 3). When Vicky messed up Robert's business deal, Robert had many options for response. He could have noted his concern assertively and lovingly, hinted indirectly, sulked, blown up or remained silent. He chose the latter. Objects, in contrast, have no choice. Calling services follow a computer program to dial up sport shirt buyers, and our own answering machines click in on the fourth ring (or wherever we've set them). When our talk with others assumes that they have no options, we objectify them. "May I come by on Tuesday or Thursday to show you those knives, Mr. Peterson?" sounds like he's got a choice. But it's a loaded question. What if Mr. Peterson doesn't *want* the salesperson to drop by at all?

People are addressable. By saying humans are addressable and objects are not, we mean that one can speak *with* a person, but only *at* an object. This is what Stewart and Buber say distinguishes humans from animals. By speaking *with* someone, we engage in communication of similar kind and mutuality; we engage their personhood, and they engage ours. Animals, and especially pets, seem to take on this "almost human" addressable quality. But no matter how tender a response from my dog Brindle, her actions are not of human kind nor mutual. Animals remain objects.

Just because people are addressable though doesn't mean we engage this quality with every word. A critical moment in the film *The Fugitive* illustrates this point. Bad guy Dr. Nichols is giving a speech to members of the medical community regarding his new miracle drug. From the audience's nodding heads and respectful silence you can tell that Nichols is connecting well with them. Then good guy Dr. Kimble (played by Harrison Ford) enters the back of the banquet room. Kimble knows that Nichols jimmied his research for the new drug, and Nichols knows that he knows it. When Nichols' eyes meet Kimbles' he loses concentration and looks down at his manuscript. Any connectedness he enjoyed with his admiring audience evaporates as he no longer addresses them but mumbles at them. Eventually he quits trying altogether. Most of us have mumbled at audience members due to other sources of stress, but the effect is the same. We lose them.

INTERPERSONAL COMMUNICATION IS ABOUT CONTACT AND RELATIONSHIP BETWEEN HUMANS

Stewart, Fisher and Adams would all agree that when we stop communicating we stop relating. Again, Stewart writes, "For me interpersonal communication is the type or quality or kind of *contact*..."[10] He could have said *relationship*. Fisher and Adams write, "A relationship is not a 'thing.' When you are not interacting, the...relationship...[is] not occurring."[11]

To illustrate this point, think back about someone you considered a friend in elementary school but not since then. For me that person would be John Werner. John and I played dodge ball together, ate in the cafeteria, and stayed over at each other's homes. We talked a lot. We had a relationship. Today I have no idea where John lives. All I recall is a newspaper announcement of his engagement that showed him balding and stating he was an accountant. Any relationship we once had is but a memory.

This is the rock-bottom truth that the transactional model (charades metaphor) offers us. Interpersonal communication is not about the mechanical conveying of words; it is about creating, enacting, and becoming in relationship. I used to teach this model for years to my students with little further reflection. As a believer I appreciated its implied call to treat people humanely and invest in community. More recently I have begun to think that "heightening each others humanness" makes good advice as a process but not as an end. What I mean is that how we relate with others should affirm the qualities Stewart outlines, but our goal in relating should be something different. Paul's words to the church at Ephesus comments on process and end. He wrote, "Instead, speaking the truth in love [the process], we will in all things grow up into him [the goal] who is the Head, that is, Christ" (Ephesians 4:15). To me this speaks of redeeming the communication process and the person, the relationship and the relaters. I want to acknowledge your fallenness in how I speak with you, but I don't want to enhance your vice. I want you to be redeemed to every corner of your person.

Redemptive Interpersonal Communication

In our postmodern culture it isn't cool to impose your ideas on others, much less think that your ideas hold for everyone everywhere. Postmodernists call for a hands-off model of relating. "Live, and let live," is their motto. They prefer that we affirm how people are, and not pretend that there's a better way to be. No one has the right to say that one cultural identity or personal identity or type of relationship is more accurate or desirable than another. Truth is what we make it because we are products of our environment. (Recall Chapter 3 on self-concept.)

Even still, most postmodern thinkers will admit that evil is less desirable than virtue, even if these ideals are "constructed" by our society. We would all prefer a world where a counselor can talk a serial killer into a new identity so he doesn't kill again. Where we may differ is whether his conversion requires God or just good psychiatric care. In either case he's a new man — a redeemed man in terms of his identity and behavior.

So there is a basis for wanting others to change, to be redeemed for the better. In biblical terms redemption means deliverance and freedom from sin. If you believe that sin affects the whole person, you can see how redemption in turn makes the whole person new. And this, I suggest, is the believer's purpose of interpersonal communication — to inch people closer to the new life, whether in spiritual conversion or human relationships. It's a both/and proposition.

One author to change my mind on these issues was Charles Kraft. His research into why and how God communicates with us provides a model for humans too. He writes,

> The Scriptures provide us with communicational models to imitate. We see there a God who refuses to stay on the other side of an enormous communication gap. He seeks a relationship with us that will elicit from us a commitment to himself and his cause. To bring this about he develops a strategy to assure that he will be understood on our side of the gap. In this strategy he is receptor-oriented, entering our frame of reference in a trusting, dependent, even vulnerable manner to show his love, acceptance, and respect toward us in a way that we cannot misunderstand. God is personal and identifies with us by incarnating himself and himself becoming the message he sends. Furthermore, God assures that his messages come with impact. He develops high credibility, deals specifically with his receptors and the issues that concern them, leads his receptors to discovery, and trusts them to carry on the cause.[12]

It seems that God's way and a transactional way of communicating share much in common. God values relationship. His strategy is receiver-centered. He respects us, trusts us, and loves us. He identifies with us through incarnation (coming in the flesh), and he deals with us uniquely, one by one.

Where the models differ is in purpose. God bridges the gap so he might "elicit from us a commitment to himself and his cause." God communicates redemptively in order that we might grow up in Christ and help others do so as well.

This book, however, is about communication, not spiritual growth. So let us consider our primary question: What does redemptive communication look like for people such as Robert and Vicky? You and me? I think the answer extends to four areas, namely, how we 1) perceive others, 2) speak with others, 3) deal with conflict, and 4) listen to each other.

GRACIOUS PERCEIVING OF OTHERS

In Chapter 3 I suggested that you do the twenty statements exercise for self-perception. What if your best friend wrote down twenty statements that describe you? Would his or her list match yours? Probably not. What you wrote down about you is what scholars call your *private self*, but what others see on the outside is what they call the *public self*.[13] We've all done a little acting around others, and this is the stuff on which they base their impressions of us. There's also the tendency for us to process this information in less than rational ways. It may be of no surprise therefore to learn that "Researchers have found no correlation between confidence in our perceptions of others and the accuracy of those perceptions."[14] Robert and Vicky may have thought they knew each other as they dated, but if either was putting on a front, those impressions were but sand castles.

Research indicates that we can improve our accuracy in perceiving others by being more realistic about ourselves, by not seeing things in black and white, and by becoming better at inferring traits from behaviors.[15] If we're unsure about our own self-concept, we best not make outlandish claims about our friends. Chances are, we'll be off target. Also, if we've grown up in a strict, authoritarian home, we're prone to think that we can peg our friends into sharply cut wholes—she's proud, he's a jerk, she's totally neat, and he's a complete catch. But as we noted in the last chapter, we are more complex than that, and so are others. Making better inferences from behaviors may take some practice. The key is remembering that the same behavior can indicate a variety of causes. Our best friend may be having a conversation with the person we just dated last night for completely innocent reasons.

Christ's call to take the log out of our own eye before we complain about the sawdust speck in someone else's (see Matthew 7:3) is more a caution not to judge than a rule for how to perceive others, but there's a principle that still holds. It is this: Acknowledging that we are complex and not perfect will help us exercise empathy and extend grace when trying to understand others. To use Kraft's terminology, we will probably be more receptor-oriented and able to enter their frame of reference if we recognize that we often don't make sense either. Unfortunately, we fail miserably at empathizing with others and understanding them as they do. Research testifies to a long list of perceptual biases. Be aware of these.

Our first impressions of others go deep and die hard.[16] This is called the *primacy effect*, because we tend to weigh early information about others more heavily than later information. A short-term memory exercise I do with my students hints at why this might be true. I ask my students to listen as I read off a list of ten words. After the tenth one I pause and then say "go." Their task is to write down as many words as they can recall in the right order. Without fail, the most remembered word is the first one (usually 95% get it right), then the second word (about 90%) and then the last word (about 85% score a ringer). Between words two through ten there's a big dip, like a grin from left to right. The smile is actually a smirk, because the poorest recall is on word seven. What happens, it seems, is that people rehearse or dwell on the first words more than the middle ones, so these ideas stick. The upswing at the end may explain the *recency effect*, or the tendency for us to form impressions of people based on what they did today while ignoring previous behavior (especially if enough time has passed that we forget early information). Both findings remind us that we're not likely to consider everything we know about someone when perceiving them in the immediate context. No wonder we're not accurate with our general impressions much of the time.

Our first impressions guide future perceptions. That is, once we think a person is "funny" or "sloppy" or "liberal," we look for behavior that confirms our impression, even if it means ignoring contradictory information. Once again, a classroom exercise comes to mind that illustrates this. By using the overhead projector and asking students to look and not look at certain times, I show them two words in two orders:

Side A of the class sees "kind," then "dishonest" about a minute later.
Side B of the class sees "dishonest," then "kind" about a minute later.

After exposure to each word, I ask them to form an impression of an imaginary person who has this trait. After they've seen both words and formed a melded impression, I ask them whether their image is more like Robin Hood (a good guy who does dishonest things to help the poor) or a con artist (a bad person who does kind things for dishonest gain). Each year the results indicate that the word seen first weighs more heavily in their impressions. Most of the students who saw "kind" first and "dishonest" second say their impression resembles Robin Hood; most students who saw the terms in reverse order see their person like a con artist. This gives us good reason to be careful about how we present ourselves when doing job interviews and going on first dates. It's also a reminder that we should hold off on cementing first impressions of others until we see the entire load.

We are prone to pay attention to the intense, novel, and beautiful.[17] Every semester professors look out on a sea of faces in large lecture classes knowing that they will befriend only a handful of those students. Which ones is somewhat predictable, everything else being equal: the guy wearing the purple sweater and sporting the two-tone buzz cut, and the gal with red lipstick who answers two questions the first week of school. Both students stand out against the backdrop of their less active classmates.

In conversation the same trend occurs. If your friend has a new hairdo or fidgets with her sleeve or tells you she just got accepted into medical school, you're more likely to zero in on these intense and attractive matters and forget the friend you knew yesterday. In the chapter on nonverbal communication we highlighted the benefits we extend to attractive people in particular. This is a good place to remember that we should guard against doing so at the expense of our more drab friends.

We allow negative information about others to outweigh the good.[18] If you have ever sat on a pastoral search committee at your church, you have a good sense of this tendency. A couple years ago I found myself sifting through eighteen resumes pregnant with personal information about the candidates. But it took only a month for our committee to narrow the field to eight and another month to whittle it down to three. How'd we do it? For good or for bad, we let negative information take its course. When two applicants had similar strengths but one had a stark weakness, we axed the poor guy. Even if a candidate had fifteen positive traits and two negative traits compared to someone who had just ten positive traits but no negative ones, we tipped our hand in favor of the second applicant. After the fact, it's easy to speak words of caution, but I'm convinced that we should recognize that even "all positive" people have their vice and that "one negative trait" people may just be more honest. A follow-up "interview" with a friend that garners more information may help us overcome this tendency to jump on negative information.

We see ourselves as responding to our environment, but see others as choosing to act as they do.[19] In other words, we are more likely to say, "I swore because he provoked me" but "You swore because you're that kind of person." This is called the actor-observer difference in attribution-making, because as social actors we tend to see other people "directing" our behavior, but as observers we see friends choosing their own role.

Consider Vicky and Robert again. When Vicky got involved in Robert's business deal, she probably attributed her behavior to his need for help or companionship. "I got involved because Robert needed me." But you can bet that Robert, who observed her behavior, attributed it to Vicky's aggressive personality. "She butted in because she's controlling!" Both could be right, because in human affairs it is not easy to determine what we *chose to do* or what we *were caused to do*. As gracious perceivers, we need to balance the two and acknowledge that other people feel just as constrained by their environment as we do.

We take credit for our good behavior and blame our environment for our bad behavior, but do just the opposite for people we dislike.[20] If there were any proof that we are essentially selfish, back-side saving creatures, this is it! Consider these typical patterns:

I consoled my arch rival after we won the game *because I'm a loving person.*

She consoled me after my dad died *because everyone expected her to.*

I failed to comfort her after her car accident *because I had such a hectic week.*

How others see us.   How we see ourselves.

She failed to comfort me after my backpack was stolen *because she doesn't care.*

The pattern to blame others in conflict situations is particularly strong. What did Adam say when God asked him "Have you eaten from the tree that I commanded you not to eat from?" He said "The woman you put here with me — she gave me some fruit from the tree, and I ate it." And what did Eve say when God asked "What is this you have done?" She answered, "The serpent deceived me, and I ate" (see Genesis 3:1-14). They both responded with blame, blame, blame. Better that we own up to our responsibility.

GRACIOUS LANGUAGE WITH OTHERS

Perceptions pave the way for words. If I think that you can't be trusted, I'm probably going to leak my distrust in words. If we are genuine in our desire to redeem our talk and our relationships, we will consider what we say to one another.

If I had to grade Robert and Vicky's language the past ten years I'd give them a "C." Their public language was not bitter or calloused or attacking or explosive, but neither was it affirming, empathetic, trusting and loving. It was blah talk — lots of factual talk about other people or issues, but little inter-human sharing.

The biblical record gives evidence that from our mouths come life and death for those around us. Even a short study demonstrates how "mere words" form powerful speech acts to nurture or destroy relationships.

The Power of Gracious Language

Words can bring healing (Prov 12:18)
Kind words bring life (Prov 15:4)
The right words bring joy (Prov 15:23)
Careful words keep one out of trouble (Prov 21:23)
Apt words are beautiful (Prov 25:11)
Words can bring help, encourage and comfort (1 Cor 14:3)
Helpful words build up and provide what is needed (Eph 4:29)
Speaking the truth in a loving manner encourages Christ-likeness (Eph 4:15)

The Power of Ungracious Language

Thoughtless words wound (Prov 12:18)
Cruel words crush the spirit (Prov 15:4)
Gossip separates close friends (Prov 16:28)

Answering before one listens is unwise (Prov 18:13)
Insulting and obscene talk are to be ridden of (Col 3:8)
Lying is bad (1 Peter 3:10)
Slander is to be avoided (James 4:11)

Maybe these verses underscore the obvious, but so often we treat words like computer bytes — weightless and dimensionless, therefore harmless. I recall hearing on the radio a report about a University of Washington study that hints at this mentality. The researchers recorded the conversations of engaged couples over several hours and coded them for type of discourse. They also asked couples to complete a self-report questionnaire that included questions about how much they felt "in love" and "romantic" toward each other. Years later the researchers went back to see which couples were still married and which were divorced. They found that the degree of love or romantic behavior couples reported while engaged did not forecast marital longevity. But the couples' talk did. Those who broke up used insults, put-downs, and subtle undercuts five times more frequently than those who were still married. Ten percent of what they said to the woman or man they would soon marry was some kind of put-down! (Only two percent for the still-marrieds.)[21]

Insults and put-downs at least recognize that the other person exists. Ignoring a friend entirely or denying her perceptions can be even more damaging. Consider the times when we have

...chosen not to return a phone call
...avoided saying "hi" to someone
...said "don't be silly — you don't really feel that way."
...changed a topic abruptly with no regard for what a friend just said

The first two shout "you don't even exist" or "you don't matter to me." The third example suggests that others are oblivious to their own emotions (a rather presumptuous suggestion!). The last example implies, "you may have said something, but what I've got to say is more important." All are cases of *disconfirming messages. Confirming messages,* in contrast, are words and behaviors that 1) acknowledge our friend and our relationship, 2) show a relevant response to what he or she said, 3) affirm our friend's experience, and 4) indicate a willingness to become involved with him or her.[22] It bears repeating. Interpersonal communication is about creating, enacting, and becoming in relationship. How we talk influences how we become together.

GRACIOUS FIGHTING WITH OTHERS

What has just been said sheds a lot of light on dealing with conflict. If Robert and Vicky had listened enough so they could confirm each other's life experience, their marriage might have survived. Or, if Robert had spoken his mind instead of shoving resentments down deep, Vicky would have had more to go on. Or, if Vicky had not bulldozed Robert under a mountain of monologue.... Very quickly we could make a list of do's and don'ts for conflict management, but each would capture but a sliver of the solution. There may be no one solution to a problem, but I'm convinced that managing conflict is not about technique so much as having a right heart before encountering the storms. In Colossians, Paul challenges us to closet our earthly nature and "clothe yourselves [rather] with compassion, kindness, humility, gentleness and patience. Bear with each other and forgive whatever grievances you may have against one another. Forgive as the Lord forgave you. And over all these virtues put on love, which binds them all together in perfect unity" (Colossians 3:12-14). He calls us to be virtuous.

It may be too simple to point out, but compassionate people rarely treat others as objects. Kind friends rarely use words that wound. Humble individuals rarely judge others. Gentle folks rarely cuss out others. Patient people rarely open their mouths prematurely. Being a godly person may be half the battle in managing our wars with each other.

The other half of the battle is to know practical tips that work. Carole and Jack Mayhall offer some biblically informed advice for how to manage conflict.[23] Here are their insights.

Keep your cool. Quick tempers are like hydrogen-filled blimps: one spark and the whole thing can blow! The proverbs remind us that quick-tempered people act foolishly (14:7) and stir up strife (14:18). Righteous people, instead, think before they answer (15:28), and step away from quarreling in the heat of the moment (17:14). As long as that stepping away doesn't lead to avoidance of the issue, the idea of a cool-off period for reflection makes a lot of sense.

Keep short accounts. Robert's 31-year grudge is a sober reminder to not let the sun go down on our anger (Ephesians 4:26). If we nip it in the bud, an issue will never have time to blossom. Some married couples make a pact that they will not let a day end without addressing an issue. We can all benefit from that strategy. It may mean we make a phone call later than usual or getting together for coffee at one of those 24-hour joints, but when the account has been credited with attention and discussion, there's little fear of a major blow-up later.

Act wisely, not foolishly. This gets back at that idea of being and acting virtuously. I know that sounds high and lofty, but what are the alternatives? One is to treat problems rationally. A century ago John Dewey, the father of modern education, suggested that the best way to solve problems was by systematic method. First you define the conflict, then examine possible solutions, and then debate the feasibility of each solution. After that you judge which solution is best, reject the bad ones, and implement the one you chose. John Dewey was no fool, but he certainly put more faith in reasoning than wisdom to solve our problems. Reasoning plays an important role, but we're more than brains. And that's what the Mayhalls mean by wisdom. Managing conflict is a matter of heart and spirit as much or more than one of smarts. Too many brains puff up (1 Corinthians 8:1), but a wise person considers whether a solution meets people's needs.

Make understanding your aim. If you're at all competitive, you'll have the urge to beat your opponent, not understand him. Men in particular have this urge to win verbal duels rather than connect in understanding.[24] As long as we're in control, we feel we're managing conflict just dandy. This attitude may win us the battle but it will lose respect with comrades. We might succeed in window dressing the problem or determining a Band-Aid solution, but we sacrifice mutuality. Solomon put it bluntly, "A fool does not delight in understanding, but only in revealing his own mind" (Proverbs 18:2). Understanding begins with listening.

David Augsburger suggests that when we enter conflict we should "carefront." He coined this word by joining "caring" and "confronting" to capture the notion that we need both. We should show love, but also address our differences.[25] Part of that process is knowing when to say "I messed up, will you forgive me?" It also means having the guts to say, "And you hurt me too." If that person denies doing anything wrong, or denies your feelings, you still have to make a choice. Is that person's denial a reason to harbor bitterness, or should we still forgive him or her? Alice Morgan had to make this tough decision. She writes,

> As a small child I was brutally sexually assaulted by my father, who is both alcoholic and mentally ill. To this day he is not able to admit that he even did anything wrong.
>
> There were terrible consequences in my own adult life — chronic depression, substance abuse and blatant self-destruction patterns that would not let me go until I sought spiritual and professional help.
>
> Should I forgive my father? I knew Christ wanted me to. And what other choice did I have, unless I wanted to be ruled by the abuse for the rest of my life?

Alice found God's grace sufficient to forgive her father. As Neil Anderson writes, that act of release was as much for her as it was for her father.

You don't forgive someone for their sake; you do it for your sake so you can be free. Your need to forgive isn't an issue between you and the offender; it's between you and God.

Forgiveness is agreeing to live with the consequences of another person's sin.... You're going to live with those consequences whether you want to or not; your only choice is whether you will do so in the bitterness of unforgiveness or the freedom of forgiveness.... All true forgiveness is substitutionary, because no one really forgives without bearing the penalty of the other person's sin.[26]

What emotion do you think Alice felt upon forgiving her father? She says:

Compassion. Almost in spite of myself, I began to feel sorry for my Dad, a broken man who has never allowed God to touch or heal his deeply fractured soul.... To paraphrase scripture: How many times shall I forgive my father? As many times as it takes.[27]

Alice's experience is a good example of how words and speech acts change our social reality. Not only is forgiveness a redemptive communication act, it also leads to a more redeemed person in the sense of being whole and made right with others. Listening leads to that kind of change as well.

GRACIOUS LISTENING WITH EACH OTHER

Recently I had the privilege of attending a dedication kick-off assembly for the new elementary school building where my children attend. Five hundred children and eight hundred adults packed the gymnasium to hear the principal, vice-principal, board chair, local politicians, staff, and committee chairs extol the facility and the people who made it happen. Speakers were given 3-5 minutes to say their due. The temperature rose, a few speakers spoke long, and soon the seventy-five minute program expanded to ninety. As you can sense, I struggled to hang in there and listen actively.

Interestingly, research suggests that trying to listen—and remember—what a friend said interpersonally may be even more difficult than mass listening like at a lecture.[28] At least in a lecture our roles are well defined as speaker and listeners, but in interpersonal encounters we are speaker *and* listener. To make matters worse, we are often thinking about what we want to say next, and this garbles incoming messages.

Our entire relational attitude with friends can be summed up in one question: are we willing to listen to them? Really listen? The problem is that we are trained early in life, and right on through university, to value speaking, writing, and reading, not heartfelt listening. What does it mean to listen? The basic building block is that we first *hear* the other person. Hearing is the physical receiving of someone's vocal sound waves. It's also a plus if we can *see* the other person so we might interpret their nonverbal behavior as well.

We hear and see millions of sounds and sights a day, but *attune* (or attend to) a mere fraction of them. As you read this, pause for a minute and listen to the sounds around you. Maybe there's a whir of a computer or the buzz of a florescent lamp, the muffled voices of people next door or the shuffling of feet in the hall. By choice though you are attending to these words visually and blocking out a good deal of the noises aurally. We attune to friends by dropping what we're reading, giving them eye contact, turning our bodies toward them, and leaning forward. These behaviors cue them that we're ready and focused on them.

But of course we also need to *understand* them. We need to grasp the meanings of their words and the tone of their emotions. Is it possible to hear and attune but still not understand? Consider this sentence: "I'm feeling like ya' know, like I could do it if I had to, but so many things can, well…it's hard to say, ya' know…it's not easy." What does this person mean? The abstract words ("it," "things") and halting delivery make us strain to

"What do you mean Molly? I can hear you."

eke out some meaning. Sometimes the context and topic don't even help. Here is where responding comes in.

Listening isn't passive receiving, it's also heart-and-mind *responding* with appropriate questions and nonverbal affirmations. Asking "What do you mean by 'it' Susan?" or "What kinds of 'things' make it difficult?" may keep you and Susan on the course to understanding. Furthermore, your quizzical look and thoughtful pause after you pose your questions will inform Susan that you await clarification.

Hearing, attuning, and understanding may seem like a sufficient definition of listening, but some scholars suggest that the process is not complete unless we *remember* what was said.[29] The percentages cited in footnote 28 suggest we are pretty lousy at this. I must admit that once a month or so I will ask Shelaine about an upcoming event or present issue and she will graciously respond, "We've already discussed that, William—the answer is...." Making notes or repeating ideas after we hear them the first time helps long term memory, and simply remembering is one way we can tell others "I was not only present, but I was all systems go, too!"

We are our own worst enemies when it comes to listening to others. I think the following examples crystallize how we should *not* listen if we want to engage in redemptive communication. Suppose a friend sat down with you and remarked, "I can't believe it! My sister is getting married and she isn't including me in the wedding party. Maybe I should just volunteer to park cars!" Consider how friends might respond.

The Pseudo (Fake) Listener: "Uh huh. Yeh, marriage...it can be quite a party or a lot like parking cars." (The pseudo-listener is clueless to the intended meaning but has obviously heard something.)

The Selective Listener: "I didn't know your sister was getting married! Who's the lucky guy?" (The selective listener picks out only a portion of the meaning rather than the larger picture.)

The Monopolizer: "Ah, sister behavior!! Sisters can be so wrapped up in their own worlds sometimes. My own sister, Louise, once said that..." (The monopolizer takes over the conversation rather than allow the speaker to finish or expand on ideas or feelings.)

The Fixer: "You know what you should do? You *should* volunteer to park cars and she will feel so ashamed I'm sure she'll ask you to be in her wedding party. She'll figure out what's right, and you'll get what you want!" (The fixer seems to understand the speaker, but intends to fix the problem, not simply hear out the issue and emotions.)

The Ambusher: "I was just waiting for you to criticize your sister's wedding plans, and there, you've done it! Well I'll have you know that your life plans have not always pleased your friends and relatives either!" (The ambusher looks for opportunity to criticize the speaker, rather than support the speaker.)

The Defensive Listener: "So are you implying that I had something to do with it? I may know your sister, but please don't blame me!" (The defensive listener interprets descriptions as personal evaluations, rather than taking them at face value.)

These examples might make us chuckle, but, sadly, they're representative of how we sometimes respond to others. James, the brother of Jesus, encouraged believers to be "quick to listen, slow to speak, and slow to become angry" (James 1:19). If we live out that second challenge — to be slow to speak — we will probably have time and heart to listen. Active listening is considered an ideal by many communication practitioners. We listen actively when we reflect back to people what we believe they meant and felt as they spoke. Whether we do this by paraphrasing what they said or by affirming them nonverbally, we show them the respect and space they need to voice what's down deep. Sounds redemptive to me.

Summary

In this chapter we likened interpersonal communication to bowling, Ping-Pong, and charades. "Bowlers" picture communication as a one-way process that is largely dependent on their hurling messages at passive recipients. "Ping-Pong players" acknowledge that receivers provide feedback, but still assume a primarily predictable process of give and take until meanings are scored. "Charade players" view communication as a transaction where not only messages become created and shared through joint effort, but relationships are strengthened or weakened due to the communication type. I then suggested that God communicates to us for the purpose of relationship so he might enlist our efforts for his cause. The cause is to redeem our talk so we might redeem our walk with him and others. It suggests that God is serious about redemption of others as spiritual, emotional, and relational beings.

Redeeming our dialogue with others means guarding against nasty perceptual biases. We should guard against letting early, recent, novel and negative information overshadow other things we know about friends. We also need to guard against rationalizing that what we do is driven by our environment, but others are driven by their choice; both are likely at work.

Redemptive dialogue also means that we engage words that edify or confirm, not tear down or disconfirm. It means seeking understanding, not winning, as we experience conflict, and dealing with issues sooner, not later. Finally, I suggested that our entire relational stance with friends is measured by our willingness to listen to them with an empathetic heart. Listening takes much mental effort and requires an appropriate response. Active listening requires that we reflect back to the speaker what we hear him or her saying rather than charge off on our own agenda.

Many of our closest and most trying relationships occur with blood relatives. We turn to the family context in the next chapter to see how redemptive communication often does *not* happen.

Worth the Talk

1. Do you agree or disagree with Stewart and Buber that we should heighten each other's unique, unmeasurable, choice-making, and addressable qualities? What features would you remove? Add? Why?
2. Do you agree or disagree with the point in this chapter that interpersonal communication should be viewed through the lens of relationship (the transactional/charades model), not the lens of effects (the linear/bowling or interactive/Ping-Pong models)? How does a "relational lens" or an "effects lens" influence your view of friendship?
3. The underlying world view of the transactional model is existentialism, or the basic belief that whether there is a God or not, we still define ourselves largely through our interaction with others around us. Therefore, the role of a good communicator is to affirm another person's experience and identity. What is the truth value of this perspective? What cautions would you have about this perspective?
4. Under the topic of gracious perception of others, I described six ugly tendencies. Which perceptual trap or traps are common among college students? What strategies would you suggest to guard against them?
5. An old saying goes "Sticks and stones may break my bones, but words will never hurt me." After reading the section on "gracious language with others," what do you think is true about that old saying? Does it hold true sometimes? Never? Always?
6. I make the assumption that if we are people of compassion, kindness, humility, gentleness and patience, then we will have much of what we need to deal with conflict. Other people say we need to learn conflict-resolution skills and theories. What do you think?
7. What do you think are the top three barriers to active listening? How can we minimize them?

Consider the Walk

1. Keep a journal about your interpersonal communication with one other person (for instance, your roommate, your girlfriend or boyfriend, your mom or dad, your spouse). Choose someone you see regularly or some-

one with whom you think you have poor communication. Use the ideas in this chapter as a backdrop for your reflections. Ask:
   a. to what degree do you admit your humanness? To what degree do you seem to treat others like objects?
   b. to what degree does our communication encourage spiritual growth. In what ways do you discuss spiritual concerns?
   c. how do you perceive this person? Are any biases at work?
   d. what kind of language typifies your talk?
   e. how do you manage conflict? Do you seem to fight fair?
   f. what is the quality of listening in your relationship?
2. Write a paper that reports and analyzes your findings from the journal noted in number one. Or, if you have not written a journal, use the same questions listed there to analyze your communication with one person or with people generally. The paper could accomplish two goals. The first is that it describes your communication habits with others (both the good and the bad). The second is that it prescribes rules or goals you want to set for yourself to make your relating more redemptive.
3. Watch your favorite soap opera or prime-time drama and analyze the interpersonal communication between characters. Use the criteria noted in number 1. You will have to speculate about some of the dynamics because you are not one of the interactants.
4. Interview a person whose work is largely interpersonal communication (e.g., student affairs staff, a counselor, a salesperson, a visitation pastor), and ask what role interpersonal communication plays in that person's work. Write up your findings and share them in class with your classmates.

NOTES

1. These metaphors for interpersonal communication come from E. Griffin, *Making friends (and making them count)*, InterVarsity Press, Downers Grove, IL, 1987, Chapter 1.
2. Works that typify the linear view include Harold Lasswell, "The Structure and Function of Communication in Society," pp. 37-51 in Lyman Bryson, (Ed.), *The communication of ideas*, Institute for Religious and Social Studies, New York, NY, 1948, and Claude Shannon and Warren Weaver, *The mathematical theory of communication*, University of Illinois, Urbana, IL, 1949.
3. For a good overview of the interactive model, see David Berlo, *The process of communication*, Holt, Rinehart, and Winston, New York, NY, 1960.
4. See Dean Barnlund, "A Transactional Model of Communication," in Kenneth Sereno and David Mortensen (Eds.), *Foundations of communication theory*, Harper & Row, New York, NY, 1970.
5. Griffin, p. 16.

6. B. Aubrey Fisher and Katherine L. Adams, *Interpersonal communication: Pragmatics of human relationships*, (2nd ed.), McGraw-Hill, Inc., New York, NY, 1994, p. 18.

7. John Stewart, "Interpersonal Communication: Contact Between Persons" in *Bridges, not walls* (5th ed.), McGraw-Hill Publishing Company, New York, NY, p. 13.

8. See Martin Buber, *The knowledge of man*, (edited by Maurice Friedman and translated by Maurice Friedman and Ronald Gregor Smith), The Balkin Agency, 1965. Excerpt titled "Elements of the Interhuman" may be found in John Stewart, pp. 450-460.

9. Stewart, p. 18.

10. Stewart, p. 18, italics added.

11. Fisher and Adams, p. 30.

12. Charles Kraft, *Communication theory for Christian witness*, Abingdon Press, Nashville, TN, 1983, p. 34.

13. For a full treatment of this idea see Erving Goffman, *The presentation of self in everyday life*, Doubleday, Garden City, NY, 1959.

14. Stewart L. Tubbs and Sylvia Moss, *Human Communication* (7th ed.), McGraw-Hill, Inc., New York, p. 57.

15. In addition to these factors, research indicates that people with higher intelligence are more accurate people perceivers. See Tubbs and Moss, p. 57.

16. D. E. Hamachek, *Encounters with others: Interpersonal relationships and you*, Holt, Rinehart and Winston, 1982, pp. 23-40 as cited in Ronald B. Adler and Neil Towne, *Looking Out/Looking In* (6th ed.), Holt, Rinehart and Winston, Inc., Fort Worth, TX, 1990, p. 98.

17. See Adler and Towne, p. 98.

18. See Adler and Towne, p. 99.

19. Cited in Fisher and Adams, p. 78 from E. Jones and R. Nisbett, *The actor and the observer*. General Learning Press, Morristown, NJ, 1971.

20. T. Pettigrew, "Three Issues in Ethnicity," in J. Yinger and S Cutler (Eds.), *Major social issues*, Free Press, New York, 1978 as cited by William B. Gudykunst and Young Yun Kim, *Communicating with Strangers*, Random House, New York, p. 91.

21. Try as I may, I am unable to locate where this report was published.

22. These criteria are from Evelyn Sieburg, "Interpersonal Confirmation: A Paradigm for Conceptualization and Measurement," Paper presented at International Communication Association, Montreal, Quebec, 1973, as quoted in Kathleen Galvin and Bernard Brommel, *Family communication: Cohesion and change*, Scott, Foresman and Company, Glenview, IL, 1982, p. 88.

23. Jack Mayhall and Carole Mayhall, *Marriage Takes More Than Love*, NavPress, Colorado Springs, CO, 1978, p. 83-85.

24. See Deborah Tannen, *You just don't understand me!*, Wm. Morrow, New York, NY, 1990, especially the section "Put That Paper Down and Talk to Me!," pp. 74-95.

25. David Augsburger, *The love fight*, Herald Press, Scottdale, PA, 1973, p. 3.

26. Neil T. Anderson, *Living free in Christ*, Regal Books, Ventura, CA, 1993, p. 294.

27. Alice Morgan, "Seventy-seven times: The thorny issue of forgiveness," *Christian Info News*, Counselling Supplement, November 1994, p. S5.

28. See Steven Beebe, Susan Beebe, Mark Redmond, and Carol Milstone, *Interpersonal communication: Relating to others*. Allyn and Bacon Canada, Scarborough, Ontario, 1997, p. 103. For example, twenty-four hours after listening to someone give a speech, we remember only 25% of what was said. However, in a study where married couples were asked if they had discussed a certain topic "in the last six months," wives often said "yes" (71-91% depending on the topic) but husbands rarely said "yes" (15-19% depending on topic). The researchers interpret this finding to suggest that men may have a more difficult time remembering conversations.

29. See, for example, Joseph DeVito's model in *The interpersonal communication book* (7th ed.), Harper Collins College Publishers, New York, NY, 1995, p. 71.

CHAPTER 5

Power Systems That Fail
When Family Communication Goes Awry

[An overseer] must manage his own family well
and see that his children obey him with proper
respect. If any one does not know how to manage
his own family, how can he take care of God's
church?

1 Timothy 3:4, 5

So far I have been positive about the mystery and joys of communication. I've suggested that our language, nonverbal cues, sense of self, and connection to friends is mainly due to healthy communication. That is good news.

But if there are any bad news chapters in this book, this is one of them. Not because I'm down on families, but because I'm aware of their destructive potential. A communist leader once said that if he could mold a child from infancy to age five, he would have that child for life. He's right, and that's why our type of talk in the family is critical to personal health, our identities, and our outlook on life.

If you have ever been frustrated with how communication happens in your family, this chapter is for you. Even robust families experience patterns of interaction that can drive us batty at times. To understand these dynamics we will look at two concepts — systems and power — and the light they shed on family dynamics. We will also consider how poor biblical doctrine combined with our sinful tendency to look out for ourselves can make other people's lives miserable at home.

To get us started I want to begin with a story based on what I know to be the experience of many families. But you should know that I've created this story for the sake of insight. My fictional family is the Douglases, and its members include Susan (the daughter), Glenda (the mom), and Brent (the father and ex-husband).

THE BIRTHDAY DINNER

Susan was not looking forward to the weekend. It had been two years since her parents' divorce, and this was the first time that all three of them would be together again. To make matters worse, it was supposed to be a happy occasion — her twentieth birthday party.

Glenda said the little party would be an opportunity for everyone to "show some maturity" and "help healing happen." Susan marveled at her optimism and resilient spirit. Susan was less so. She still resented her father and did not trust him. She was still trying to figure him out and determine his role in their family's disintegration. If nothing else, she mused, the evening could provide her with one more piece to the puzzle.

On the day of the dinner, Mrs. Douglas busied herself with setting the china, arranging a silk flower center piece, and preparing steak, rice pilaf, snow peas, Caesar salad, and Susan's favorite frozen chocolate cheesecake. Susan returned home, an hour before her dad was to arrive, to join in her mom's effort. Soon the women completed the finishing touches — glasses and silver, candles, balloons, streamers, and light classical music. They sat down to chat and wait for Brent Douglas. They waited. And waited some more.

Half an hour late, Mr. Douglas cruised up to the house in his Lexus. He took his time to locate a gift and bouquet of flowers, and made his way to the front landing. Susan answered his knock.

"Hello Suz!" he beamed, handing her the items. "For you — my little Suzie."

"Hello Dad," Susan replied, managing a smile.

"No, no, no. It's *Daddy* to you, kid. Always has been, always will be."

"Hello *Daddy*," Susan repeated tensely.

Brent Douglas entered the home and kept his distance from his ex-wife. "Hello Glenda," he said soberly. "Guess you two are wondering where I've been? Big client called about noon; asked if we could meet from three until five. We just went long, but hey, now that I'm here — let's eat."

The remainder of the evening progressed a lot like it had started. Susan's father controlled the floor of conversation and directed it toward his own activity and accomplishments. Mrs. Douglas carefully chose her words and conversation topics according to her ex-husband's need to be center stage. Susan could hardly believe that the mother with whom she had just shared a delightful hour preparing the party was now cautiously subdued with every sentence. Brent Douglas joked all evening: he even took a jab at Glenda by insinuating that she should have made *his* favorite dessert instead of Susan's. He asked Susan how her studies were going at the college, and then promised her a trip to Southern California if she graduated on the dean's list. Later still, Susan opened the gift he gave her — a handsome tote bag, complete with his company's logo.

After he left, Susan and her mom had a long discussion. *He didn't take responsibility for his tardiness,* they agreed. *He is a self-absorbed person,* they lamented. *He hides strong, domineering messages behind sugar-coated terms and joking,* they realized. *He controls the type of talk allowed in the family,* they determined. *All of us are affected by his presence.* The puzzle was coming together.

The Family as a System

We too can put the puzzle of family communication together when we recognize that family members do not act nor respond in isolation. For example, how Brent Douglas treats his ex-wife affects how Susan sees her mom which affects how Susan responds to her dad which affects how Mr. Douglas treats his ex-wife. Scholars call this patterned entanglement a *system*.

In *A First Look at Communication Theory*, author Em Griffin provides a vivid example of the family-as-system:

> Picture a family as a mobile suspended from the ceiling. Each figure is connected to the rest of the structure by a strong thread tied at exactly the right place to keep the system in balance. Tug on any string, and the force sends shock throughout the whole network. Sever a thread, and the entire design tilts in disequilibrium. The threads in the mobile analogy represent communication rules that hold the family together.[1]

In more academic terms, a human system is the combination of three or more people, their characteristics, and one or more rules that guide their interaction. If everyone is playing by the same rules, the system is said to be *homeostatic*, that is, in balance. Even if those rules do not encourage personal growth or moral discipleship, the system is still said to rotate in harmony. By now you've figured out that the Douglas family rules are unhealthy. However, unless these rules are acknowledged and recast in new forms, this system can hum along in *deadly balance* as its structure slowly destroys the people in it. Some call this pattern *dysfunctional,* for it does not allow members to meet other members' needs for love, acceptance, and control. Dysfunctional communication fails to edify others; it tears them down.

THE CHRISTIAN FAMILY: HAVEN OF REST?

My own upbringing in a functional, loving home gave me the sense that my bliss was due to God's blessing. I'm sure it was. But does choosing God to be overseer of one's family guarantee a life without dysfunctional family communication? I think you'll agree that the answer is no—even believers still struggle with working out their salvation in their family relationships. Even still, most Christians probably believe that their life-in-Christ translates into some baseline benefits in family communication. Others believe that we are still no better off than average non-Christians. Richard Stellway, a sociologist at Northwest Nazarene College in Nampa, Idaho, summarizes these views well:

> In the absence of available and reliable data on the state of the Christian family, pronouncements have tended toward extremes. On the one hand there are those who maintain that Christian marriages are not only different from, but far superior to, all other (non-Christian) marriages.... On the other hand, there are those who insist that such assertions are merely a sales pitch. They see Christians as people afflicted with the same shortcomings as their non-Christian neighbors, and believe any semblance of superior well-being among Christian couples and families is superficial at best.[2]

People who have a more skeptical view of faithful families suggest that theological rigidity, authority-model fathering, and gag orders on talking about sex contribute to an unhealthy family life.[3]

As equally diverse as these opinions is the research that attempts to prove who's right. For example, Stellway cites a 12,000-person study by Philip Blumstein and Pepper Schwartz who report that "only a few of our findings indicate that relationships can be affected by attendance at church or synagogue."[4] However, the well-known "Middletown" study of residents in Muncie, Indiana by Theodore Caplow and his associates "found that church attendance to be related to both marital happiness and marital stability."[5] In order to answer the question for himself Stellway did an in-depth study of believers living in Wheaton, Illinois. Did he find that support for the haven hypothesis or the hell hypothesis? Consider these results he found and then you be the judge.[6]

1. 65% of Christians surveyed indicated that their marriages were "very happy" compared to 68% of a general population study.
2. the majority of those surveyed indicated that they enjoyed "calm discussion" (82%) and "laughing together" (81%).
3. 87% fell into the "good" and "very good" categories of marital adjustment—a percentage that was on par for the national average.
4. their adjustment was strongly correlated with companionship and communication: the more time couples spent together, the better adjusted they were.
5. Christians with conservative beliefs did not report experiencing significantly happier marriages nor greater marital adjustment than Christians with more liberal beliefs.
6. Church attendance related positively to marital happiness, but not to companionship or adjustment.
7. Christians with conservative beliefs were as likely or even more likely to report that they and their spouses communicated freely about sex: the more communication they had, the better sex life they said they experienced.

Keep in mind that Richard Stellway's findings are correlational. That is, he measured how variables tend to go up and down together (or inversely), but not, necessarily, whether one causes the other. So, for example, spending a lot of time together with a spouse or family members may nurture companionship and communication, or the need for companionship and communication may cause people to spend time together. Which causes which isn't clear, but the two tend to rise and fall together.

No matter how you take these findings, I think it is fair to say that becoming a believer does not transport one's marriage and home life to seventh heaven bliss. What we can say for sure is that critics of the Christian family should take a hard look at the evidence: the life-as-a-living-hell hypothesis does not seem to hold water. With this said, however, we should realize that dysfunctional communication goes on to greater and lesser degrees across all family types whether religious or not, single or double parent, black or white or other racial background. A closer look at dysfunctional communication may help you recognize destructive relational patterns in your own family or a friend's.

Dysfunctional Communication: Tearing Others Down

Broadly speaking, dysfunctional communication is the use of words or actions that fail to edify others physically, socially, intellectually, and spiritually. Dysfunctional talk and behavior hammers people's spirits, constrains their options, subverts their intelligence and rattles their emotions. To use the mobile analogy again, dysfunctional communication is a sign of less-than-redemptive "threads" or rules at work. Those rules, while rarely articulated, govern the twirl and twist of the entire family structure.

Scholars call these threads *regulative rules* because they guide what the family considers appropriate behavior. Unhealthy families often have a battery of rules for keeping their system in balance—rules that may seem odd to other families but which make sense to unhealthy families in light of their history. Consider the following rules and how they get expressed in families such as the Douglases.

Dysfunctional Communication Rule[7]	Resulting Communication
1. Yelling is acceptable. It shows you care.	A lot of yelling, in earnest.
2. Withdrawal is acceptable. It shows you know how to submit and admit that you are wrong.	Concessions (e.g., "You're right, I'm wrong), and subsequent silence.

Dysfunctional Communication Rule	Resulting Communication
3. Critical joking is acceptable. It shows that you don't take yourself or others too seriously.	Jabs, ridicule, sexist jokes, ethnic jokes, comments that the perpetrator is "just joking."
4. Children should be seen, not heard. To speak only when one is asked is a mark of good training.	Silent children who may use disruptive behavior to gain attention.
5. Don't air personal problems nor expect an empathic ear. Strong people work out emotional issues on their own.	Talk that denies emotions ("You don't really feel that way"); children who turn to peers for support; a sense of not being loved.
6. Don't talk about sex. Sex is a natural thing that happens wonderfully when you get married and until then needs no discussion.	Confused children, especially during the hormonal years; children who meet their curiosity about sex by talking with friends and turning to media sources.

Sometimes parents lay down these rules in Technicolor (for example, "I don't ever want to hear you talking about sex again!"). Other times, rules emerge through patterns, including patterns of silence. I recall how little my birth family engaged in talk when a girl at church became pregnant. The girl's parents shuffled her away to have the baby in another town, and all we heard was, "Tina's going to have a baby and give it up for adoption." We heard no wrestling with the issue of motherhood or adoption. No discussion of our need to be sexually responsible. No discussion that Tina's boyfriend was as much responsible. Therefore, despite my belief that God made us sexual creatures (something I learned at church), the lesson I learned from Tina's case was that sex was best left not discussed at home.

The previous chapter described how silence between partners may communicate indifference. But silence is only one form of *disconfirming messages*, only one sign of a family mobile that orbits in cold, black space. Let's look at other forms of disconfirming messages.

DISCONFIRMING MESSAGES: SIGNS OF A JILTED FAMILY MOBILE[8]

As a reminder, "social scientists use the term *confirming communication* to describe messages that convey valuing, and *disconfirming messages* to define those that show a lack of regard."[9] This lack of regard runs contrary to the principles we find in God's word to love, honor, and value others as made in his image. Consider these fallen communication habits.

Verbal abuse: communication that is meant to cause psychological pain. The verbal abuser may attack another person's competence ("You are an idiot"), role ("So all you do is run a cash register?"), perceptions ("You're wrong to feel that way"), sex ("Yes, you're a stupid blonde!"), body type ("Come here, fatso"), or race ("He's a honky [nigger, dago]"). The messages sent are "You are worthless" and "I am more powerful than you."

Complaining: communication that persistently finds fault with someone's behavior. Brent Douglas uses complaining when he suggests that Glenda should have made *his* favorite dessert. In effect, he has told her "you blew it." Even if a complainer justifies his or her complaining with a righteous motive ("I nag about your dirty room because I want you to be responsible"), the receiver can interpret the tone of the complaint as meaning "you can do little right."

Impervious responses: communication that ignores the other person. The impervious responder gives the "silent treatment" or turns a "cold shoulder," whether in brief conversations or over a span of weeks or months. The dominant message received is "you don't exist."

Interrupting: communication that breaks into someone else's floor space. Verbal interruption is equivalent to stepping in front of someone on a sidewalk. Interrupters may be forgiven on first occasion, but repeated interruption sends the message that "my ideas and agenda are more important than yours."

Irrelevant responses: communication that is oblivious to what the other person just said. Irrelevant messages tell the listener "Your message wasn't worth attending to" or, again, "my agenda is more important."

Tangential responses: communication that takes the speaker's comments in part, but shifts the topic down the responder's bunny trail. Suppose Glenda says "We need to talk about whether we'll ski or not this weekend." If Brent answers "Yeh, speaking of skiing, you should see the snowboard I just bought," he has in effect disconfirmed Glenda's suggestion.

Impersonal responses: communication that responds in the abstract or with clichés. Suppose Susan says "Dad, I really need to talk about how I feel about you and mom," and Brent Douglas responds "Glad to hear it. We all need to talk things out," he has, in effect, turned Susan's need into a statistic about everyone. If he followed up with a statement such as, "So what do you think? I'm ready to listen," he's back on track.

Ambiguous responses: communication that can be taken more than one way, leaving the receiver unsure of what is meant. Suppose you say to your professor "Could I come by tomorrow to talk about my grade?" Your prof might respond with an ambiguous (but oddly welcoming) statement such as, "Uh, maybe so. Grades are important, and you have a right to ask about yours. Tomorrow's not too full." Does this mean "yes" or only "we'll see." If it means "we'll see," you still don't know if the professor plans to contact you later about a time to meet.

Incongruous responses: communication that contains two contradictory messages, one usually verbal, the other nonverbal. Suppose someone like Glenda Douglas asks her husband "Honey, do you love me?" only to receive an angry "Of course I do!" We know the wife will pay attention to the tone of voice, but the words will irk her silly.

What makes disconfirming messages so insidious is that they inflict personal pain. Researcher Anita Vangelisti examined *hurtful messages* from family members and outsiders and their effect on our psyche. She found that attacks from family members registered just as hurtful as criticisms from non-family members.[10] Just because we're family doesn't lessen the pain level. Vangelisti also found that hurtful messages create a distancing effect between recipient and attacker. Interestingly though, she found that we lose less social intimacy when family members hurt us than when outsiders do. Maybe this finding indicates that "blood is thicker than water," but the results are still disturbing. Like a dance with a beloved porcupine, we keep closely in step with parents and siblings even when our faces are bloodied by prickly barbs. Some family members, especially women and children, know no other family life but an intimately abusive one.

VERBAL ABUSE: A CLOSER LOOK

Three books that shed much light on the plight of verbally and physically abused family members include *Families that Abuse* (W. W. Norton, 1992), *The Verbally Abusive Relationship* (Adams Media Corporation, 1996), and *Verbal Abuse* (Servant Publications, 1992). I want to review some of their insights and then the role that power and theology might play in abuse.

Firstly, how prevalent is verbal abuse? In a recent study involving 6,000 families representative of the United States population, about 75 percent of husbands and wives indicated that they were the targets of verbal abuse in the previous year.[11] While seventy-five percent seems high, keep in mind that it represents an entire year of a couple's interaction. What must be understood as well is that verbal abuse is not just tongue lashings and yelling profanities. It can include subtle diminishing (of one's partner), cool indifference, one-upmanship, witty sarcasm, silent withholding, manipulative coercion, and unreasonable demands.[12] Patricia Evans, author of *The Verbally Abusive Relationship*, gives us a scenario described to her by Cora, a woman married to Curt for 22 years. As you read, take note that Curt's words are innocent enough—it's his attitude and speech acts that do the damage. Curt has just joined Cora outside. Cora writes:

> I had noticed clouds moving in, and the cool moisture in the air, and I thought, "Maybe we could get a little thunder shower." I thought of the cold front moving in and turned to Curt saying, "I think maybe when weather changes rapidly from hot to cold, there's a greater chance." I was angrily interrupted with, "It's not COLD. It's COOL." "Oh," I said, "I didn't mean it's cold here." "You said cold!" Curt glared. I tried to explain, "I know it's not cold. I was thinking of weather in general and changes in the atmosphere." "Well, you didn't say atmosphere!" he raged, spitting the words out. I tried again: "What I was trying to..." I was interrupted again: "Will you just drop it. It's impossible to talk with you!"
>
> I had a sick feeling in the pit of my stomach. [This is a definite sign of abuse.] I wondered, "How come I can't get Curt to understand what I'm saying? Why is it so hard? Maybe if I'd just said I thought there was a chance of thundershowers, he would have understood." [13]

Cora's first statement was, admittedly, a bit ambiguous. When she said "I think maybe when weather changes rapidly from hot to cold, there's a greater chance," Curt didn't know she was thinking about thunderstorms. But, rather than ask her, "...a greater chance of what, dear?" Curt attacks her with an arsenal of disconfirming messages. He interrupts Cora (he stole her conversational floor); he corrects her perceptions ("It isn't COLD, it's COOL) despite the fact that her use of "COLD" was referring to atmospheric temperature, not their backyard temperature; he's tangential in noting that Cora did not say "atmosphere" (this may be true, but it was beside her point about the probability of thundershowers); and he complains ("It's impossible to talk to you!"). He doesn't even qualify his complaint to this one case of misunderstanding—he blankets her as "impossible."

The case of Cora and Curt mirrors an ugly set of patterns in unhealthy marriages and families. Patricia Evans contrasts these patterns with those in healthy relationships. These lists may help you determine if you or someone you know lives with a verbally abusive family member.[14]

Abusive Relationships Exhibit	Healthy Relationships Exhibit
Inequality	Equality
Competition	Partnership
Manipulation	Mutuality
Hostility	Goodwill
Control	Intimacy
Negation	Validation

For whatever reason, abusers have a strong need for being "one-up." They need to feel that they are the superior partner (inequality), the winner (competition), and the relational oarsman (control). To acquire these positions, the abuser twists words and perceptions (manipulation), blasts others in rage (hostility), and refuses to acknowledge the victim's feelings, perceptions, values, and accomplishments (negation). What really irks the victim is that an abuser's words are sometimes accompanied by seemingly loving and sensitive nonverbals. The result is what some authors call crazy-making—the sense of being confused, lost, off balance, and generally bugged by double messages.[15]

Power is key. Patricia Evans uses the concept of power to explain these dynamics. She writes, "There are two kinds of power. One kills the spirit. The other nourishes the spirit. The first is Power Over. The other is Personal Power. Power Over shows up as control and dominance. Personal Power shows up as mutuality and co-creation."[16] Verbal abusers relish Power Over. They feel that the family exists to meet their needs and they demand respect by virtue of their status. Family members who exhibit Personal Power thrive on mutual trust and assume good will. They value legitimate authority, but do not abandon their need to earn respect.

Dividing power into two types may be a bit simplistic. But what Evans is onto, and what others confirm, is that power is a telling feature of the family relational matrix. Power does not belong to a person; power is *a property of relationship* among all group members. To use Griffin's mobile analogy again, a member who yanks rank on his or her relational string shocks the entire system.

Scholars who write in the area of interpersonal persuasion typically distinguish among more than two types of power. Family communication authors Galvin and Brommel summarize six bases for power. As you read them, consider what types are at work in your family.[17]

Punishment or coercive power. Punishment power is at work when family members promise or threaten physical or psychological pain. Parents may resort to name-calling or threaten to not pay tuition "unless you straighten up." Children may use punishment power when they threaten to run away from home or crank the CD so loud the foundation cracks. Coercive power is the *modus operandi* of the verbal abuser. It communicates, "Do as you're told, or else...."

Positive reinforcement power. Positive reinforcement is at work when family members promise or deliver something you desire. Brent Douglas' attempt to motivate Susan toward the dean's list with the promise of a Disneyland trip is a good example. In dysfunctional relationships, however, such an offer may be taken as bribery or pure manipulation. I know of a case where a not-at-home dad made grand promises to his son to buy him an expensive birthday gift (to earn the son's love) but never followed through. Consider the head games that move represents.

Expertise power. Expertise influence is at work when we believe another family member knows more than we do. Young children are particularly suspect to expertise power because they in fact know less than their parents, but also because they believe that their parents know everything. Humility on part of the parents is crucial if the child is to learn that everyone is finite and fallible. Abusers typically lack this humility, even over-claiming what they know. Abusers often see themselves as experts on almost everything.

Legitimate or position power. This power comes when we acknowledge that some roles carry certain responsibilities and privileges. My wife is our family bookkeeper, and so her opinion about financial matters carries clout. If she says "Sorry, but we can't afford that this month," I listen. As noted above, abusers exercise legitimate power as an inherent right. If anyone ever said to you, "Why should you obey? Because I'm your father (or mother), that's why!" you've experienced legitimate power by mere role, not reason.

Identification or referent power. Identification power serves as a base when you see yourself as similar to someone else and desire to be like him or her. The Susan character I created identified with her mom, but not her dad. She is more apt to take her mom's advice on a wide range of issues because of her mom's similarity. Identification can boomerang though, as in the tendency for children to take after their parents in a host of destructive habits.

Persuasion or information power. Persuasion power is at work when family members offer sound reasons and values for why others should agree with them. Abusers would likely abuse less if they imitated God's call to "Come now, let us reason together" (Isaiah 1:18). Offering reasons based on logic and values is usually considered a highly ethical way to persuade others. However, its method can still be exploited. Consider someone who says, "You have two options: get a job or go to school. If you go to school, you'll cost me money, need to move, get homesick, and probably flunk out anyway." Their reasons may be true, but they limit choice and fail to acknowledge the plusses of college (for example, character development, vocational training, relational enrichments). Abusers in particular can be very bright, persuasive arguers, but their aim is not to reason together. Their goal is to win arguments with vice-grip logic.

This list makes it sound as if every type of power is an incarnation of evil. Not so. How we use power determines its moral force. Our choice is whether we regard power as a right (to lord over others) or as a responsibility (to meet family needs mutually). *Power-as-right* leads to domineering communication; *power-as-responsibility* encourages mutuality where everyone pulls their weight within their role.

In traditionally conservative Christian homes the role of leader has fallen to the husband. Advocates see this model as biblical and healthy as a father provides resources, protection and care for his wife and children. Critics of the *Father Knows Best* model point out that in some cases it tends toward theological rigidity and power-as-right. As already noted, Richard Stellway suggests that both may be right.

Without getting into strong prescriptions of do's and don'ts, however, is it worth asking how family members ought to relate? I would like to answer this question in part by looking at the role of men and what constitutes a functional family.

Men as Relational Key

Right off the bat some of you might ask, "Why focus on men when the goal is to encourage functional family communication among all members?" Good question. I was always taught that marriage requires a 100% effort by both partners and that families thrive from mutual effort. Three things make me focus on men. The first are these sobering statistics:[18]

1. Children raised with no father in the home have been shown to exhibit more antisocial behavior than their raised-with-dad counterparts.
2. Children from broken homes suffer from illness twenty to forty times more often than children raised in intact families.
3. Fatherless children are more likely to do poorly at school and are doubly at risk of dropping out of school than kids with dad at home.
4. Even among children with fathers at home, the average time spent in conversation with their father is eight minutes, and only four minutes if their mother holds a job outside the home too.

5. Many men involved in the current men's movement attribute their sense of lost identity and confused views about masculinity to their father's absence during childhood.

This evidence suggests that when men split the home scene, they contribute to the disintegration of families. And since more men leave the home than women, it seems justified to suggest that a family's relational health depends on dad's commitment and effort.

The second reason I focus on men is because of a claim I read by Richard Halverson, Chaplain of the United States Senate. Halverson may be no family communication expert, but his wisdom from forty-some years of marriage and family life give reason to pause. He wrote,

> It is my deep, settled conviction that *one hundred percent* of the responsibility for the sustenance of the marriage relationship belongs to the husband. The scriptures tell us that as husbands we need to model ourselves after Jesus Christ, who gave Himself up in every way in order to present His bride to Himself without blemish or stain or spot or wrinkle![19]

The first time I read this I was so shocked I read it again. The husband is 100% responsible for sustenance of the marriage, and by implication, the family relationship? What did he mean? As I reasoned through it, I saw his point. Whether because of nature, nurture, or our sinfulness, men are inclined toward tasks and hierarchy, assertiveness and competition — things you need to build an army, not a family. Women have a tendency toward relationships and context, nurturing and intimacy — qualities that make a family mobile turn in positive balance. Left to their customary leanings, many men are less relationally savvy than their wives. Therefore, as Halverson argued, the soundness of a man's marriage and family life is dependent on his commitment to relationships and mutuality — two qualities of the charades model of interpersonal communication we noted in the previous chapter.

The third reason I address men may come as no surprise: men are more likely to abuse others verbally, and women and children are their most common victims.[20] What Halverson intimates, therefore, I call straight up — men should not be less like men, but men should attempt to be more like women in terms of relational sensitivity.

Accepting this idea as a biblical truth has become easier for me after reading Jack Balswick's book *Men at the Crossroads: Beyond Traditional Roles and Modern Options*.[21] Balswick suggests that some believers have bought into a flawed theology that fuels men's beliefs that women and families are to be dominated, not nurtured. First he clarifies what "helper" means in Genesis 2:18: "The LORD God said, 'It is not good that man should be alone.

"Because I said so!"

I will make him a helper as his partner.'" The root for the term "helper" here is used fifteen times in the Old Testament, *always in reference to God.* Balswick concludes, "Needless to say, it would be a gross misinterpretation of Scripture to think of God as subordinate to humankind because the Bible says he is our helper."[22] The operative word in Genesis 2:18 is not "helper" but "partner." Just as God is our helper but not subordinate to us, so it is possible for a woman to be a helper but not subordinate to her husband in the negative sense. She is his partner.

Second, he explains that Eve's sin was the sin of going beyond the *dominion* given to her. She had already been given the whole of Eden except the tree of good and evil. For overstepping her God-given *dominion*, God's punishment to Eve was that she would be *dominated* by Adam. God said "Your desire will be for your husband and he will rule over you" (Genesis 3:16). Balswick observes that "many have interpreted this sentence to mean that God *intends* (desires) for Adam to lord it over his wife—and that, therefore, Christian men today should dominate their wives as well. Within the context, however, God's statement is better understood as a consequence that will come from the curse placed upon Adam as well as Eve."[23] Adam's curse was that he would *want* to dominate Eve, but this was not God's original design.

Finally, Balswick turns to Jesus Christ as a role model for men today. To make his point he asks the reader to do an activity. I'm going to repeat it here because it's a real eye-opener. I hope you'll do it like I did.

First, locate a pencil and a piece of paper. Then take five minutes to list one-word descriptors of Jesus' characteristics. Base your list on what you know of his life on earth. (These words might include terms such as "loving" and "just.") Make your list of Jesus descriptors now.

Once you've made this list, reflect on how our society today typically defines "masculine" and "feminine" qualities. Now go back to your list and consider each descriptor one at a time. If a term seems to fit the "masculine" ideal, mark it with an "M." If it fits the "feminine" ideal, mark it with an "F." If it doesn't seem to fit either stereotype, skip it and go to the next word. Do this now.

What I found, and what Balswick has found time and time again, is that the "male" traits and the "female" traits come out about even. Jesus showed power, might, determination, and skill, but he also showed love, compassion, emotion, and concern. Balswick concludes, and I heartily agree: "A masculinized or feminized image of Jesus is not supported by the scriptural narratives. Taken alone, each view is incomplete. But taken together, they suggest the rich depth that characterized Jesus' human life. So we men need to turn to Jesus to find liberation from sterile, restricted definitions of manhood that are prevalent in modern culture."[24]

Imitating Christ. That theme runs throughout this book. Just how that looks in your family may be a little different from mine, but the result should be the mutual creation of a robust atmosphere for growing up in God. Let's finish with a look at that kind of functional family.

The Functional Family: A Goal Worth Pursuing

Put in the negative, a functional family avoids hurtful games based on dysfunctional rules, disconfirming messages, and a power-over mentality. Put in the positive, they strive for validation, intimacy, goodwill, mutuality, partnership, and equality.

David Miller is a professor of Counselor Education who also counsels families in the pit of divorce. He can recognize negatives a mile away. He also knows what's nurturing. In his book, *Counselling Families After Divorce*, he offers six traits of the functional family, Christian or not. They serve as an encouraging finish to a chapter filled with examples of ugly communication habits.[25] He offers more than insights on communication, and I like that. Home life is about more than talk.

Healthy relationships. Functional families develop relationships that are characterized as "affiliative, trusting, positive and optimistic, warm, unconditionally accepting, and relaxed."[26] Obviously, communication is key to establishing these relational traits. In my Douglas family fiction, Brent Douglas fails to build these kinds of relationships. He's too full of self-centered talk, a critical spirit, conditional love, and a need to be independent.

Servant power. Functional families ask "What can we do to meet each other's needs," not "How can I get what I want?" Families who exhibit servant power acknowledge that someone needs to lead, but not the same person day in and day out. Servant power allows every member to have a say in how the family is run, but still acknowledges that dad and mom are most responsible and that dad is accountable before God for the whole package. A father's accountability to God by grace is no basis for power-lording but rather humble stewardship.

Clear role differentiation. Healthy families talk about who does what, when, where, and why. In our home, I manage the lawn, the garbage, the repairs, and the shop projects. Shelaine manages the finances, the social calendar, the laundry, and the medical needs of our children. Together we share vacuuming, gardening, and planning vacations. As our children mature we want to extend their responsibilities beyond cleaning their rooms. These roles aren't in stone though, and we negotiate new ideals in family councils and spousal chats.

Freedom to express emotions. Who expresses emotion and how they do so are strongly influenced by our birth family and cultural heritage. Part of men's history has been the rule to suppress their emotions and play poker face. However, healthy families acknowledge that life has its joys and stresses with resulting elation, sadness, peace and depression. Healthy families realize that emotions are not right or wrong, but that they are foundational to being human and an important outlet for understanding each other. Men who hug sons and women who cheer on daughters in sports show emotional aptitude.

Good problem solving skills. Healthy families talk through their problems and solve them. Less functional families do not. Healthy families focus on the problem, not the person. They are more likely to use a win-win framework for discussing issues rather than a win-loss one. That is, they try to meet both party's needs fully rather than one person's needs at the expense of the other. Sometimes they compromise and meet half way. Other times they graciously agree to disagree on matters that don't matter.[27] They look out for each other.

Communication. We are not surprised by this final trait of healthy families. Functional families exhibit open, frank, and respectful talk about issues and needs. And as Miller writes, "Healthy families speak the truth in love, and parents and other older family members are willing to listen to the words spoken by 'mere children.'"[28]

Summary

The family should be our first and favorite harbor amidst the gales of life. In families, we have the opportunity to nurture children and affirm developing adults. Families begin with parents, and we reviewed that Christian couples appear to be on par with the cultural norm for reported marital happiness, adjustment, and healthy communication.

Exceptions to this standard include families where rigid, critical, and domineering webs of entrapment snag children, teens, and parents. The presence of dysfunctional rules, disconfirming messages, and verbal abuse usually means that some or all family members are hung up on powering over others rather than serving others. Abusive environments are characterized by inequality, competition, manipulation, hostility, control, and negation. Men are more likely to verbally abuse others and leave home. For these reasons this chapter encourages men to seriously consider their talk and how they may conform it more to the richly balanced manner of Christ. Men, and families, who want to nurture a healthy home environment will communicate equality, partnership, mutuality, goodwill, intimacy, and validation. By God's grace the outcome will be the functional family, parents and children who serve one another within clearly defined roles where problems are addressed cooperatively with emotional freedom. How we talk with each other contributes to the successful construction of this social reality.

Some people have left their birth families so long ago that the lack of communication effectively frees them from its bounds, but this doesn't mean they live as hermits. Rather they surround themselves with friends and find new identities by joining other groups. College students are prime examples. Examining the dynamics of non-family groups is the topic to which we now turn.

Worth the Talk

1. Can you give personal examples from your own family experience that family communication is well understood as a "system"? Discuss with others how the words or behaviors of one person have a rippling effect throughout your family and on future communication.

2. How significant is Richard Stellway's finding that Christians who hold conservative Christian beliefs were not necessarily any more happy in their marriages (and presumed, family life) than Christians with less conservative beliefs? What other criteria for a "successful Christian marriage" could we use in addition to "happiness?" Are these other criteria more or less important for how God would have us experience family life?

3. What types of power do others exercise *over* you? *With* you? (The difference indicates whether they engage a Power Over approach or Servant Power approach.) Closer to home, what types of power do you exercise *over* others? *With* others? (Do you more commonly engage in Power Over or Servant Power?) You may want to refer to the six types of power reviewed in this chapter to aid your discussion.

4. Do you agree with the statement made by Richard Halverson, that 100% of the responsibility for marriage sustenance [and family functionality] belongs to the husband? Why or why not? Is it fair to expect so much of men?

Consider the Walk

1. Dysfunctional communication begins with dysfunctional rules. Analyze your own family for dysfunctional communication by making two lists, one for rules, the other for resulting messages. Consider the ones that you might be most responsible for establishing and maintaining. Some time after you have made your analysis, sit down with your family (or one on one if necessary), and discuss what you have discovered. In a spirit of grace and reconciliation, admit where you are not serving the system well. Invite others to contribute their ideas, but don't force or demand change from them. Work cooperatively toward a new set of rules and how your family talks.

2. Verbal abuse can be a slippery term unless we can recognize its various forms, both in our own communication and in others. In *The Verbally Abusive Relationship*, Patricia Evans lists eighteen verbal abuses. They include: withholding, countering, discounting, abuse disguised as jokes, blocking and diverting, accusing and blaming, judging, criticizing, trivializing, undermining, threatening, name calling, forgetting, ordering, denial, and abusive anger. Write a paper about verbal abuse that defines these terms, and exemplifies what they look like in family relationships. As part of your work, address whether or not power misuse is the underlying problem. As a case study, you may want to analyze your own communication with others or interview friends (with guaranteed confidentiality) to provide some original research for your writing.

3. Use ideas from this chapter to analyze how the characters of your favorite soap opera, situation comedy, prime-time drama, or feature film relate to each other. You might consider what rules are being followed, what disconfirming messages are typically sent, what types of power are being abused, and what hope there is for functional communication. Try to give representative dialogue as proof of your analysis.

Notes

1. Em Griffin, *A first look at communication theory*, 2nd ed., McGraw-Hill, Inc., New York, 1994, p. 185.
2. Richard Stellway, *Christiantown*, USA, The Haworth Press, Inc., Binghamton, NY, 1990, p. 2.
3. The three studies Stellway cites include J. K. Hadden, "Televangelism and the Mobilization of a New Christian Right Family Policy," in W. D. D'Antoni and J Aldous (Eds.). *Families and religions* (pp. 247-266), Sage, Beverly Hills, CA, 1983; J. A. Larsen, "Dysfunction in the Evangelical Family: Treatment Considerations," *The family counselor*, Vol. 27, No. 3, 1978, pp. 261-265; J. Scanzoni,, *Shaping tomorrow's family: Theory and policy for the 21st century*, Sage, Beverly Hills, CA, 1983.
4. Stellway, p. 31-32. See Philip Blumstein and Pepper Schwartz, *American couples: Money, work, sex*. William Morrow, New York, NY, 1983.
5. Stellway, p. 32. See Theodore Caplow, H. M. Bahr, B. A. Chadwick, R. Hill, and M. H. Williamson, *Middletown families: Fifty years of continuity and change*, University of Minnesota Press, St. Paul, MN, 1982.
6. These findings are reported in Stellway, 1990, as follows: Item 1, p. 22; Item 2, p. 26; Items 3 & 4, p. 28; Items 5 & 6, p. 34; Item 7, p. 42; Item 8, p. 44; Item 9, p. 47; Item 10, p. 44, and Item 11, pp. 56 & 60.
7. I constructed these rules, in part, based on features of the *functional* family as described by Kathleen Galvin and Bernard Brommel in *Family communication: Cohesion and change*, (2nd ed.), Scott, Foresman and Company, Glenview, IL, 1982, pp. 283-289.
8. Ronald Adler and Neil Towne, *Looking Out, Looking In* (8th ed.), Harcourt Brace College Publishers, New York, 1996, pp. 369-370
9. Adler and Towne, p. 367.
10. Anita Vangelisti, "Messages That Hurt," (pp. 53-82) in W. R. Cupach and B. H. Spitzberg (Eds.) *The dark side of interpersonal communication*, Lawrence Erlbaum Associates, Publishers, Hillsdale, NJ, 1994.
11. I am indebted to Adler and Towne, p. 369, who cite this study by M. Straus, S. Sweet, and Y. M. Vissing, "Verbal Aggression Against Spouses and Children in a Nationally Representative Sample of American Families." Paper presented at the annual meeting of the Speech Communication Association, San Francisco, CA, 1989.
12. This list is provided by Patricia Evans in *The verbally abusive relationship*, Adams Media Corporation, Holbrook, MA, 1996, p. 17.
13. Evans, pp. 51-52.

14. Evans, p.
15. See George R. Bach and Ronald M. Deutsch, *Stop! You're driving me crazy*, G. P. Putnam's Sons, New York, NY, 1980.
16. Bach and Deutsch, p. 29.
17. Galvin and Brommel, p. 126-127.
18. Items 1-3 reported in Charles Colson, *A dance with deception: Revealing the truth behind the headlines*, Word Publishing, Milton Keynes, England, 1993, p. 187-188. Items 4 and 5 are reported in Colson, pp. 185-186.
19. Richard Halverson, *No greater power*, Multnomah Press, Portland, OR, 1986, p. 118. I am indebted to Stu Weber's *Tender warrior*, Multnomah Books, Sisters, OR, 1993, p. 118 for his citation of Halverson's book.
20. Though not documented with scholarly studies, the premise that men verbally abuse women more than vice versa is quietly assumed in Evan's *The verbally abusive relationship*, and Grace Ketterman's *Verbal abuse*, Servant Publications, Ann Arbor, MI, 1992.
21. Jack Balswick, *Men at the crossroads*, InterVarsity Press, Downers Grove, IL, 1992, p. 30.
22. Balswick, p. 54.
23. Balswick, p. 56
24. Balswick, p. 59
25. David R. Miller, *Counselling families after divorce: Wholeness for the broken family*. Word, Incorporated, Dallas, TX, 1994, pp. 268-272.
26. Miller, p. 269
27. I was reminded of this important rule recently while reading Romans 14. The issue Paul addresses is how to deal with differing opinions over types of food. Paul concludes, "Let us therefore make every effort to do what leads to peace and to mutual edification. Do not destroy the work of God for the sake of food. All food is clean, but it is wrong for a man to eat anything that causes someone else to stumble. It is better not to eat meat or drink wine or to do anything else that will cause your brother to fall" (verses 19-21).
28. Miller, p. 269.

CHAPTER 6

The Good Group
More than a Committee

*Let us consider how we may spur one another on
to love and good deeds. Let us not give up meeting
together, as some are in the habit of doing, but let
us encourage one another.*

Hebrews 10:24-25a

It was late November and our church council members were huddled around our conference table in an attempt to hammer out an overdue vision statement for our local assembly. The previous evening the vice president from my school spoke to our council about vision-setting and planning. Now it was the next afternoon and we felt the time crunch to put the VP's ideas to pen and get on with our task.

We had just returned from lunch when Jack—a successful middle-aged real estate developer—proposed an unexpected turn. "I don't know about you folks, but I'm wondering if it's premature for us to discuss God's vision for our church before we examine how we stand before him and each other. Are we right with him? Are we right with each other? I think we need to settle these issues before we can discuss vision."

Several members glanced at the chairman for his response. He commented that we had sloughed off the vision task long enough and that our two-day retreat was intended to help us nail it down. But Jack's point was hard to ignore. If we harbored bitterness or unconfessed sin, how could we lead?

Then Lynn spoke up. "Maybe God would still honor our task even without a long confession-and-tears time. Maybe God can work through our good intentions and thoughtful discussion if we give it a try." From the nod of heads I could see a fence line go up mid-table. On Jack's side were those wanting to get relational, confess to each other, and bond in spirit. On Lynn's side were those wanting to pursue the task, trust in God's grace, and let cohesion take care of itself. We were at a standoff.

My council experience and the research of group communication schol-ars confirm a hunch you may have as well: groups can make you or break you—and they're practically unavoidable. We took a candid look at the family group in the preceding chapter. Now it is time to examine groups we choose to join, namely, task groups, relationship groups, and influence groups.[1] Let's begin with features that define small groups generally.

Defining Groups

Take a minute to consider the groups you have chosen to join. These might include the student newspaper staff, a sports team, or a college and career class at church. By conservative estimates, about 33 million U.S. citi-zens have a meeting on any given day at their workplace, and about 80 million people attend groups each week for personal support and care. In fact the majority of groups that meet for support and care stem from churches and synagogues.[2] What distinguishes these kinds of small groups from the people who mingle around a coke machine?

The answer, in part, is in how we define them. One definition is that a small group is "a limited number of people who communicate face-to-face, share a common understanding of an interdependent goal, influence one another, and express a sense of belongingness to the group."[3] These fea-tures are broad enough to include your college student newspaper staff and care group, but narrow enough to exclude the coke crowd and those cheering on a football team. Let's examine each feature.

A LIMITED NUMBER OF PEOPLE

How limited? Scholars don't always agree, but most see small groups as consisting of 3-20 members. What's true of a dyad (twosome) may be true of some groups, but what's true of a triad (threesome) better captures the group dynamic. Some add that an odd number is better than an even num-ber if your group votes a lot and where one vote either way will swing it. Depending on a group's purpose, too few members (3 or 4) may mean too few resources. Your newspaper staff would be stretched with only three writers and one editor. But too many members (12-20) may create other concerns such as *coalitions* and *deadwood*. Coalitions are clusters of indi-viduals who form cliques and nettle the nest with their own agendas. Dead-wood members are usually isolates who fail to contribute for reason of boredom, personal insecurity, or simply lack of time. There is no perfect number for how large a group should be, but conventional wisdom and research indicate that somewhere between 5-11 members there resides much potential for a good group.

WHO COMMUNICATE FACE-TO-FACE

We take this for granted, for without symbolic action among its members, a group could not function. However, trying to measure or describe group communication has proven to be a complex task. The sheer number of messages that could be sent appears daunting, even in a small group.

Suppose only two writers, Allen and Betsy, show up for a newspaper staff meeting one week. The number of possible actions (messages sent one way) is 2: A to B and B to A. If Carla, the editor, shows up the next week, the number of possible communicative actions shoot up to nine: 1) A to B, 2) A to C, 3) B to A , 4) B to C, 5) C to B, 6) C to A, 7) A to B & C, 8) B to A & C, and 9) C to A & B. And if that's not enough, groups of four yield 28 possible actions, groups of five 75, groups of six 186, groups of seven 441, and groups of eight 1,056.[4] It's no surprise that we say eight is enough! Numbers like these may look onerous until we recognize that each utterance comes to us one at a time and probably makes a lot of sense in context. But how can we categorize what gets said?

One way to organize communicative behavior is by *direction of contribution*. We've all experienced groups where two or three people hog the limelight and others are left off stage or in the balcony. To measure direction precisely, researchers typically videotape a group's interactions and then go back and systematically count who spoke to whom. The tally might be the tale to be told. In our fictional newspaper staff, we might find that Carla and Allen talk the most and usually to each other, while Betsy speaks the least and only to Doug, who usually makes comments to the whole group. Such patterns may prove interesting and helpful, but most of us want a feel for whether what got said contributed to the good of the group.

One way to answer that question is to observe the way comments and behavior function to fulfill group goals. We will look at goals in the next section, but here it is enough to say that most groups exist to solve problems, whether task, relational, or personal. Two group communication scholars, Randy Hirokawa and Dennis Gouran, suggest that members are more apt to solve problems with quality decisions when their interactions perform four important functions: 1) they show a thorough and accurate analysis of the problem, 2) they express criteria that frame their ideal goal, 3) they identify as many alternative solutions as possible, and 4) they evaluate the pluses and minuses of each alternative in light of the criteria frame.[5]

My church's council members had long expressed the problem: we had no statement of mission, vision, or core values. We felt rudderless. Our goal was also clear: we wanted to write a mission statement, vision statement and set of core values that would give focus to our programs and initiatives. The night of our major impasse, we eventually split into four sub-groups to discuss alternative statements. Four groups of three members each toiled over their own versions of these statements. Finally, in future meetings, we returned to debate the two most likely proposals.

Although Hirokawa and Gouran's functions capture the rational decision-making process much more than interpersonal squeaks and squawks, you might use their model to figure out why your group flounders relationally. Group members who offer up irrelevant comments, false information, biased opinions, and mere silence may frustrate others and create conflict. On the other hand, that members fail to engage in vigilant, mindful discussion may explain the eerie sense that the group is getting along too well, and is on it's way to a lousy decision.

Who Share a Commonly Understood Interdependent Goal

All groups do not pursue the same goal, yet their varying goals often determine the kind of talk and behavior members consider appropriate. Some, like a newspaper staff or church council, gather to get work done (the *task* or *decision-making* group); their meetings smack of all business. Others gather for friendship and fellowship (the *relationship group*); their meetings seem all fun. Still others come together for personal healing and growth (the *influence group*); their times can be emotionally charged.[6] In each case though, members realize that none of them can accomplish these tasks alone. They share an *interdependent* goal—something no one person can achieve alone.

The task or decision-making group. Classic examples include school and work committees who manage programs and budgets. My church council is a task group with a relational overlay. Here is its purpose:

> *Church Council:* to provide administrative and visionary oversight to the policies, personnel and programs of our local church so that we might extend the work of God's kingdom in spiritual depth and numerical breadth.

You can bet that this calling influences our communication significantly. We hear a lot of reports, debate what our church members want and need, and vote on recommendations to take before the entire church body. All the while we manage courteous civility and a little fun too. As you see, task groups are mainly work and occasionally play.

The relationship group. Relationship groups consist of people whose main goal is to enjoy each other's company, but not by accident like the coke machine gang. Their interaction is planned and purposeful, as in youth group fellowships and adult care groups.

Four years ago my wife and I helped begin a gourmet club among some couple friends. We meet four times a year in each others' homes. Life would go on without the Lundbergs, Camerons and Sawatzkys, but life is richer with them. Here is the purpose of our club:

> *The Gourmet Club*: to prepare and consume delectable international delights in the company of long-time friends, and to encourage each other in our marriages, family life, and Christian walk.

We don't have this goal written down in a manual, but we act as if we share it. For example, one night we got onto the topic of how we met our spouses. Ned told us of his initial attraction to Kim and his fear that she might be too good-looking for him. We didn't psychoanalyze Ned after his disclosure (despite there being four licensed psychologists in the group!) We simply chuckled and smiled our approval of Ned's willingness to be honest, and then affirmed that Ned and Kim were highly suitable for each other.

The gourmet goers represent what some describe as a good relationship group. In varying degrees we show committed volunteer attendance, affirmation of members, confidentiality of what is shared, open and honest self-disclosure, empathy for each other, accountability with each other, and prayer.[7] Relationship groups play with a purpose and their connecting is three-quarters the fun.

The influence group. Robert Wuthnow asked a U.S. sample of over 2,000 people the following question: "Are you currently involved in any small group that meets regularly and provides support or caring for those who participate in it?"[8] Exactly 40% said "yes." The faithful and irreligious alike join influence groups because they recognize the need for changed attitudes and habits. And that's what the influence group's purpose is: to help people change their views of themselves and their relationships so they can move up the ladder of personal development.

For some people their ladder is already in a very deep hole, and change means struggling back to ground level where life is "normal." For example, consider the purpose of groups such as Alcoholics Anonymous and Weight Watchers.

> *The Self-Help Counseling Group*: to help people who are caught in addictive and abusive behavior to accept this dependence and to assist them in moving toward a new identity with new expectations and behaviors towards others and the addictive substance.

Counseling groups like AA and WW require a skilled leader who understands the plight of group members and what they need for physical and emotional healing.

Other people's ladders are on firm ground, but they desire to go beyond the third rung spiritually or developmentally. Discipleship programs, such as the Navigators' 2:7 series, fall into this category. Members are not drug dependent; they seek God-dependence. What's their purpose?

> *The Discipleship Group*: to foster an environment where people can study God's word thoroughly and be given encouragement and accountability to apply spiritual principles and practices to every sphere of life.

The key is that members choose to be involved, desire to change, and are willing to do the homework and activities required to encourage spiritual growth. Influence groups represent the intriguing mix of serious relating toward the goal of spiritual and social health.

WHO INFLUENCE EACH OTHER

The reason my wife and I do dinner with friends regularly is because our friends are good for us. To modify Wuthnow's book title, "We Come Away Stronger." Becoming stronger means change, and change means being persuaded. Although entire books have been written about persuasion, it seems prudent to highlight leadership and conflict resolution as they pertain to the small group.

Leadership.[9] Without someone at the helm, most groups would veer off course and float adrift. One researcher found that ninety percent of group members say their current group has a leader, more than those who say they have a stated purpose (84%), name (76%) or agenda (75%).[10] The questions are, Who will lead, or Who should lead?

We used to think that leaders were born, not made. You either had leadership *qualities* or you didn't. Of little surprise, we found that leaders were more intelligent, knowledgeable and self-confident than followers as well as more attractive, taller, and verbally adept. The problem was that as the list of traits got longer and longer, the likelihood of finding anyone with each trait became slimmer and slimmer. In addition, many a short guy and average-looks gal who led groups admirably blew the whole formula.

What followed was an attempt to describe leadership *styles*. Autocratic leaders who cracked the whip and announced self-made decisions usually engendered aggression or apathy, depending on the followers. Laissez-faire leaders who took a "hands-off" approach did little to motivate, cohere, or even upset group members. Democratic leaders who encouraged group discussion and group decision-making were most likely to instill group satisfaction, cohesiveness, and quality decisions. But we have since discovered that the democratic leadership style doesn't work in some situations. If the college newspaper is two days overdue and the printer says she is about to go on vacation, what's needed is not a so-what-do-you-think-let's-take-a-vote democratic leader. The situation calls for a strong autocratic voice that can move sluggish writers to their computers!

So came a shift to our search for *situational* factors that allowed for leadership. Later this approach was modified in *contingency* theory. This view combined the styles view with the situational view to suggest that effective leadership depends on both variables. Contingency researchers showed that leaders who are most motivated to meet interpersonal needs are best qualified to lead less-than-enthusiastic followers who face a complex, unstructured task. Leaders who enjoy pushing for task accomplishment perform best with admiring followers who undertake less complex, more routine jobs.

Today one of the most popular views of leadership is the *functional perspective*. Its advocates suggest that being a leader is different than leadership. Leadership is *any behavior that helps the group accomplish its goals*. If our council chairperson misses two meetings in a row, the other eleven members will still get the job done. They might be *leaderless*, but not *leadership-less*. If you read between the lines of the functional approach, you can see a biblical theme, namely, *she or he who serves the needs of the group, leads*. The functional perspective endorses servant leadership.

Leadership style may conflict with group goals.

Conflict. Two chapters ago we discussed how we might manage conflict with friends, but I never defined conflict outright. Let's do that here. Conflict can be defined as "an expressed struggle between at least two interdependent parties who perceive incompatible goals, scarce rewards, and interference from the other party in achieving their goals."[11] Jack and Lynn expressed competing goals. Jack wanted to come clean with God and each other before we discussed what the church's vision should be. Lynn wanted to discuss vision straightway. Most group members sensed that we had scarce rewards, such as time, and wanted to avoid costs, such as an extra meeting. We were also interdependently linked by our desire to arrive at a unanimous decision. Jack saw Lynn as interfering with spiritual renewal. Lynn saw Jack as blocking task accomplishment.

Some believers like to think that life in the body is (or should be) a life of peace only. But that denies our fallenness. All human groups experience conflict, but Christians might be particularly uneasy with it. Why? I think it is because of at least three myths we hold dear.

Myth #1. Conflict is a sign of unhealthy diversity; the scriptures call us to unity.

Reality. Paul for one called us to unity (see Romans 5:5-6), but not unity in all thought and behavior. He called us to unity in spirit for the purpose of glorifying God. I know Lynn and Jack. They want to glorify God through their actions. Their clash probably led us to a more robust group experience than had either kept mum. Unity, like harmony, requires two different voices with the same musical score. Unity does not mean sameness just as harmony does not mean monotone.

Myth #2. Conflict is sin. Or, where there is conflict, sin must be present.

Reality. Conflict can be due to sin, but not all conflict is sin. Carla's call for more advocacy writing in the newspaper differs from Allen's goal for straight news, but both are legitimate newspaper philosophies; neither is immoral. Carla's hurling insults at Allen to win the argument would be sin.

Myth #3. Nice people do not conflict. (To be read: Holy people always agree.)

Reality: Many godly people conflict. Consider Jesus and Peter (see Matthew 16:23 where Jesus says, "Get behind me, Satan!) or Paul and Barnabas (Acts 15:39 "They had such a sharp disagreement that they parted company."). Peter's devotion to Christ (that led him to say No, you won't die!) earned him a stern reply. And Paul and Barnabas only had different views for how to launch the faith. The point is that even exemplars of our faith experience conflict.

A lot of advice has been given as to how we might manage conflict. In chapter four I repeated the Mayhalls' advice that we keep cool, address issues early, act wisely, and make understanding our aim. Here we may add that we speak the truth in love. Truth seeks justice in human affairs and love provides the grace to heal the wounds of truth. We might be passionate about our principles, but that doesn't mean we can clobber others enroute to advancing them.

And that's what seemed to transpire in the church council meeting. Our senior minister suggested that we first spend time in personal reflection and public confession, and then divide into work groups to draft separate vision statements. Jack's side of the table appreciated the pastor's sensitivity to relational and spiritual matters, and Lynn's side saw that work groups of three or four members could accomplish more than our clunky group of twelve. We met the true needs of each group member in a civil manner.

AND WHO EXPRESS A SENSE OF BELONGINGNESS TO THE GROUP

Feeling a sense of ownership is the last key to defining a small group. When we don't feel like we belong, our experience drags along. Several years ago the students on my school's student newspaper staff felt like spare wheels. The editor was a top-down, opinionated individual who did little to instill a sense of team work and group identity. Attendance at staff meetings plummeted and morale sunk to an all-time low. The group resembled a loose bunch of rag tag, individual reporters more than a *staff*.

Most small group scholars would say the newspaper staff lacked cohesion. One writer defines cohesion as "the total field of forces acting on members to remain in the group."[12] That's a broad definition, but it accounts for how groups as diverse as hockey teams and Weight Watchers can feel pulled to the center or repelled to outer orbit. What are some of those forces?

John Cragan and David Wright suggest four important forces: 1) the communication that occurs (or doesn't) and its quality, 2) the roles people play, whether contributing or detracting from the group's goals, 3) the norms or rules for behavior that the group establishes for itself, and 4) how members manage conflict. It may go without saying, but a lack of quality talk, competing roles, uncertain norms, and habitual conflict spoil any hope for cohesiveness. I think the first and fourth of these factors squelched belongingness for the newspaper staff. The top-down edicts from the editor-in-chief stymied group discussion, and, because no one "carefronted" the editor, everyone suffered.

Groups are more likely to experience cohesiveness when members know their roles, play by the rules, manage conflict well, and keep their talk and walk consistent. Cragan and Wright report that a cohesive blend leads to three desirable outcomes: productivity, consensus, and member satisfaction.[13] The more cohesive your group, the more likely it will get the job done, agree by consensus (everybody supports ideas), and enjoy themselves. Cohesion sounds like the holy grail of good groups. Find it, and you succeed.

. . . .

A few people. Face-to-face communication. A common goal. Influence. Belongingness. You will find these criteria in most standard textbooks that explain small group communication.

What believers might be asking is whether Christian groups experience any more bliss than other groups for reason of our shared faith and spirit. It'd sure be easy to think so, but it's tough to make absolutist claims when comparative data are hard to find. Besides, what a small group of believers considers bliss may differ from what newspaper staffers consider a good group.

What we do know is that small groups thrive when group members feel that their needs are being met. In one recent study researchers found that Christians who joined a weekly care group were largely motivated by the desire "to become more disciplined in [their] spiritual life."[14] And their small group experience seemed to meet that need. After participating in the group, 56% said spiritual matters were more important to them now, 53% said church or synagogue were more important, 63% said prayer was more a priority, and 48% valued Bible study more. A considerable majority of 84 % confirm that their faith and spiritual walk have been influenced positively by participating in a small group.[15]

What might be better than data on the devoted is a conceptual and biblical understanding of groups. There's nothing wrong with describing groups with criteria such as number of people, type of interaction, common goals, influence and belongingness; there's just the itch to ask, What's missing? Does our faith contribute a theme or criteria that explains why Jesus modeled his ministry after twelve disciples or why church growth pundits praise the small group movement?[16] Several authors who write about small groups in the church believe they are on to such an idea. What's missing is *community*.

The word "community," like "communication," derives from the Latin word *communis*, which means *to share in common*. We speak of urban communities (where we live together), but we can also speak of spiritual community (how we commune with each other). First century witnesses of new Christians said, "look how they love one another." Love for one another is the basis for *koinonia*, or believer fellowship. It's an ancient theme.

Before the Beginning There Was Community

Religious thinkers make some intriguing observations about God, earth-lings, and how we connect in community.[17] Their ideas apply not only to the small group context, but to our very definition of a person as self-in-community (see Chapter 3). Consider this theology of community — why group life reflects God's design locally and globally, whether that be on the level of committee, newspaper staff, or church life.

1. *God is community.* "From the beginning, God has existed as a commu-nity of Being. In human history God has revealed this community of Being as Father, Son and Spirit, an eternal small group, a Trinity of Being and relationship, around whom the greater community of be-ings is gathered, both angelic and resurrected."[18] The mystery of com-munity in the Trinity has baffled theologians for centuries, but most recognize the Trinity as *one* community.

2. *God desires community with us and among us.* Despite the perfect com-munity within the Godhead, God chose to create us — people — for fel-lowship with him. Everyone "is called to live in intimate, reciprocal, dialogical and growing relationship" with God.[19] Even if we have not found God, only through life with each other do we come to know who we are. Even if we reject God, our life with each other images the com-munity of the Godhead.

3. *God established a special community with and in his chosen people.* In the time before Christ, God entered a covenant relationship with the na-tion of Israel. A covenant is a promise, and God's promise to Abraham was that he would prosper and be blessed. God's requirement for Is-rael was that they be his people, his holy nation, his priesthood who would realize that individual-in-community was God's chosen design for human-human and human-divine relationships.

4. *Jesus Christ came to re-establish community between us and God.* The Jews struggled to maintain their integrity with God. We struggle to main-tain our integrity with God. God knows that we fail again and again. Therefore, in his desire to re-establish divine-human community, God walked on earth in the form of Jesus Christ. In Christ we have a God model for how we ought to live with God (vertical community) and with each other (horizontal community). Jesus used the twelve dis-ciples to epitomize the power of community and to establish his church.

5. *The church locally and globally expresses human and divine community.* Upon Christ's resurrection and ascension to God the Father, God sent his Holy Spirit to enable us to live out community in ecclesia — the church — and in the culture at large. We are called to love, honor, disciple, serve, wait for, care for, comfort, build up, maintain the peace with, be sub-

ject to, forgive, confess to, and extend hospitality to all people, especially those in the body. God's spirit binds all ecclesia together worldwide and some day Christ will return to unite with us.

To summarize this theology of community, I think Julie Gorman puts it well when she writes: "However much we may think of our relationship in individual terms, we are always seen by God as family, networked, honeycombed, related to one another as His children, His bride, His building."[20]

So What Really Is Community?

Good question. If we apply the term to everything from prayer with God to lunch with the girls, we may ruin the term's usefulness and spiritual insight. With this said, let's be honest: trying to define community is akin to defining time or justice. All are elusive ventures.

One person who has chosen that venture, however, is Scott Peck. In his popular book *The Different Drum: Community Making and Peace*, this Episcopalian medical doctor and psychiatrist wrestles for the defining features of community.[21] Although his ideas may apply to lovebirds and large organizations, keep in mind that Peck is mainly interested in the small group of 3-20 people. As you read these features below you might reflect on whether the groups to which you belong exhibit these qualities. If you can answer "yes" to a number of them, you will begin to see the centrality of community to group communication.

A place where everybody is welcome. Peck calls this "inclusivity," but it boils down to a welcoming spirit. Inclusivity is not an absolute though; it's something your group must negotiate, especially in fellowship and care groups. If you let *anyone* in, you could kill the group. If you let *no one* new in, you could kill the group. The key is finding the balance between an open field and a brick wall.

I recall some acquaintances that struggled with inclusivity. Their growth group was into its third month and bonding nicely through Bible study and mutual encouragement. Then a new couple arrived that had a different purpose in mind, namely, to question the faith. The original members thought their purpose was to edify believers, not attract disagreeing dissenters. The group limped along for a few weeks and then breathed relief when the couple failed to show one night. Sadly, the group's leader reported that the newcomers left because they felt coldly unwelcome. Your group members may need to discuss what your purpose is and how obviously they want to hang the sign "newcomers welcome."

Whether we intend to or not, we convey welcoming and distancing messages to outgroup members with our nonverbals.

A place where people are committed to each other. Commitment means showing up in body and putting up in acceptance. For example, the chairman of our church council relishes in tidbits of data whereas I'm a more global thinker who enjoys waxing philosophic. Both Don and I have to guard against judging each other unduly; our manner is a matter of style, not morality. We express our commitment by faithfully attending council meetings and through active listening and respect for the other guy's strengths. Don can recall obscure budget lines and important nuances of ancient conversations that I have long forgotten. We would be sunk without him.

A place where decisions are made by mutual agreement. Maybe not every time, but most of the time. I like the cartoon that shows the juror standing outside the jury room giving the bailiff the carry-out order. "Eleven hamburgers, one frank. Eleven coffees, one tea. Eleven apple pies, one chocolate cake." Juries *must* come to consensus or unanimous agreement. It's part of due process. Most groups we belong to don't have to agree unanimously, but it's wise to shoot for it. As already implicated, consensual agreement leads to a more cohesive bunch than when leaders bark orders to passive members or when voting results in a 6-4 split.[22] Consensus also takes more time and patience than a vote or leader fiat because members need to listen to everyone's view.

A place where people are realistic about the world and themselves. In other words, community encourages looking out as much as looking in, and members are not duped about either reality.

Recently the Parents Advisory Council of the elementary school where my children attend held a meeting to determine whether or not students should be required to wear uniforms. One hundred and seventy five parents showed up to speak their minds about uniforms, money, identity, choice, and convenience. The arguments stacked up about even. Just before the vote (yes, it's smart to vote with 175 people!) one mother commented that this issue could be explosive and divisive. It could turn parent against parent and destroy P.A.C. unity. But then the mother said that she didn't sense antagonism, rather passion for the welfare of the children. The vote eventually went 110 against to 65 for.

Community affords this kind of luxury. It is a place where you can be true to yourself and speak your mind without the fear of attack. At the same time, however, community requires us to listen to others. To use a political phrase, community encourages checks and balances to keep us on course with the felt needs of our members and the world at large.

A place of safety where contemplation, healing, converting, and growth occur. What Peck means by contemplation is not quiet meditation but a heightened awareness of your self and your group's purpose. Contemplation in this sense is asking, "How are we doing?" "Are we on target?" "Are we healthy?" "Where are we headed?" The key is that group members protect your right to ask these questions. John Fischer laments that in some Christian circles people are not encouraged to ask certain questions. He writes,

> Have you ever been in a group of believers when someone asked a question that didn't have an easy answer? Disapproving glances were probably thrown at the questioner as if to say, "Don't you know we don't ask such questions here?" There is a tacit understanding within many churches and fellowship groups that this gospel ship navigates best if you don't rock the boat.[23]

If your group discusses the same topics in the same patterns with the same outcomes meeting after meeting, then there's a good chance you could benefit from contemplating why you began the group and where it is headed. If you feel like you can't ask tough questions, you might ask, "What do we fear about tough questions?"

In addition to contemplation, Scott Peck also suggests that community occurs when converting and healing take place. That might mean spiritual conversion (as in finding redemption in God through Christ for the first time) or physical healing (as in release from alcoholism). But it can also mean personal discipleship in the iron-sharpens-iron manner of Proverbs 27:17. And that's what seems to be going on in many church groups. Robert Wuthnow reports in *"I Come Away Stronger"* that most members of cell groups say they feel closer to God (90%), have a deeper love for others (87%), are better able to forgive others (84%), and are better able to forgive themselves (82%).[24] Indeed, most of them joined church groups because they wanted to learn more about God and develop their trek with him.

A word of caution though. Peck suggests that a leader's attempt to *program* healing and converting can backfire. Whether due to our western sense of rugged individualism or simple fear of change, most of us do not want to be considered someone else's project. We want to change on our own accord. Research by Robert Wuthnow once again supports this idea. He writes:

> I have shown that many of the formal structures that have been discussed in the literature on small groups — such as contracts, terms, able leadership, and fixed agendas — contribute *less* to the successful functioning of groups than do informal norms and activities, such as encouraging all members to share, respecting their views, and making them feel appreciated.[25]

This does not mean that leaders should come unprepared or have a vague purpose. It means the goal should be to establish a safe place — a place where it's okay to not be okay. Communicating love and acceptance provides this kind of safe place where members can be vulnerable and accountable.

A place where people can fight gracefully, influence others equally and enjoy a spirit of unity. We talked about fighting gracefully in chapter four. Let me give you a brief example of how fighting, influencing, and enjoying unity looks in a group. Six years ago I joined up with two other men to meet every other Friday over breakfast to read and discuss books. Today we still hold to three implicit rules: read the chapter, form an opinion, and come ready to hear differing opinions! We might say that Rick is our leader because he phones us to confirm our meetings, but beyond that everyone has equal time and voice. We debate, cajole, laugh and pray over ideas such as church growth, consumer-culture, being men, and loving our wives. We jokingly acknowledge who's the liberal, the conservative, and the middle-roader. We agree, disagree, and agree to disagree on a range of issues. But we're bonded, like the *Three Musketeers*. Our threesome is so well known to Cory, the restaurant's maitre d', that on occasion he will greet the first guy to arrive with, "Table for three?"

So there's an attempt to capture community in words and link it to small groups. If its contours remain a little fuzzy, that is probably a good thing.

What we should garner from Scott Peck and others is that community is more process (how things are done) than product (what gets done), more motive than behavior, more heart than head. Authentic Christian community is about sharing life with others under Christ's lordship. "This is what *koinonia* is all about. *Koinonia*, the Greek Septuagint and New Testament word for 'fellowship,' actually means *sharing something with someone*. This kind of relationship is deeper than that of acquaintances or even friends. It is marked by the quality of sharing that *good* friends with a *close personal relationship* enjoy — love for one another. This a relationship characterized by openness, acceptance, warmth, and growth."[26]

With this said I think I hear some groans. Equating community with *koinonia* and considering them defining qualities of a good group suddenly makes for a very high standard. But if not community, what should be the acid test for the good group of believers? Should we expect church councils and newspaper staffs to be as communal as gourmet clubs and care groups? Maybe not, but a task group without community is sheer drudgery. Should we expect Christian groups to share more community than other groups? Maybe. We often share the same values, goals, and language. But before we make any claims to having more community, we better check our motives. If it's to be better than out-group members, we may kibosh a welcoming spirit. Is community any different from what others already call cohesiveness? That's a tough question. Perhaps it should remain as the springboard for future thinking about small group communication.

Summary

As we approach the turn of the millenium, the small groups movement within churches has in some sectors outpaced Sunday school classes in numbers. Whether at church on Sunday morning or in someone's home midweek, small groups seem to meet important needs for believers. This chapter presents the idea of community as a feature of Christian groups that may explain their longevity and dynamic.

We defined a small group as a limited number of people who interact face-to-face over time toward a common goal. Group members typically enjoy equal opportunity to persuade each other and find identity with each other. Group communication reflects the purpose of a group, whether it be task, relationship, personal change or a mix thereof. Leaders in groups would be wise to ask, "How can my behavior help meet the needs of the group?," not "How might I structure change?" Being organized is important, but keeping the flow of discussion open and affirming members appears to be more important for success.

The notion of community goes beyond the realm of explaining group dynamics. Community explains, in part, the mystery of the Trinity, God's desire for fellowship with his creation, and his choosing of Israel as a special people. Community helps us understand Immanuel—God with us—in his incarnation through Christ, and it deepens our appreciation of what it means to be reconciled among fellow believers, whether in our local fellowship or worldwide.

Attempting to define community is a slippery venture, but Scott Peck's description gave us a start. Community exists when people feel welcome, not shunned; are committed to each other, not dogged under gun point. Community is about making decisions together and being in tune to our purpose on earth. In community we are safe to reflect on the tough questions of life for the purpose of healing, changing and growing. Finally, community is where we can conflict gracefully, influence one another mutually, and enjoy a spirit of unity. It's about getting along despite our differences.

Whether we can expect full-blown community in task groups might be wishful thinking, but task groups with no community is conveyor-belt painful. How to nurture community without chasing it away may be our primary challenge.

Worth the Talk

1. Is there any feature of small groups that you think is missing from the definition given above? What feature would you add? Subtract? Why?
2. Do you think that the idea of "community" explains best the dynamic of God's relationship with us and our relationship with other believers? If so, why? If not, why not? What idea would you use?
3. What's the likelihood that a task group such as a newspaper staff or yearbook staff will experience community as described above? Is this a realistic goal or is it pie in the sky?

Consider the Walk

1. Consider a group to which you belong. Analyze its dynamics using the criteria for defining a small group (noted under the "Defining Groups" section of this chapter). Try to explain why your group members interact as they do. Use the criteria as a basis for suggesting ways your group might improve its experience.
2. Analyze the same group for community using the criteria under the "So What Really is Community?" section of this chapter. Suggest why you think your group suffers from a lack of community or relishes in ripe community. (Or perhaps your group falls somewhere in between.) Use these criteria for recommending attitudes or actions the group could use to increase community.

Notes

1. I take this typology from Em Griffin's *Getting Together: A guide for good groups*, InterVarsity Press, Downers Grove, IL, 1983, pp. 27-41, but need to acknowledge that various authors categorize groups differently. For example, Michael Argyle distinguishes between family and adolescent groups, work and committee groups, and therapy groups in his article "Five Kinds of Small Social Groups," in Robert S. Cathcart and Larry A. Samovar (Eds.), *Small group communication: A reader* (6th ed.), Wm. C. Brown Publishers, Dubuque, IA, 1992, pp. 18-25. Griffin's categories are preferred because they appear to be more encompassing: family and adolescent groups are examples of relationship groups; work and committee groups are examples of task groups; therapy groups are one example of influence groups.

2. The 33 million figure is cited by Stewart Tubbs and Sylvia Moss, *Human communication*, 7th ed., McGraw-Hill, Inc., New York, NY, 1994, p. 266; the 80 million figure is estimated from Robert Wuthnow, *Sharing the journey: Support groups and America's new quest for community*, The Free Press, New York, NY, 1994 where he shows that 40% of a national survey indicated they belonged to a support group. If, by conservative estimate, there are 200 million adults in the United States, the total number of people in support groups alone is about 80 million.

3. Beatrice G. Schultz, *Communicating in the small group: Theory and practice*, 2nd ed., HarperCollins College Publishers, New York, NY, 1996, p. 5. See Tubbs and Moss, p. 267, for this second definition: A small group is a "collection of individuals who influence one another, derive some satisfaction from maintaining membership in the group, interact for some purpose, assume specialized roles, are dependent on one another, and communicate face to face."

4. Robert Bostrom, "Patterns of Communicative Interaction in Small Groups," *Speech Monographs*, Vol. 37, 1970, pp. 257-263 as cited in Tubbs and Moss, p. 286.

5. This discussion of Hirokawa and Gouran's work is based on Em Griffin's description in *A first look at communication theory* (3rd ed.), The McGraw-Hill Companies, Inc., New York, NY, 1997, pp. 247-258. See also Dennis Gouran, Randy Hirokawa, Kelly Julian, and Geoff Leatham, "The Evolution and Current Status of the Functional Perspective on Communication in Decision-Making and Problem-Solving Groups," in *Communication yearbook 16*, Stanley Deetz (ed.), Sage, Newbury Park, CA, 1993, pp. 573-600.

6. Griffin, *Getting together*, pp.27-41.

7. Griffin, *Getting together*, pp.35-36.

8. Robert Wuthnow (Ed.) *"I come away stronger:" How small groups are shaping American religion*. Wm. B. Eerdmans Publishing Company, Grand Rapids, MI, 1994, p. 369.

9. This concise review of leadership theory is based on Beatrice G. Schultz, *Communicating in the small group: Theory and practice*, 2nd ed., HarperCollins College Publishers, New York, NY, 1996, pp. 94-102.

10. Wuthnow, *Sharing the journey*, p. 135.

11. Joyce Hocker and William W. Wilmont, *Interpersonal conflict*, 3rd ed., Wm. C. Brown Publishers, Dubuque, IA, 1991, p. 12 as cited in Tubbs and Moss, p.195.

12. Schachter, Stanley, "Deviation, Rejection and Communication," *Journal of Abnormal and Social Psychology*, Vol. 46, 1951, pp. 190-208 as cited in Tubbs and Moss, p. 281.
13. John F. Cragan and David W. Wright, *Communication in small group discussions: An integrated approach* (3rd ed.), West Publishing Company, St. Paul, MN, 1991, Chapter 1.
14. Wuthnow, *Sharing the journey*, p. 381.
15. Wuthnow, *Sharing the journey*, p. 382 and following.
16. Along with that praise comes a legitimate call for concern. For a balanced view of the small group movement in religious America, see Warren Bird, "The Great Small-Group Takeover," *Christianity Today*, February 7, 1994, pp. 25-29.
17. Most of these ideas come from Gareth Weldon Icenogle's *Biblical foundations for small group ministry: An integrational approach*, InterVarsity Press, Downers Grove, IL, 1994 and Julie A. Gorman's *Community that is Christian: A handbook on small groups*, Victor Books, Wheaton, IL, 1993.
18. Icenogle, p. 371.
19. Icenogle, p. 371.
20. Gorman, p. 23.
21. M. Scott Peck, *The different drum: Community making and peace*. Simon and Schuster, New York, NY, 1987.
22. See for example Cragan and Wright, pp. 20-21 and 269-270.
23. John Fischer, *What on earth are we doing?*, Servant Publications, Ann Arbor, MI, 1996, p. 35.
24. Wuthnow (Ed.) *"I Come Away Stronger,"* p. 382.
25. Wuthnow, *Sharing the journey*, p. 133. See Chapter 5 especially.
26. Thomas G. Kirpatrick, *Small groups in the church: A handbook for creating community*. The Alban Institute, New York, NY, 1995, p.5. Kirpatrick quotes Gerhard Kittel (Ed.), *Theological Dictionary of the New Testament*, Wm. B. Eerdmans Publishing Company, Grand Rapids, MI, 1965, p. 797 for this definition of *koinonia*.

CHAPTER 7

Responsibility Behind the Rostrum
The Challenge of Public Speaking

Now Stephen, a man full of God's grace and power, did great wonders and miraculous signs among the people. Opposition arose, however from members of the Synagogue....These men began to argue with Stephen, but they could not stand up against his wisdom or the Spirit by which he spoke.

Acts 6:8-10

In January of 1995, an Argentinean sports idol—Carlos Monzon—was killed in a car accident that left Argentineans reeling in grief. The boxer had led a very public and celebrated life, defending his middleweight crown a record fourteen times between 1970 and his retirement in 1977. He was undefeated those seven years.

But after his retirement, Monzon became alcoholic and violent. In 1988 Carlos Monzon killed an estranged companion during a domestic fight and was sentenced to eleven years in prison.

Fortunately for Monzon, his years in prison were not hopeless. During that time he asked Hector Gimenez, senior pastor of 'Ondas de Amor y Paz' (the second largest church in the world) to counsel him. Gimenez' own previous experience as a drug addict and thief helped him identify with Monzon. After several visits and many long talks, Monzon gave in to the love and lordship of Christ. "From the moment of his conversion he was determined to do whatever he could to help young people avoid the traps he had fallen into. He spent hours everyday reading the Bible in prison, and soon began Bible studies."[1] In the eyes of many Argentineans, Carlos Monzon was a new man.

Monzon's fatal car accident occurred when he was returning to the prison on his weekend pass after speaking at a youth gathering in his own hometown. The news of his death spread quickly. Writer Rauna May, who attended the funeral, tells the rest of the story:

> With just one day's notice, over 30,000 people flooded a small town almost 500 kilometres north of Buenos Aires for Monzon's funeral. The procession through the town filled the streets. The nation mourned the loss of an idol.
>
> Gimenez, who was asked to speak, asked the people, "How many of you want to see Carlos again?" The crowd roared. He told how Carlos had received Jesus Christ and had dedicated his life to seeing as many people as possible enter into the same relationship with the Lord he had.
>
> Gimenez explained that if the fans truly wanted to see Carlos again, the only way they could do that was through receiving Jesus Christ as their Lord and Savior. He then led the crowd in a prayer. When he finished, he told them that if they meant what they had prayed they would see Carlos again. His invitation to express that was followed by a thunderous shout, "Carlos, I'm going to see you again."
>
> Gimenez closed by saying that the death of an idol, which the enemy had meant for destruction, had been turned around for the glory of God.[2]

For Reverend Gimenez, the results of his speaking were repentance and joy for many of his listeners. For Stephen, the outcome of his speech to the Sanhedrin was his stoning at the hands of a mob. Both were willing to rise to the challenge of the situation, and both spoke the truth. Their task, like our speaking task, is a sobering one.

The Challenges and Responsibilities of Public Speaking

How willing would you be to address 30,000 people mourning the loss of someone like Michael Jordan? How eager would you be to speak with thirty atheists on a university campus? What would you say? Would you inform them, console them, persuade them, or provoke them? What type of logical and emotional appeals would you use? What types of appeals do you think would be ethical? What research would you have to do? What

Excerpt from "Death of flawed Argentine hero brought salvation," *Christian Info News*, March 1995, p. 4 by Rauna May used by permission.

things would a funeral context require you to say? A university context? Do you think you would be the right person for such a task?

Few of us will ever be in the speaking situations Pastor Gimenez and Stephen were in. But all of us will have opportunity to speak publicly before smaller groups and for less publicized events. Whether we speak to 30,000 people or to thirty, many of the challenges and responsibilities of public speaking remain the same.

One out of five students in elementary school, secondary school, and college suffer from extreme fear of speaking in public. Another one in five experience "butterflies" before speaking.[3] Why does public speaking instill so much fear? I believe the answer is that, consciously or not, people recognize the sobering challenges and responsibilities that define public address. What are those challenges? What are those responsibilities? Let's consider each.

PUBLIC SPEAKING IS A RHETORICAL AND PURPOSIVE ACTIVITY

By "rhetorical" we mean persuasive and by "purposive" we mean intentional. It's a broad claim, but some scholars suggest that all speeches convince us of something whether the speaker intends so or not.[4] Public speakers are usually very intentional about why they speak, but even those who intend to "merely inform" ultimately persuade us of something.

For example, while attending the University of Iowa I often passed the free speech quadrangle in the center of campus. There I would pause to hear the "informative" talks of saffron-robed Hare Krishna converts as they described their vegetarian diet and invited students to an informative evening lecture. Even if I ignored their long-term goal to win me as a convert, their description of a vegetarian diet came with some tacit assumptions such as our value for health and the humane treatment of animals.

Or consider the stand-up comedy routine of Rodney Dangerfield. Here's a guy who claims he gets no respect, but whose mastery of the one-liner draws our admiration. We're convinced he deserves respect. Even his jokes perform social commentary. Once he quipped, "I was at a boxing match last night, and things got so rough, a hockey game broke out." You can't help but think that hockey fights have gotten out of hand.

In terms of purpose, some speeches are more obviously persuasive than informative, or more celebratory than entertaining. Pastor Gimenez was purposeful in his talk—he wanted as many people as possible to enter into a new relationship with Jesus Christ, just as Carlos Monzon had wished. I bet he wrestled with how to present that spiritual challenge in the context of a funeral. He seems to have succeeded.

In your speech class, you are likely to give speeches for different purposes: to introduce, inform, persuade, inspire, entertain, or celebrate. I encourage you to pay close attention to your instructor's expectations. Each year I hear speeches that miss their mark. "Ten informative reasons why you should vote Democrat" is a case in point. Be mindful and intentional as you abide by the purpose of the assignment.

PUBLIC SPEAKING IS A RESEARCH ACTIVITY

Research is one of those "ugh" topics. Few of us would prefer to be in a library with books stacked high or have our noses to an Internet screen for hours upon end. We also may think that people who excel in public speaking are naturally bright or have true-life experiences that give them an edge.

While it's true that a person's fight with cancer or climb to the peak of Mt. Rainier banks him or her a rich experience for speaking publicly, the vast majority of speeches would go no where if not informed from other sources. Consider my colleague, Paul Chamberlain. Paul's mother suffers from Multiple Sclerosis, the degenerative killer that weakens a person muscle by muscle. Paul has had to ask himself, "What does 'quality of life' mean?" as he has watched his mother worsen over the years.

At the same time, Paul is an avid debater who has debated the topic of physician-assisted suicide. It would be a natural for Paul to debate his opponents from personal experience. But you can imagine the shallowness of his claims if he only had his mother's experience for proof. I had the privilege of hearing him debate a Member of Parliament before 500 students at the University of British Columbia recently. He spoke flawlessly for twenty minutes and responded to questions adeptly for ten more. Later I asked him how much time he spent in research. "Oh, about two hours a day for the last two months," he said. That's sixty hours of research for thirty minutes of talk, a ratio of 120-to-1.

You don't have that kind of time, but you do have some decisions to make as you prepare your talks. How much do you know about your topic? How can you invest your time best to garner opinions and data? How might you weave in your own experience? Unless you tap into the breadth and depth your topic represents, you might forfeit your right to be heard by your classmates. Types of evidence that you might unearth include:

Facts
Statistics
Opinions from experts
Personal knowledge
Examples and illustrations
Anecdotes and stories
Quotations
Definitions and descriptions

You can locate material from a variety of sources. Your goal should be to use the appropriate sources, not the easiest or fastest ones. Consider doing your research from:

Magazines
Books
Scriptural texts
Encyclopedias
Statistical sources
Biographical sources
Newspapers
Government publications
Computer databases
Internet Websites
Microfilm databases
Special reference books[5]

Speaking on a topic that interests you will take some drudgery out of research. Receiving positive feedback from your instructor and classmates for a well-researched speech removes even more. I encourage you to go the extra mile.

Public Speaking Is a Logical and Emotional Activity

Reverend Gimenez knew this well. He offered hope to an emotionally distraught crowd, but he conveyed that hope logically. First he affirmed the scripture's guarantee that those who die in Christ will live forever in heaven. Then he addressed how one may come to Christ. In what logicians call *syllogistic form*, Gimenez' logic looked like this.

Major Premise: Believers in Christ live forever in heaven.
<u>Minor Premise: Carlos Monzon was a believer in Christ.</u>
Therefore: Carlos Monzon will live forever in heaven.

Major Premise: Carlos awaits other believers in heaven.
<u>Minor Premise: Anyone can believe in Jesus Christ for new life.</u>
Therefore: Anyone can see Carlos in heaven if they believe in Christ.

Aristotle used the term *logos* to refer to appeals we make with logic. He used the term *pathos* to mean appeals we make with emotions. While the two look distinct, keep in mind that they overlap to varying degrees depending on the points we make in a speech.

You don't have to mention both premises in your speech however to make sense with your audience. Reverend Gimenez does this in regard to his second claim, namely, that anyone can see Carlos again if they rely on God's grace through Christ. He doesn't actually say "Carlos awaits other believers in heaven" or "Anyone can believe in Jesus Christ for new life." Some scholars feel this form of reasoning, called the enthymeme, is a more convincing way to speak because you allow your audience the freedom to create the missing assumption.[6] They create their own proof, in effect, and that persuades.

We might not think of hope as an emotion, but that's what Gimenez offered grieving Argentineans. We might imagine that the crowd interpreted this offer as an act of love. Some may have seen it as manipulation and become indignant. As a speaker you may want to make a direct appeal to emotion or an indirect one. For example, a direct appeal you might use would promise listeners personal satisfaction if they begin a regular exercise program. An indirect appeal might be to simply list the benefits of regular exercise and let the audience infer that these benefits bring contentment. Either way, your audience will have some kind of emotional response to you as a speaker and your message.

Public Speaking Is a Symbolic Activity

Do you think Franklin Roosevelt's speech after Japan's attack on Pearl Harbor would have been memorable if he had begun it with, "December 7, 1941: A date which will live in world history"? That's how his assistant first wrote it. Roosevelt made one slight change, and now most college students can repeat, "December 7, 1941: A date which will live in infamy." Or consider if John F. Kennedy had said, "Stop looking for a government handout, and find some way to chip in your own two bits." Instead he penned, "Ask not what your country can do for you—ask what you can do for your country."

In Chapter 1 we discussed the power of words to refer to and create reality. That is perhaps no truer than in public speaking. Behind the podium we *cite* incriminating evidence, *describe* war and heaven, *plead* the case of the innocent, *defend* the widow and orphan, *proclaim* God's truth, and the like. This is not to ignore the importance of vocal variety and appropriate gestures, but to highlight that without words we would have pantomime, not public *speaking*. In Chapter 1 we considered how words might be used intelligibly, culturally, graphically, worthily, and in speech acts. Here are some additional guidelines.

Find the right word. Not the *morally* right word, though this may apply at times, but the *meaningfully* right word. Meanings are in people, but the right words vibrate them. "World history" might be correct, but "infamy" captures the evil and anger associated with the bombing.

Find the appropriate word. By *appropriate* I mean words that will not offend people inadvertently. Sexist expressions such as *dame, broad, stud,* and *typical male aggressor* fail to show the respect others deserve as made in God's image. Similarly, stereotypical expressions such as *dumb blond, red neck, WASP (White Anglo Saxon Protestant),* and even *some black guy* place people in boxes. Preferred expressions convey the same meaning but don't offend, such as *woman, man, an aggressive male, a less intelligent woman with blonde hair, an obnoxious racist, a Euro-American Presbyterian* (or whatever denomination), and *an African-American man whose name I can't remember.* In culture wars today you may hear some believers using harsh terms such as *feminazi* (feminist + nazi) and *fag*. While these terms capture the disdain believers have for some of these people's activities, it's hard to imagine that God is pleased. He knows people's hearts, and he says he will judge. Should our language judge?

Avoid jargon. What would you think if your pastor began a sermon like this: "Lest our sanctification be hindered by iniquity, let us renounce our abominations and embrace Christ's propitiation." Besides being repetitive (*iniquity* and *abomination* both mean *sin*), this statement is rotten with jargon. Jargon is the specialized language used by a group or a profession. Better if your pastor simply said, "Let's admit that we've messed up and accept Christ's payment for our sins so we can grow spiritually." Even non-church-goers can tap into this line's meaning. Jargon creeps in as we learn the intricacies of our faith and its teachings. Our challenge is to translate those ideas into simple and concrete words for our audience.

Define terms early. Pastor Gimenez instructed the funeral mourners that they could see Carlos Monzon again "through receiving Jesus Christ as their Lord and Savior." But what does "receive" mean? We "receive" packages in the mail. Is receiving Christ as passive an act? What does "Lord" mean? To some it denotes a serf-and-master relationship that smells of subjugation. And what of "Savior"? Outside of Christendom you don't hear politicians or church leader calling themselves "savior." It's an elusive term. Several years ago I was pleasantly challenged by a pastor who once asked, "From what does the Savior save us?" I had always thought "from death." But then what does it mean to "work out one's salvation" while still on earth? Obviously salvation kicks in before I kick out. Our challenge is to define or describe key words in our speech early on (or as the words arise) so our audience can construct sensible meaning. Like bricks to a wall, defined terms help build our ideas.

PUBLIC SPEAKING IS ABOUT WHO YOU ARE

Or put another way, public speaking is about being someone worth listening to. In the United States and Canada, *doing* is more valued than *being*. As task masters, many folks see public address as an *activity*, consisting of topic selection, audience analysis, library research, organization, writing, practice, and performance. This is the orientation of most public speaking textbooks. Speaking is viewed as a skill, knack, or craft.

Without doubt, speaking is a craft. But if you consider the great speakers of our culture, they are more than skilled artisans; they are first and foremost great individuals. Recently our campus minister asked student leaders who they would invite to speak in chapel if they could choose anyone in the world. Their number one choice was Billy Graham, their second, Tony Campolo. To be sure, these men are fine speakers, but which came first, their speaking success or their life with God?

A negative example comes to mind. For several years my wife and I have attended music concerts at a local Christian high school. The director of the chorale struck us as highly competent but uncharacteristically cocky. His students sang gospel songs, but their message didn't seem to be his song in attitude and style. Several singers struggled with the power trip the director seemed to command over them. Then new information came

"So Ms. Everschmere, we suggest you muster a shred of common ground, milk emotional stories, and promise them the world."

to light. A twenty-something woman disclosed that the director had initiated a sexual relationship with her at age fourteen. It didn't end for ten years. Duplicity cost him his job and possibly his career. He will likely not direct or speak publicly for a long time.

You don't have to be hiding a scandalous sex relationship to feel uncertain about the public arena. Sometimes it's a matter of still developing and discovering who we are. Ever so often in my public speaking class some students will confide in me that they don't think they believe anything strongly enough to warrant convincing others of the same. "Just give me a topic," they plead. For other students the concern is not beliefs, but behavior. "There's nothing I do regularly that I think others should do too; I don't exercise, don't write for the school paper, don't work with inner city kids, nor plan to do summer missions." Fortunately for these students, one goal of a college or university education is character development. If you think your speech class is frightfully unbearable, remember that trials sharpen our faith and develops perseverance that helps us mature (see James 1:2-8).

To know who we are in God, as noted in Chapter 3, yields confidence and integrity to our speaking. Most scholars of rhetoric would say that moral character is a requirement for persuasive speaking. Consider how Plato bemoaned showmanship speaking that plagued the sophists of his day.[7] Sophists (pronounced *sah-fists*) were professional speakers who traveled the Greek islands impressing common folks with their ability to argue both sides of an issue but not taking a stand for truth. Plato likened sophists to "false lovers" — connivers who used public speaking to deceive and manipulate to make an easy buck. Plato urged would-be rhetoricians to be "noble lovers" — people who spoke the truth and allowed the audience to respond in a way which benefited themselves, not the speaker.

Similarly Aristotle made much of being a person of depth and character as a prerequisite for the public speaker. He argued that a speaker's *ethos* — that is, character, good will, and moral rightness — completed the trilogy of *logos* and *pathos*. We appeal to logic, emotions, and our own moral character to persuade others.[8]

Furthermore, around the time of Christ, Roman teacher Fabius Quintilian defined the entire rhetorical enterprise as "A good man speaking well" for what was just and honorable. For Quintilian, a person was good if he or she was "free from all vice, a lover of wisdom, a sincere believer in the cause which he advocates, and a servant of the state and the people."[9] That's quite a high calling.

Today we are likely to say that these character issues concern "credibility." Credibility is the degree to which a speaker is perceived by audience members to be knowledgeable, trustworthy, dynamic, attractive, and similar to themselves. Credibility entails more than perceived integrity. The "trustworthy" factor is most akin to moral goodness, and is commonly defined as "being honest, just, and objective."[10] The scary point is that some speakers convince listeners with a "trust me" smile while feeding them a line. Jim Jones of the People's Temple and David Koresh of the Davidian Branch of The Seventh Day Adventists are poignant examples that come to mind. Despite their unorthodox teachings, both men convinced followers to believe their claims to messiah status, only to lead adherents to their deaths in mass suicide and murder.

J. I. Packer challenges us to be a person of God through knowledge of God. He suggests that those who know God have great energy for God, have great thoughts of God, show great boldness for God, and have great contentment in God.[11] Knowing God does not mean just knowing theology however. It means obedience and dependence on him so we can see his work in our lives. From these experiences we become people of God, worthy of speaking for truth.

I propose that until we get beyond the idea that speech-giving is divorced from our character, we will continue to see it as "mere rhetoric" and "fine sounding argument." Rather, if we see it as an activity that stems from our being rooted in God and his truth, we will become sought after speakers.

PUBLIC SPEAKING IS AN ETHICAL ACTIVITY

I'm certain that God has Reverend Gimenez in his firm grip, but I'll be honest: upon first reading how the minister handled the Monzon funeral situation, I felt miffed. Thirty thousand mourners tormented with heartache seemed too easy targets for an evangelistic invitation. Was their decision for Christ based on understanding or on a knee-jerk desire to see their star soccer player again? It just didn't sit right. In a phrase, I questioned his ethics.

Ethics is the area of philosophy that addresses rules for right behavior. Ethics are based on moral maxims—tungsten pylons that guide the manner by which we rivet our speech and behavior. A maxim such as "Integrity is more valued than image" might render the ethic (behavioral rule) "Don't make up proof to prove your point." Ethics pose a significant challenge for people who are rootless in their moral understanding, and this rootlessness contributes to their fear of speaking. It is desirable, therefore, that you define and use a moral code in your speaking.

In our postmodern culture it is not fashionable to suggest that any one ethical maxim reigns supreme. Consider, for example, that the authors of a long-running speech textbook say, "No one can presume to tell you what ethical codes you ought to adhere to when giving a speech."[12] The result is a moral maxim smorgasbord of values and "-isms" which students are encouraged to recognize and adopt when they speak. As believers we may value a biblical ethic over a non-biblical one, but even here one single ethic doesn't float to the surface. My desire therefore is to briefly introduce you to several non-biblical maxims, and then take more space to suggest a particular Christian ethic. You'll see though that God has spoken to the conscience of "secular" thinkers as well (see Romans 2:14 & 15).

Moral Codes for Ethical Public Speaking[13]

1. Aristotle's Golden Mean: Communication is ethical if it reflects moral virtue. Moral virtue is that which is situated between excess and deficiency. For example, arguing for complete government control of media content is excessive; arguing for no government control is deficiency. Arguing for moderate involvement would be considered virtuous, hence ethical.

Did Reverend Gimenez hold to a Golden Mean? It's not clear-cut, but one could say an excessive strategy would have been to demand that his listeners confess and convert to Christ; a deficient one would have not even addressed their grief. Perhaps his offer of hope, and their freedom to choose for or against Christ, made his speech virtuous.

2. Situation Ethics: Communication is ethical if it is the most loving thing to do and if it adheres to the ethical maxims of a given place or culture. Therefore, there are no universal rules for ethical behavior, only cultural or situational ones. To speak ethically in Argentina would mean understanding Roman Catholic belief and Argentinean culture and what "to love" means in that culture.[14]

Culturally Argentineans rank moderately high on their desire to avoid uncertainty and relationally prefer achievement and assertiveness over nurturance and support.[15] They prefer speakers who take charge and lay out their ideas in black-and-white—no beating around the bush with "ums" and "maybes." If so, then Pastor Gimenez is speaking their language. His if-Jesus, then-Carlos claims cut through the underbrush to guaranteed hope. Perhaps they read him as ethical and loving.

3. The End Justifies the Means: Any communication strategy (the means) is ethical if the speaker believes her goal (the end) is noble and just. Quintilian, for example, believed it would be okay to lie to an audience if this strategy diverted an assassin from a victim, deceived an enemy to save one's country, or comforted a child who is sick.

This maxim implies that as long as Gimenez was being true to Monzon's wish to see "as many people as possible enter into the same relationship with the Lord" as he had, no amount of emotion manipulation was out of bounds. What concerns many believers and non-believers alike is that the likes of Adolph Hitler and Ganges Kahn have used what they believe to be a moral end to perform heinous acts of brutality as well as manipulative rhetoric.

4. Mill's Principle of Utility: Communication is ethical if it brings the greatest good for the greatest number of people. Typically "greatest good" has been defined as the presence of pleasure and the absence of pain. Other scholars say that what's "good" includes the entire package of beauty, economic gain, honor, and the like. Believers would likely include redemption and eternal life.

This is the ethic used to justify electronic evangelism. If great good occurs with great numbers, then a strong radio transmitter must be of God. Pastor Gimenez may have been thinking similarly. What better opportunity to bring about spiritual good than to offer 30,000 destitute people God's good news through Christ? To not bring them into God's fold of salvation nor encourage them in their search to see Carlos again would have left them in a hopeless, sorry state.

5. Kant's Categorical Imperative: "Categorical" means "all" and "imperative" means "essential." Therefore ethical communication is speaking in a manner that you believe is essential for everyone, not just yourself. Suppose I make up some statistics to pad a weak section in my speech. If I think this is okay for me but not okay for you, I've broken Kant's maxim. He suggests that behavior is ethical only if it is considered okay for everyone, not a select few.

I recall a discussion about premarital sex among high school students on television. One guy said, "How can you know if you're compatible with someone unless you get to know her sexually?" When asked if he encouraged his younger sister to know guys sexually, he said "no." Why? He retorted, "Well, that's different!" Kant would not be pleased with this double standard. Unless we're willing to say that everyone should abide by rule X, we're probably just making excuses for our own behavior.

6. Legal Perspectives: Communication is ethical as long as it is legal according to civil law. For example, since there are laws against libel and defamation of character, these are unethical. However there are no laws against profanity, so its use is ethical.[16]

To my knowledge, there are no laws in Argentina against proselytizing—any religious group can work to win converts within the acceptable norms of the culture. In some people's eyes, this means Gimenez was speaking ethically; he broke no law. The idea that our laws cue us to immoral actions dates back at least to Old Testament times where the purpose of the law was to alert the Israel nation of sinful behavior (see Romans 3:20). We know, however, that a system of laws may not cover every speaking situation, and we are still left to ask what is ethical. Jesus said that the commandments to love God and our neighbor as ourselves sum up the entire law (see Matthew 22:37-40). Asking whether a speech is charitable or not puts the burden on us, rather than the law, to determine its moral value.

7. Rationalist Perspectives: Communication is ethical if it conforms to what rational people would say and allows people the freedom to reason with your claims. "Rationalists view persons as primarily rational beings. Anything that is not rational does not fit with or subverts a person's basic nature and therefore would be unethical."[17] Examples of unethical communication techniques include "illogical appeals, strong emotional appeals, heavy reliance on style for persuasive impact, appeals to the character of the speaker, or any technique that bypasses or demeans a person's ability to reason."[18]

This is the basis on which I question brother Gimenez' manner. Can distressed people think clearly? Do strong emotions cloud our ability to reason? If the answer is "yes," then ministers should be slow to strike while the emotions are hot. Better to come to God with a warm heart and cool head than with a hot head and cold heart. I realize others disagree and

"Well, I heard it was illegal to shout 'Fire' so I shouted 'stampede!' and look at that, there was one."

suggest the stakes are too high. Why quibble over method when the difference is heaven or hell? My response is that if God made us rational and emotional, what is ethical will speak to both, not one or the other alone.

8. Democratic Perspectives: Communication is ethical if it mirrors "equality of opportunity, free and open discussion, equality of individuals, belief in the inherent dignity of all human beings, [and] the right of freedom of information."[19] As public speakers this translates into the right for everyone to speak their mind and receive our respectful attention. It means speaking in a manner that invites discussion rather than squelches it, and acknowledges that we as speakers do not wield ultimate expert authority.

It's hard to tell if Reverend Gimenez meets this criterion. Funerals aren't typically the place for round table discussion. Do you suspect anyone felt free to holler, "Wait a minute sir, I don't agree with your view of the after life. Let's debate that point before you proceed." It's a corny example, but you get my point: one-way speaking that discourages audience feedback isn't democratic, and some people consider it unethical.

9. Dialogical Perspectives: Communication is ethical if it adheres to the rules of dialogue, not monologue. Dialogue resembles the charades model of interpersonal communication we discussed in Chapter 4. People who dialogue are genuine, empathetic, show unconditional positive regard for the other, promote a spirit of equality and emotional support. This ethic suggests that you should be audience-centered and audience-sensitive as you prepare and deliver your speech.

I bet Gimenez would go to the gallows saying he had nothing but love for those mourners in January of 1995. His heart was broken like theirs over the tragic death of his good friend Monzon. We can imagine that he felt that his evangelistic call was their route to comfort, both immediately and long-term. As noted above, however, he probably did not expect to enter into genuine dialogue with dissenters during the speech—something true of most speakers in formal settings.

10. Religious Perspectives: Communication is ethical if it adheres to the commandments or edicts in any number of books considered holy. Ethical frameworks are assembled around a set of scriptural passages. Sometimes adherents to a particular faith perspective cling to one or two passages to guide a wide band of behavior. Using the ninth commandment ("You shall not bear false testimony against your neighbor," Exodus 20:16) or Ephesians 4:15 ("speak the truth in love...") are examples. Other religious perspectives look more like a theology of communication than a chapter-and-verse list of prescriptions. This is the type I introduce below.

Each of these maxims is intended to define ethical behavior. While we might haggle over whether they shed light as God would have it shed, we will likely agree that most are not an affront to Christian belief and practice. Where they differ from orthodoxy is in their casting of people as primarily rational, social or political rather than spiritual or religious.

A CHRISTIAN ETHICAL PERSPECTIVE

A refreshing Christian perspective comes from professors Daryl Vander Kooi and Charles Veenstra at Dordt College in Sioux Center, Iowa.[20] It is outlined in Table 7.1. Their moral maxim is that *God must be honored in all communication*. Like St. Augustine who said, "Love God and do what you will," these scholars are convinced that if we aim to please God, we can do no wrong with people.

Vander Kooi and Veenstra begin by observing that we are essentially religious creatures, made in his image. That means we are intelligent, morally aware, and originally righteous and holy (in the case of Adam and Eve). They also point out that God made us for fellowship with himself. In short, we were made to respond to him in prayer, worship, and in how we live our lives. Finally, they observe that we are God's ambassadors whose role is to assist him in redeeming others and the culture.

From these initial insights into human nature and purpose, Vander Kooi and Veenstra suggest three basic principles. First, we should have a high view of communication. God proved that he values communication when he gave us language and when he bridged the gap between us and himself through his life in Christ. Second, we should have full respect for others in our communication. Gossip, name-calling, and slander don't belong in a believer's verbal repertoire. And third, we should "recognize the direction of people's lives" as we speak with them. That means doing ample audience analysis and being sensitive to our listeners' needs and world view.

On these basic principles Vander Kooi and Veenstra build a set of five sub-principles — nitty-gritty rules for speaking well: be honest, have a correct attitude toward others, choose your words wisely, respect people's intellect, and try to meet their needs. From these subprinciples spill many examples of ethical speech which you can see at the bottom of Figure 7.1.

The only element that I would add to this ethical framework is that we respect listener choice. Free will is so critical to a Christian picture of human nature that Em Griffin suggests it should be the fulcrum of any persuasion ethic. In *The Mind Changers: The Art of Christian Persuasion* he writes: "As ambassadors for Christ, we need to have an ethical standard which guides our appeal regardless of how people respond. I believe there is such a standard. Simply stated it is: Any persuasive effort which restricts another's freedom to choose for or against Jesus Christ is wrong."[21] Verbally abusive speeches that coerce listeners to "choose Christ, or else" obviously fall outside Griffin's rule. Christ *calls* us to himself; he doesn't use a cattle prod.

The Image of God in Human Beings				
A Religious Being Created for Response to God. God's Representative on Earth				
Principles and Subprinciples Which Guide Communication				
Over-arching Principle (the moral maxim): GOD MUST BE HONORED IN ALL COMMUNICATION				
Basic Principles:				
High View of Communication		Recognition of the Direction of People's Lives		Full Respect for Others
Subprinciples:				
Honesty	Correct Attitudes Toward Others	Proper Word Choice	Respect for People's Intellect	Attempt to Satisfy Needs
Examples of Practices of Principles for Ethical Communication				
tell good and bad	combine tact with honesty	eliminate profanity	use good reasoning and evidence	analyze audience
make faith assumptions clear	care for others	build others up	make emotional appeals consistent with evidence and reasoning	don't simply tell others what they want to hear
fit organization with content	ensure other's well-being	correct bad word choice		consider needs
	promote others' reputation			
match verbal and nonverbal		avoid flattery	confess truth	speak only on beneficial topics
	be gracious	improve language	avoid fallacies	speak at their level
etc.	etc.	etc.	etc.	etc.

Figure 7.1.   Christian Ethical Perspective for Communication

Christian Ethical Perspective for Communication in *Responsible Public Address*, 3rd edition, by Daryl Vander Kooi and Charles Veenstra © 1996, used by permission.

What you will find from Vander Kooi and Veenstra's model is that determining what is ethical is not always cut-and-dried. For example, we might praise Gimenez for calling Argentineans to respond to God, attempting to satisfy their emotional needs, and using respectful language, but we may still feel uneasy about his emotional appeal that potentially subverted reason. Of note is that Gimenez speaks directly to the "honor God" maxim when he closed the eulogy by declaring that God was glorified in seeing many turn to repentance even when the enemy meant Monzon's death for destruction.

You may never preach a sermon, but you will likely have opportunity to give persuasive speeches throughout your adult life. Even if you prepare informative talks, you will ultimately convince your listeners of something. As you do, consider this checklist. It may spur you on to ethical excellence.

CHECKLIST FOR ETHICAL PUBLIC SPEAKING

As you prepare your speech, ask yourself:

✓ Am I honest with myself? Am I telling the truth to my listeners?
✓ Do I have correct attitudes toward my audience? Can they tell it?
✓ Have I chosen the best words to express my message?
✓ Do I show respect for my audience's intellect and emotions?
✓ Do I want to meet their needs? Have I analyzed them well enough to do so?
✓ Am I allowing them free will in how they respond to my speech?
✓ Will God be honored with what I say and how I say it?

Summary

If the tone of this chapter has seemed a little onerous, you're right. But it's burdensome for a purpose. I want us to wake up to the challenges and responsibilities of public address. Sometimes I sense that students take speech courses for the same reason they sign up for bowling: to improve their delivery. Delivery is important, but I've chosen not to focus on that here. Rather, my conviction is that people fear public speaking because it requires mettle, not improved methods. By mettle I mean character and knowing yourself.

Some speakers have mettle, but vague purpose. Can you spell out your purpose in one sentence? My purpose for this chapter has been to convince readers that public speaking presents unique challenges and responsibilities that give most of us the willies. (Have I succeeded?)

One of those challenges is research. Few of us like to do it, but without it we're sunk. The same goes for our logic and emotional appeals. As God said to his nation Israel, "come, let us reason together." We ought to reason together too. In regard to emotion, our appeals to love and hope, disgust and fear should be appropriate and not keep our listeners from reasoning clearly. God has made us complex creatures—a single slug to the heart or the head is cheap.

Perhaps most significant is that speaking is an ethical and symbolic challenge. We choose what we say, but do those choices honor God and respect others? For example, do we ever have the basis to call a political opponent a "twit"? May we harangue believers to jump even higher? Can we say, "none of my research supports the opposing view" when we've looked at just one book? Do we ooze, "you've been a great audience," when they've been our absolute worst? By now I hope you can wrestle with the answers.

Worth the Talk

1. What is the relationship between our speaking efforts and God's work through his Spirit to change people? This chapter may make it sound like it's all up to us. What do you think?
2. Do you see any similarities between the ten ethical maxims described in this chapter and the Christian perspective outlined by professors Vander Kooi and Veenstra? What are their differences?
3. Can you think of instances where a speaker used strong emotions to persuade you? Do you think the speaker acted ethically?

Consider the Walk

1. Listen to a classmate's speech or another person's speech and analyze it from several ethical perspectives described in this chapter. Answer the question: Did the speaker use ethical means to accomplish an ethical end? The means of a speech deal with how it was organized, worded, researched and argued. The end of a speech is its goal. Did the speaker encourage the audience to adopt an ethical behavior?
2. Write a research paper where you examine the ethics of a well-known speaker in world history. Some examples include Abraham Lincoln, Patrick Henry, Susan B. Anthony, Winston Churchill, Adolph Hitler, John F. Kennedy, Mother Teresa, Billy Graham, and Chairman Mao. Be sure you research more about ethics from other sources, and try to explain how this speaker's ethics enhanced or inhibited his or her success as a speaker.
3. Study the following cases. Write a one-paragraph response to each of the questions asked. Be prepared to discuss and expand on your answers in class.[22]

a. A student in a speaking class has been assigned to give an informative speech in one week. He is very busy with required assignments in other courses and puts off the preparation of the speech until the night before it is due. He has great difficulty finding a topic and finally resorts to using extensively an article from *Reader's Digest* as the basis for his speech. He makes no reference to the article in his speech. What are the ethical questions involved in this case, and how do you think they should be decided?

b. Is it ethical for a speech student to give a speech that was written by her roommate? Is it ethical for a politician to give a speech that was written by her speech-writer?

c. Is it ethical for a speaker to read her entire speech in a speech class? (Or, is a speaker acting ethically if she engages in no eye contact with the audience in this same class?). Would you make the same judgment for a preacher? Explain.

d. Are we ethically bound to listen to all persons who desire to speak to us? If not, why not, and when, if at all, should we refuse to listen to a speaker?

NOTES

1. Rauna May, "Death of flawed Argentine hero brought salvation," *Christian Info News*, March 1995, p. 4. Used by permission.
2. May, p. 4
3. For an excellent chapter on oral communication apprehension and how to deal with it, see "Anxious Communicators," in Donald W. Klopf and Ronald E. Cambra, *Personal and public speaking*, (5th ed.), Morton Publishing Company, Englewood, CO, 1996, pp. 77-88.
4. See Richard Weaver, *Language is sermonic*, in James L. Golden, Goodwin F. Berquist, and William E. Coleman, *The rhetoric of western thought (5th ed.)*, Kendell/Hunt Publishing Company, Dubuque, IA, 1992, pp. 201-213.
5. Most public speaking texts provide a full description of types of evidence and sources. These lists were created with the help of Rudolph Verderber's *The challenge of effective speaking*, (9th ed.), Wadsworth Publishing Company, Belmont, CA, 1994, pp. 84-99.
6. See Lloyd Bitzer, "Aristotle's Enthymeme Revisited," *Quarterly Journal of Speech*, Vol. 45, 1959, p. 409 as cited in E. Griffin, *A first look at communication theory*, (2nd ed.), McGraw-Hill, Inc, New York, NY, 1994, p. 301.
7. For a good overview of Plato, Aristotle, and Quintilian's teachings on rhetoric, see Golden, Berquist, and Coleman, chapters 2-4.
8. Golden, Berquist, and Coleman, chapter 2.
9. Golden, Berquist, and Coleman, p. 50.
10. Bert E. Bradley, *Fundamentals of speech communication: The credibility of ideas* (6th ed.), Wm. C. Brown Publishers, Dubuque, IA, 1991, p. 69.

11. J.I. Packer, *Knowing God*, InterVarsity Press, Downers Grove, IL, 1973, pp. 20-28.
12. Bruce E. Gronbeck, Kathleen German, Douglas Ehninger, and Alan H. Monroe, *Principles of speech communication* (Twelfth Brief Edition), Harper Collins College Publishers, New York, 1995, p. 9.
13. This list was compiled from several sources. I recommend that you consult a standard communication ethics text such as Richard Johannesen's *Ethics in human communication*, 3rd ed., Waveland Press, Prospect Heights, IL, 1990, for an introductory overview.
14. This description of situation ethics is based on Joseph Fletcher's ideas as described by Bradley, p. 57. The work by Fletcher to which Bradley refers is J. Fletcher, *Situation ethics*, Westminster Press, Philadelphia, PA, 1966, p. 26.
15. See Geert Hofstede, *Culture and organizations: Software of the mind*, McGraw-Hill, Inc., New York, NY, pp. 113 & 84.
16. The legal, rationalist, democratic, dialogical, utilitarian, situational and religious perspectives are described in Darryl Vander Kooi and Charles Veenstra's *Responsible public address* (3rd ed.), 1996, custom published at Dordt College, Sioux Center, Iowa.
17. Vander Kooi and Veenstra, p. 16
18. Vander Kooi and Veenstra, p. 16
19. Vander Kooi and Veenstra, p. 17
20. Vander Kooi and Veenstra, pp. 23-28.
21. Em Griffin, *The mind changers: The art of Christian persuasion*, Tyndale House Publishers, Inc., Wheaton, IL, 1976, p. 28.
22. These examples are taken from Vander Kooi and Veenstra's *Responsible public address* 2nd edition, 1988, pp. 19-20.

CHAPTER 8

Connecting with Strangers
An Incarnational Approach to Intercultural Communication

*Though I am free and belong to no man, I make
myself a slave to everyone, to win as many as
possible. To the Jews I became like a Jew, to win
Jews. To those under the law I became like one
under the law...so as to win those under the law.
To the weak I became weak, to win the weak. I
have become all things to all men so that by all
possible means I might save some. I do this for the
sake of the gospel, that I may share in its blessings.*
1 Corinthians 9:19-20, 22-23

My cultural upbringing was very narrow. From age four to eighteen, my stomping ground was Jackson, Minnesota, population 3500—a town nestled in the west fork of the Des Moines River valley. About that valley laid green-gold fields of corn and soybeans and the outcropping of farmstead windbreaks. Half the students in my school were farm kids, the other half, town kids. The Worthington Trojans were our arch rival in football, the Windom Eagles in basketball. The first African-American I ever saw lived thirty miles away. In my early years a big trip meant visiting the Twin Cities three hours northeast. During high school a band trip to Disney World brought the same sense of new and different.

My college years were spent ten hours from Jackson in the Chicago suburb of Wheaton, Illinois, and while the miles were great, the feel was the same. Eighty-five percent of my classmates were white like me, and most from middle- or upper-middle class homes. During those years I toured with a male choir that sang in Europe for six weeks. But even England, France, Switzerland, Germany, and the Netherlands looked safe from the elevated angle of a monster bus. I needed a change and a challenge.

So after college graduation I decided to work overseas, and within three months I was on a plane for India as a short-termer. Boy, did I get change and challenge.

Surrounding the orphanage where I worked were okra fields and orange orchards and the occasional mango tree. Rather than football, I played *kubadi*, a form of chain-gang tag-and-tackle. I needed no big trip to get a buzz for the different. In nearby Chandur Bazaar, merchants sold freshly butchered goat and chicken, though a live chicken was preferred. Hindu shrines and naked Jain priests that journeyed enroute to temples offered religious comment on beggars in shredded clothes and lepers with fingerless hands.

One warm summer night I was reminded of how India's ways extend through their modes of communication. I had just played a board game with Joy Meshramkar, the son of the orphanage director. (Christians in India often choose biblical terms as first names. Two of my students were named Prakash—"Light."). Joy began walking me back to my bungalow, and as he did, he reached his hand for mine. I had seen schoolboys holding hands in town, but this was different, I thought. We joined hands palm-to-palm and proceeded down the road. A few seconds later he adjusted his grip, placing his fingers every-other between my own. To a Minnesota boy, this meant "going steady." As a college graduate I knew it meant "a cultural expression of friendship." You might imagine my ambivalence. A hundred steps later we arrived at the guesthouse and Joy let go. I was free at last. Twenty years later I can still recall my relief.

You might smile with me over such a little thing, but it was huge to me then. Showing friendship is a little thing, a godly thing. But *the manner* in which we show friendship is a cultural thing, and sometimes, it makes a huge difference. Connecting with someone from a different background can bring much needed variety and learning to an otherwise sheltered life. It can also establish a relational bridge for us to be God's ambassador to the world on our doorstep. Understanding how we might connect interculturally is the focus of this chapter.

GAZING AT OUR CULTURAL NAVELS?

Today you do not have to go to India to find people of different races, cultures, and religions. The urban centers of the United States and Canada have become cross-sections of the global village. Within three houses of where I live reside a German couple from Paraguay, a couple from Brazil, and a couple from Greece.

However, despite our increased opportunity to interact with people unlike ourselves, we are far more likely to befriend people who are similar to us in age, sex, and race. We may enjoy work relationships and "activity friendships" on sport teams or in a choir with ethnic acquaintances, but we reserve relationships of trust and influence with those largely like ourselves.[1]

This pattern of whites befriending whites, blacks linking with blacks and the like is important communicationally. We're more likely to develop a coherent personal and group identity, and experience harmonious use of language and nonverbals, within a single ethnic tradition. No one should blame anyone else for desiring these benefits. The problems arise when we begin to believe that how one group thinks and lives culturally is the only acceptable way. If I judge okra thumbs-down because it doesn't rate with Iowa corn, it's only a step away to judge Joy Meshramkar for being "forward" because he failed to befriend me the Illinois way. Doing so suggests that I've gazed too long at my own cultural navel.

For believers, the urge to judge may be doubly strong, because we are tempted to equate what is culturally acceptable with what is morally (or even biblically) permissible. The two may overlap at times, but not always. For example, in Chandur Bazaar the Christian women worship on the left side of the church sanctuary and the men on the right. Is this biblically required? I don't think so. Is it culturally expected? I think so—the same pattern is repeated in East Indian movie theaters. Should I judge this split arrangement as evil? Hardly. What I might do is ask a local in-the-know Indian where this behavioral pattern came from and then learn to live within its parameters, both good and bad. Doing so helps me, like Paul, to become all things to all people that I may influence some for God. Observing others and asking questions make us a student of their culture.

Understanding Culture

When we think of "culture" it is easy to conjure up images of burial site artifacts, painted masks, and dugout canoes (or for that matter, cemetery headstones, Avon cosmetics, and Ford Windstars). These are physical features of culture, but they are only a slice of its meaning. *Culture* is the total life way of a people: how they think, how they behave, and what they create.

This definition is a composite of three aspects: the cognitive, the behavioral, and the artifactual. *Cognitive culture* is in our heads. It consists of our world view, values, beliefs, and typical ways of thinking. An Indian student's value for family enmeshment compared to a Canadian student's value for personal independence is a good example of cognitive culture. *Behavioral culture* is what we do, whether individually or as a group. It includes our micro use of space (proxemics), body movement (kinesics), and time (chronemics) as well as macro behaviors such as sports, driving styles and how people celebrate holidays. Sunita's choice to go home over break, but Susan's desire to spend time with friends on a road trip, reflect behaviorally what each woman values. *Artifactual culture* is what we build, sculpt, design, plant, and create. In Sunita's home town, stone and corrugated steel buildings, oxcarts, open air markets, black bicycles and *Tata* trucks (a company name) are the norm. In Susan's city you'll find brick and steel buildings, import cars, cement walks, malls, and multi-colored mountain bikes.

Culture is passed on through our language, behavior, and experience. We learn at our parent's knee to love or hate God, play football or *kubadi*, and build homes from brick or bamboo. The process of learning our original culture is called *enculturation*, and the longer we spend time in that culture, the harder it is to adjust within another one.

Is Culture Good or Bad, of God or of Humans?

In Minneapolis, Minnesota the Mall of America boasts 1000 plus stores for your shopping pleasure. In all of Chandur Bazaar the local merchants number about sixty. Both are cultural efforts to meet material needs. Is one good and the other bad? Would it be okay to establish a church that meets near the Mall of America's food court? In the Chandur Bazaar business district?

Marvin Mayers, past Dean of the School of Intercultural Studies and World Missions at Biola University, wrestles with the question of whether culture is evil, neutral, holy, or what. To answer, he first grapples with the question of biblical truth and cultural reality. We know that the scriptures call us to holy living, but we also know that we live in an okra-and-football world. Where is the truth for how we should live? In *Christianity Confronts Culture*, Mayers suggests a matrix for picturing how Christians may look at biblical truth and cultural reality.[2] We can look at both through the eyes of *absolutism* or through the tinted glasses of *relativism*. Together these two responses form four categories of thought (see Figure 8.1).

Bible and culture as absolute. Position 1 is taken by many conservative believers. They hold that the Bible and culture are both absolute, that is, complete and unchanging. Biblical mandates are interpreted as having one cultural expression, so to change that expression is to question the authority of the scripture as containing the principles for guiding life and behavior. For example, some believers interpret the command to "not make for yourself an idol" in Exodus 20 a call for barren worship halls. Even a simple wooden cross or embroidered banner is forbidden. Such a view produces what Mayers terms cultural exclusivism, where "all other cultures and their life-ways are approached from the point of view of the person looking in."[3] Growing up in one culture within one religious denomination tends to create Position 1 thinking. Such individuals use scripture and their own culture to evaluate what is good and bad in other people's cultures. The academic word for making such judgments is *ethnocentrism*.

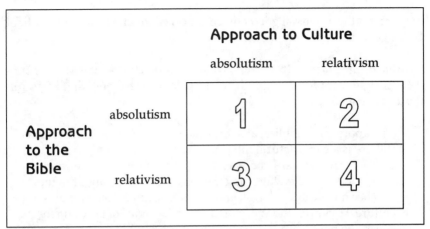

Figure 8.1   Four Ways of Thinking About Biblical Truth and Cultural Reality.
(See Mayers, 1987, pp. 247-249)

Taken from Christianity Confronts Culture by Marvin K. Mayers. Copyright © 1974 by
The Zondervan Corporation. Copyright 1987 by Marvin K. Mayers. Used by permission of
Zondervan Publishing House.

Bible as relative, culture as absolute. Position 3 is held largely by hu-
manitarians who regard culture as the sole determiner of what to regard as
truth and responsible behavior. In earlier chapters I have referred to these
people as postmodernists. Postmodernists regard cultures as complete,
whole systems that define and guide each cultural group toward their construction of truth and moral behavior. They believe that no outsider has
the right to alter a culture's principles or lifestyle. The Bible is considered
one of many sacred and secular texts that contribute to cultural life. The
Bible is not considered the rule of life and behavior for all cultures, because
it is the product of one culture—the Jewish, Greek, Roman mix of 1st Century Palestine.

Bible as relative, culture as relative. Position 4 is held by many professors in the social sciences. Mayers cites Clyde Kluckhohn, Margaret Mead,
and Ruth Benedict as examples, as well as Christian anthropologists
Bronislaw Malinowski, A. R. Radcliffe Brown, and Robert Redfield. In this
view, "culture is a dynamic [not absolute] process that is internally self-
correcting and can be relied on to produce decisions that aid the society as
well as the individual within society."[4] The Bible is regarded as one of
many texts for moral guidance that helps people communicate and act re-
sponsibly. Position 4 is similar to Position 3 in spirit but not degree. Position 4 Christians believe that we can rise above our cultural entrapping to

understand the universal good and communicationally prudent in light of God's general revelation to everyone on earth.

Bible as absolute, culture as relative. Position 2 is the one Mayers suggests is significant for the church worldwide. It is the view that I favor in this book. He writes:

> The approach of biblical absolutism and cultural relativism affirms that there is a supernatural intrusion. Truth is from God. Truth does not change. [However,] the way truth is communicated in a given culture and language will change. Even as Christ through the Incarnation became flesh and dwelt among us, so truth becomes expressed in culture. However, the Word made flesh lost none of his divineness, and truth is not corrupted or changed necessarily by its expression via human sociological forms. It is always full and complete as truth. The moment truth is wed to [only] one cultural expression, there is a high potential for falsehood.

Culture as good. What Mayers means, by a Position 2 stance, is that culture is at least neutral, or perhaps even a good tool for the expression of biblical (and other) principles for responsible living. If any thing or any one is evil, it's people, not culture, so it's quite possible to convey God's unchanging message through cultural forms. Women sitting on one side of the sanctuary and men on the other may reflect cultural sex roles, but it doesn't undermine God's call that we treat each other as sisters and brothers in the Lord. Likewise, a church that holds its services in the Mall of America milling area is simply playing Minnesotan. If Jesus lived a cultural life as a Jewish carpenter-gone-rabbi, we too can convey God's message to others through local forms. In short, Mayers is saying that most cultural forms are neutral or even good because they are created by made-in-God's-image people, and capable of communicating his truth.

Culture as bad. Sherwood Lingenfelter, a colleague of Marvin Mayers, would underline "most cultural forms." He may even say that only a few cultural forms are so blessed. He reasons that if culture is the cognitive outpouring of sinful people into behavioral and physical forms, then some cultural patterns (if not a good many) are fallen too. For example, if we are "locked" into a Mall-of-America way of thinking, we are apt to worship money, not God eternal. Our cultural habits, though common place to us, are essentially keeping us from communion with God. He refers to Paul's writings to make his point that culture might be a "pen of disobedience:"

> Paul suggests that human beings are in a prison, a cell of disobedience: "God has imprisoned all human beings in their own disobedi-

ence only to show mercy to them all" (Romans 11:30-32 NJB). He re-
peats the same theme in Galatians 3:22, paraphrasing Psalm 14:1-3.
He observes that "the whole world is a prisoner to sin." God has
penned up all people in their self-created cells of culture, including
Jew and Gentile, pagan and missionary.[5]

Taking Mayers' analogy of culture as a tool, Lingenfelter uses the same
analogy with a different result:

> Using the tool analogy, culture is more like a "slot machine" found
> in Las Vegas' gambling casinos than a wrench or screwdriver. Cul-
> ture, like a slot machine, is programmed to be sure that those who
> hold power "win" and the common players "lose"; when or if the
> organized agenda is violated, people frequently resort to violence to
> reestablish their "programmed" advantage.[6]

Insofar that worship services in a mall mock the Creator, they are pens of
disobedience. To the extent that dividing women and men in worship leads
to the stereotyping of the other, it is a fallen cultural form.

Some people believe that certain cultural practices and technologies are inherently stacked toward evil.

So who's right? That's a tough one. Frankly, I don't think we should ask this question, because both perspectives deserve merit. Jesus didn't ignore the cultural means available to him, but neither did he involve himself in every cultural practice. Professor Mayers' optimism is based on Christ's use of first century cultural forms to convey his life-changing message. Professor Lingenfelter's pessimism stems from observing sinners who get side tracked by attractive, sinful forms. Some forms, like slot machines and inhumane housing complexes and nuclear bombs, are bent toward evil: the first two are designed to soak others for an easy profit and the third to wipe out an enemy rather than turn the other cheek. Determining what forms may pen us in and which ones bring new life may not be easy. What we do have is the life of Christ as a model for being spiritual and cultural earthlings. His method was to bridge the culture of heaven with the culture of earth through the mystery of the incarnation. That's a model worth considering.

What Is Incarnational Communication?

Put simply, to communicate incarnationally is to imitate the strategy of God in Jesus Christ. While it is similar to redemptive interpersonal communication (see Chapter 4), its scope is intercultural. As Rene Padilla writes, "All authentic communication of the Word is patterned on the incarnation and therefore, seeks to find a point of contact with [people] within [their] own situation."[7] It is receptor-oriented communication that respects the receiver's frame of reference and life experience. And its primary motivation is love.

Love "Them" at the Expense of "Us"

If God had not chosen to love us, had not chosen to bridge the gap to redeem us at the price of Christ, we might still be living under the law. But he didn't. While we were still broken, pathetic individuals, Christ came and died for us. God loved us at the expense of his son. Heaven would have been a safer place for Jesus.

We are safest, most comfortable, when we surround ourselves with same-race friends. Remember though, that when we identify with an ingroup, we often do so at the expense of outgroups. We favor our own buddies when dividing up resources like money and affection, and we usually rate our own group more positively, even when the lines of distinction between "them" and "us" are minimal and arbitrary.[8] As one author concludes: "Because we evaluate ourselves partly in terms of our group memberships, seeing our own group as superior helps us feel good about ourselves."[9] Professor Lingenfelter might suggest that this kind of thinking is a pen of selfish disobedience.

Christ's example is so different. While he surrounded himself with close disciples, he did not shy from those unlike himself. Jesus was not a tourist to earth, content with an impersonal speaking circuit agenda. Nor was he on a short-term summer mission project. Jesus was into Jewish culture and world change for the long haul. His position toward people, whether poor or rich, Jew or Samaritan, was love and humility. As Paul writes, "make my joy complete by being like-minded, having the same love, being one in spirit and purpose. Do nothing out of selfish ambition or vain conceit, but in humility consider others better than yourselves. Each of you should look not only to your own interests, but also to the interests of others. Your attitude should be the same as that of Jesus Christ" (Philippians 2:2-5). Our first inclination may not be to barbecue with our Paraguayan, Brazilian, and Greek neighbors, but at least our attitude toward them should reflect humility and service, not judgment and avoidance.

Loving people who think and live differently than we do is not a natural thing, and the edict to love them sounds difficult and concocted. How can liking them become as normal as phoning a friend? Here are some guidelines based on research and biblical insight.

Befriend people of similar socio-economic status. The three neighbors I mentioned are all retired, but suppose one couple owned a clothing store and the other couples worked in the berry fields around my city. The odds are that I would have more in common with the retailers than the tillers.

Making contact with those of similar economic background may strike some as snobbish and unchristian. Jesus didn't seem to hold to this pattern. But research in ethnic relations shows that strangers get along best when they hail from similar strata in society.[10] Jesus' blue-collar roots as the son of a carpenter made him a shoe-in with the likes of fishermen Peter, James, and John. His knowledge of the law made him attractive to Nicodemus (the Pharisee, see John 3) and Luke the medical doctor. Our own social status may be more uniform, but it's no sin to stack the deck in the direction of status as we seek to influence others for God.[11]

A debate that continues in some Christian circles concerns the role of ethnic churches. Some suggest that dividing churches along ethnic lines sends the wrong message to outsiders. It makes us look like we preach love but practice racism. Murray Moerman disagrees. As president of the Council for Christian Churches of Greater Vancouver, British Columbia, Murray has seen a lot of good in ethnic churches. He writes, "Anglo churches are best at reaching Anglos. Spanish churches are best at reaching Spanish people. Chinese churches are best at reaching Chinese people. Not only that but professional athletes are best at reaching professional athletes, media people at reaching media people, yuppies at reaching yuppies, men at reaching men, women at reaching women and so on."[12] His examples highlight the wisdom of befriending people from similar socio-economic backgrounds when possible. Their culture may differ, but their lifestyle and values likely align with our own.

Pursue a common goal. A veteran missionary to India, John Seamands, writes of his encounter with a boxer named Gunboat Jack in his book *Tell It Well.*[13] When John asks Gunboat "how are you getting along in the ring of life?", Gunboat laments, "I've been knocked out again and again by the devil" through gambling, sex, and booze. Seamands had a choice to make just then. He could have railed on Gunboat Jack to clean up his life, or he could have focused on their mutual enemy, the devil. He chose the latter.

Research indicates that when two cultural groups join hands to defeat a common enemy or accomplish a common goal, then relations between them are more harmonious.[14] The opposing attitude is to make each other the problem. Rather than criticize with, "If you were less lazy, you wouldn't go thirsty during drought," a more cooperative spirit is to say, "Let's figure out a way we can save water during the rainy season." The problem is drought, not the people.

On most college and university campuses, international and English as a Second Language (ESL) students struggle with English. A native English speaker who asks "How can we tackle subject-verb agreement?" is water to a thirsty spirit. I have heard more than one report of good friendships developing between English tutors and their students when this attitude is taken. Working together directs us away from thinking "me" against "them." It helps us think "we" against "the problem."

Spend time together. This point may seem like common sense and moot, but consider Jesus' manner. After growing up thoroughly Jewish, he began his formal ministry by choosing twelve men with whom he spent the next three years. He walked, ate, joked, fished, preached, worshipped, philosophized and in every other way hung out with them. As Donald Smith suggests in *Make Haste Slowly*, communication boils down to involvement in other people's lives.[15] It means developing an experience base over coffee and *kubadi* so we can share meaning more easily. Involvement means bonding over mundane things, not squirming under the pressure of a slick gospel presentation. Other things equal, spending time together decreases stereotyping and prejudice, and increases attraction.

BE TEACHABLE AS TO THEIR CULTURE AND LANGUAGE

It's hard to love others when you don't understand them. Worse yet, we tend to fear people whom we can't figure out. So it is not surprising that the second element of incarnational communication is to know our audience thoroughly. It means becoming observers of their culture.

Some time back I had opportunity to do just that. In 1987 I packed all my earthly belongings into a rusted Dodge Aspen and drove 1880 miles from Iowa to the province of British Columbia on the West Coast of Canada. Having already visited sixteen countries, and studied intercultural communications at the doctoral level, I felt overly confident that adjusting to life in Canada would be a breeze. Canadians, I believed, were just Americans who hadn't rebelled against the British in the 1770s.

I was wrong. Within a couple years I had opportunity to observe five-party politics, constitutional struggles (Canada still has no constitution), the French fact (six million francophones in Quebec province), a First Nations and Canadian military standoff (at Oka, Ontario), Canadian-rules football (a 130 yard field, and three downs) and the unsettling attitude that some Canadians don't like the United States as much as I thought they did. My previous intercultural experiences in India, East Asia, and Europe still rendered me an *Americanus Ignoramus* in the land north of the 49th parallel.

Despite my lack of knowledge, however, I did not lack the spirit to learn. I watched nothing but Canadian Broadcasting Corporation (CBC) news, read the local paper religiously, and quizzed my colleagues. A year later I married a Canadian woman and, after a decade, still live in Canada. Even though I hold U. S. citizenship, I'm more apt to think like a Canadian. I have been told, by Americans, that I "sound" Canadian. Your understanding of an international friend or your adjustment to a new culture will come over time as well, but what practical guidelines can guide us along the way? I can think of at least four.

Develop the sense of "different and good." When we encounter strangers and enter new cultures, we are prone to focus on how they differ from our roots, and evaluate those differences negatively. Consider the last time you visited another country. What did you take pictures of? Many a short-term missionary returns to show slides of crowded sidewalks, open air meat markets, shantytown poverty, and religious architecture. Audience members ooh, ha, and ugh their way through these pictures, and resolve that life is better in North America. These surface differences may cue us to significant world view themes, but it's hard at times to get past the blood-drained goat at the meat shop to understand the butcher.

Become a student of their culture. In my Canadian experience, I now understand that five-party politics symbolizes a strip of Canadian cultural diversity. It reflects Pierre Trudeau's push to make multiculturalism Canada's state policy, not the exception to the rule. (Quick. Who is Pierre Trudeau?) I'm not sure what Canadian football rules suggest, but I've interpreted the three-down rule as one way Canadians gently say, "We are not Americans."

We can make sense of another culture's habits and forms of communicating once we understand what guides them. This is the logic behind the concept of *cultural relativism*: behavior makes sense in light of the underlying structure of society; what's meaningful depends on societal context. Behavior is like the tip of an iceberg with its own peculiar shape and look. If we understand the sub-aquatic factors, we'll understand why the tip leans and dips like it does. Figure 8.2 pictures this relationship.

Studies in acculturation inform us that plugging in to local media is a safe way to acculturate to local culture, especially if we watch news shows rather than entertainment shows.[16] In the long run though, you will need to make friendships and "do culture" interpersonally. When in India for six months, I did not have a television or a radio. Instead, day after day, night after night, I got to know Indian culture by interacting with my carpentry students, the boys' home staff, and local merchants. Personal contact is more draining than watching television, but you gain more than information; you begin to establish trust.

Become a student of their religious views. Recall how Paul argued his case on Mars Hill? After strolling through the streets of Athens and seeing it filled with idols, he began his speech by noting "I see that in every way you are very religious. For as I walked around and looked carefully at your objects of worship, I even found an altar with this inscription: TO AN UNKNOWN GOD. Now what you worship as something unknown I am going to proclaim to you" (see Acts 17:22-34). First he observed their reli-

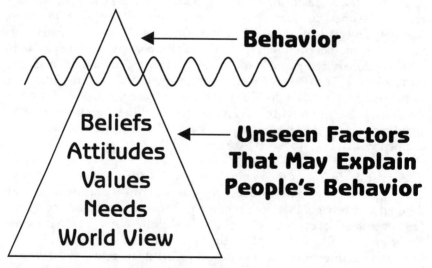

Figure 8.2.   The Iceberg Analogy: People's Behavior Makes Sense When We Understand What Lies Beneath the Surface.

gious practices; then he spoke to their spiritual need. Peter used the same method when speaking with Jews in Acts 2 to explain why believers were "drunk" with the Holy Spirit at Pentecost. He quotes Joel and David—two men they respected and whose teachings they knew well—to explain the outpouring of God's Spirit.

Without understanding a friend's religious beliefs in even a rudimentary, Religion 101 way, we will fail miserably at sorting out the specifics of his or her particular convictions. A comparative religion course that covers the tenets of Islam, Buddhism, Hinduism and New Age thought could prove invaluable in the future. Getting a hold of a classic, such as Huston Smith's *The Religions of Man*, may be a close second option. Knowing religious thought shows respect for someone else's convictions. It also helps us establish points of contact for communicating Christian truth.[17]

Learn the language of those you want to befriend and influence. This is especially important if you want to live abroad. Too many cross-cultural efforts have failed because English-speakers have bought into two myths. The first is that most everyone in the world wants to learn English anyway, so using English does them a favor. The second myth is that the demand for English education must indicate that English is better at conveying truth than other languages. While it's true that English education is in demand world wide, the motive behind it is largely economic, not cultural. The international business elite require a single language, and English became the expedient choice after it was imposed by the British during their imperial conquests. In terms of being a "better" language, English gets a "D" for lack of consistency. (Where else can you spell fish, *ghoti*? It's possible with phonemes such as enou<u>gh</u>, w<u>o</u>men, and lo<u>ti</u>on.) Linguists are now convinced that there are no " primitive languages." Many languages spoken by "less developed" people—such as Spanish and Indonesian—are more consistent than English.[18]

Far beyond the transmission capacity of a language is its potential for identification. When we speak someone else's language, something clicks. One semester while teaching at the University of Iowa, an East Indian woman looked back at me on the first day of class and smiled. I asked her where she was from and she said Bombay. Bombay folks speak Marathi (one of thirteen languages and 600 dialects in the country), and lucky for me, it was the language of Chandur Bazaar. "Kussa kai, teek ahay?" I asked her. She beamed, "Teek ahay." She hadn't heard Marathi in months, and her shock that I spoke a bit of her language soon turned to solace. All from asking, "how are you, fine?"

Use Their Cultural Forms

In addition to loving dissimilar others at our own expense, and humbly learning about their culture, we know we communicate incarnationally when we succeed in discovering the cultural forms that convey God's truth and establish responsible relationships least obtrusively. As Wycliffe translator and scholar Eugene Nida puts it, "Our fundamental task is to 'relay' this communication [or truth] in still different forms, but with essentially an equivalent content, so that men in other times and places may be put in touch with the infinite God."[19] Those forms vary from culture to culture, but somehow, some way, God is able to use these forms — whether neutral or fallen — to show himself to others. Non-westerners do not have to give up their cultural heritage to live redemptively with each other and know God's grace. Cultural forms are means to impute God's message, and God's message is able to redeem fallen cultural forms. Let's consider what this implies for us as his ambassadors.

Recognize that you are the message. It's been said that Christians are the only Bible some people will ever read. That is, what many unbelievers know about God is what they see in us. That's a little scary.

A true-life example strikes this home. E. Stanley Jones, author and veteran missionary to India, said that the attack against Christianity there came in three waves. First Hindus claimed, "It isn't *true* (i.e., these are the wrong truths), then, it isn't *new* (i.e., Hinduism has the same truths), and finally, it isn't *you* (i.e., you aren't living the truth). The last of these was the most damaging, for it suggested that some Christians in India looked rather unGod-like.[20]

Are you fit for intercultural ministry? When I was finishing my college work, some guys in my dorm asked me what I was planning to do after graduation. I told them that my uncertainties about graduate school and the workforce were influential in making me consider short-term missions. It was true, but I wish I hadn't phrased it that way. Later one of them joked to another friend, "After finishing school you can either go to grad school or get a real job. But if all else fails, you can do what Strom did and become a missionary." I laughed it off, but the attitude there is a common one. Some believers feel that intercultural work is for those who can't hack it at home. Twenty years later I know better. Missionaries, relief workers, and civil diplomats are among the most well educated and morally alert people I know. One reason why they may look out of place in Des Moines is because their heart is in Dhaka.

One of the mysteries of our faith is how God not only lived with us as Christ, but that he lives in us by his Holy Spirit. Despite our fallenness, we have God's Spirit to help us witness a life for him. That is our hope as messengers for him.

"I understand, Bobby, but this isn't Rome."

Tap into the "flow of truth." In addition to living the truth, we need to figure out how a culture pursues truth, for every cultural group has its ways of determining what is true and what should be done about it.

Western cultures use democratic politics, university systems, the mass media, and sometimes the church to meet this need. We are more likely to agree with the results of a scientific study about cancer covered on the six o'clock news than embrace the ranting declarations of a scruffy psychopath atop a soapbox labeled "healer" in Central Park. To put it another way, we need to discover the structure of decision-making and work within it. As Mayers notes, "The truth of God must come to each man completely and effectively in keeping with what he is socioculturally."[21] If we impose electronic media on people who value a shaman (holy person) atop a stump in the village center, there's a good chance they will miss our message for all the noise of the medium. Will they respect a message that comes by way of television when they are used to receiving truth from the shaman?

In certain agricultural cultures, information travels quickly along the path enroute to the rice fields. If you want to be in the know, *get on the path.* If you want your message known, *get on the path.* Donald Smith notes that once we know the structures by which truth and decisions are determined,

our strategy for reaching people in that culture should vary accordingly.[22]
We do it their way.

Find the right words and nonverbals. This was the wisdom of Chapters
1 and 2, and yet interculturally it takes on monumental significance. Our
language and body cues convey the bulk of our message. And, conversely,
what we think, and how we think, is intimately linked to our words and
actions. Both views remind us that managing symbols requires responsibility, especially when working within someone else's code.

How would you express that you feel tired and worn out? In English we
might say "I'm bushed" but a Korean might say, "I want to die." How do
you indicate your name to someone? You probably say, "My name is
_____," but a French-speaker would say, "I name myself _____." How
do you express "yes" with your head? In the United States and Canada we
nod our heads up and down, but East Indians wag their heads back and
forth. How might you beckon someone to you? Probably by holding your
hand out, palm up, and "hooking" him towards you with your pointer
finger. In India, the palm faces down and you "scoop" people toward you
with all your fingers.

The challenge is to find the *functional equivalent.* That is, you want to
find the word or action in the receptor's culture that creates the meaning
you hope to import from your home culture. If a "scoop" functions to create the equivalent meaning of a "hook," then use a "scoop."

Bible translators know the principle of functional equivalence well. For
example, in some cultures, the part of the body used to refer to the soul is
not their word for "heart" (as in North America). Some language groups
use the word "abdomen," "throat," or "liver" to mean soul. "Hence, certain familiar passages must be rendered in quite different ways, e.g., 'Let
not your liver be troubled' (John 14:1), 'So you have sorrow now, but I will
see you again and your livers will rejoice' (John 16:22), and 'These people
honor me with their mouths, but their livers are far from me (Matthew
12:34)."[23] For Position 1 Christians who may dispute such "tinkering" with
scriptural texts, the Position 2 believer asks, "What has changed?" The
words, yes. God's Word, no.

Meet human needs, find points of contact and use redemptive analogies.
These are three particular strategies for making the gospel message intelligible. The first is to recognize that people everywhere have basic life needs,
and a message that meets a need will be more readily considered.[24] Missionary Seamands realized that Gunboat Jack was a hurting man. He also
sensed Gunboat's sensitivity to spiritual things when the boxer said the
devil had knocked him down again and again. Seamands responded by
saying, "Gunboat Jack, may I introduce you to the best Manager a person
can have? His name is Jesus Christ. If you follow his instructions, you can

land a knockout blow to the devil every time." We may question the missionary's claim that believers beat Satan every time, but his heart is in the right place. Likening Christ to a manager met Gunboat's need for help from someone in his fight for life.

Second, our message will be more likely considered if it engages our listener with a slice of shared experience or a conceptual container. These *points of contact* serve as the basis for meaningful dialogue. For example, Muslims believe that God reveals himself to us, but that he would not become human to do so. Christians believe that God reveals himself to us, and in his omnipotence is able to visit earth as a human. The concept of "revelation" is therefore a point of contact with a Muslim, even though the full-fledged doctrines behind this term share no common ground.[25] But we can enter meaningful dialogue about revelation generally.

Third, we can further link with culturally different others by employing *redemptive analogies*. Like points of contact, redemptive analogies compare aspects of the gospel message to some ritual, practice, word, or behavior in the receptor's culture that opens the floodgate of understanding to what God has done for them through Jesus Christ. Don Richardson's book, *Eternity in their Hearts*, provides example after example of how God has prepared many cultures with such a comparative vehicle.[26] Among the Sawi of New Guinea, the floodgate opened when they saw Christ as their "peace child." Sawi chiefs from warring tribes exchange one of their children as a sign of trusted truce. As long as each child is alive and well, the two chiefs' tribes live in peace. If either child dies or is mistreated, there are grounds for war. Richardson developed the analogy that God and the Sawi were once at war, but God has now given them his peace child. As long as Jesus is alive and well among them, peace reigns. This comparison brought such understanding that Richardson witnessed hundreds of Sawi people trusting Jesus. Today two-thirds of the Sawi profess Christ as their Lord.

What If We Do It the Old Way?

Valuing "less developed" cultures and their modes of communication typifies the incarnational model. This culturally sensitive approach has been encouraged by Christian missionary scholars such as Donald McGavran, Alan Tippett, and Eugene Nida since the 1960s, and echoed by a second generation, such as Paul Hiebert, Charles Kraft, and Marvin Mayers. Their books are worth considering.[27]

However, for many years — even centuries — many Christians have taken a strong Position 1 approach, the old approach, to convey God's message across cultures. Viewing the Bible as their guide for holy living (a good thing) and adding the view that Western culture is superior to others (a bad thing), yesteryear attempts to reproduce believers interculturally has led to ugly methods with dubious results. Let's look at two as negative learning examples.

HOW NOT TO SHARE GOD'S MESSAGE INTERCULTURALLY

The first ineffective model is the head-on approach. "This is the method of aggressive refutation and condemnation of other faiths. This attitude assumes that all other religions are the work of the devil, are false, and devoid of value. There are, therefore, no points of contact or bridgepoints for preaching the gospel."[28] This method entails the condemning of idol worship, the condemning of false gods, the tearing down of pagan temples, and force-feeding the gospel. Without choice, many people in Africa, South America, and Southern Asia have become Christians not by choice but by default. They were never given the opportunity to understand the gospel message well enough to make their own decision to choose God and destroy idols. They are mere cultural Christians—people who display the outward signs of western Christianity, but have no personal relationship with Jesus Christ.

In response to the inadequacy of the head-on approach, some Christians have swung the pendulum to the other extreme and used the shake-hands approach.[29] This is the method of accommodation, that is, the watering down of the gospel so that it is easier for others to accept. For example, some believers equate material blessing with God's favor in order to attract materialistic Americans. "God *wants* you to have that new Cadillac—you've just got to trust him" goes their logic.

At a more symbolic level, accommodation of belief may occur through the words we use to convey spiritual truth. One year the student committee in charge of our school's Missions Week decided on the motto: La Mission: To Go Where No One Has Gone Before. The phrase "La Mission" was a take-off from a then-popular Labatts beer commercial, and the "To Go Where..." phrase was borrowed from *Star Trek*. While attempting to be contemporary, the phrase fumbled its meaning amidst images of Captain Kirk and other Enterprise crew members tilting back a cold one. It also conjured up the idea that some gospel crew, rather than God, draws people to himself.

The result of a coercive head-on approach and an anything-goes shake-hands approach is often the same: syncretism. Syncretism is the mixing of two religions to form a mutant offspring. As Eugene Nida writes, "Syncretism...involves an accommodation of content, a synthesis of beliefs, and an amalgamation of world views, in such a way as to provide some common basis for constructing a "new system" or a "new approach."[30] We want to avoid syncretism, but it is the risk we take when using the cultural forms of friends in a receptor culture. It was the risk Jesus took to convey God's will for us through Greek and Hebrew codes. Our goal, like his, is indigenization — to live and proclaim the redeeming message of God with local forms of communication so that others can hear God's still small voice and colossal love.

Summary

If you think about it, the principles for connecting and communicating with people from different cultural backgrounds are identical to those at home. Know your audience, form your message, use words your audience will understand, and engage nonverbal cues that lend credibility to what you say; spend time with them and develop shared experiences so you can play charades, not Ping-Pong or bowling; above all, choose to listen and choose to love. Intercultural communication requires the same principles; what changes is the content.

To know your audience means studying their culture and religious views. It may mean missing out on the service at First Baptist so you can attend First Buddhist. It definitely means that God's call for us to be in the world, but not of it, does not put us on the sideline, but in the thick of our world, always seeing culture through God's eyes and seeking to redeem it and people. Culture is his vehicle through which we create our lives and come to know God's life.

This was Jesus Christ's manner. He left the comfort of heaven to don human garb to walk dusty roads with Jews, Greeks, Samaritans, and Romans. His teaching reflected his knowledge of their history and occupations, their rituals and language. In this chapter we considered the wisdom of imitating his manner. Spending time with relatively similar others toward some common goal builds trust. Taking a stab at their language or immersing ourselves in it builds bridges. Tapping into how decisions and truths are made and communicated puts us on the right path. Discovering points of contact and redemptive analogies may help meet great spiritual need.

Worth the Talk

1. What do you think of the students' choice to use "La Mission: To Go Where No One has Gone Before" as a missions week motto?
2. One author has these tips about how to interact with people of different faiths.[31] Do you agree with them or not? Why?
   a. Be assured that Christ is the Truth, but show humility in that this is entirely God's doing, not our own.
   b. Show the attitude of tolerance (open-minded, fair-minded, sympathetic, and empathetic), but do not compromise the gospel's truth.
   c. Make love your primary manner, and respect the person's freedom to choose for or against Christ.

3. Consider Figure 8.1 again. Where do your thoughts lie on the issue of biblical truth and cultural reality? Can you figure out why you think this way?
4. It's easy for us to think that Christian faith has been communicated in North American culture by way of indigenization (the use of our local forms), with little if any syncretism (the mixing of Christian beliefs with non-Christian ones). Can you think of examples of beliefs or behaviors that we take for granted as biblically Christian that are really culturally Christian? For starters, you might consider church pews and Sunday-as-the-Sabbath.

Consider the Walk

1. Attend a worship service where your language isn't spoken. Do a little ethnography (see Chapter 13). In particular, observe communication forms and identify what function they appear to perform. Typical functions of worship include 1) to praise God, 2) to speak with God, 3) to hear from God, and 4) to fellowship with other believers. How does the church you normally attend accomplish the same purposes with different forms?
2. Interview an international student. Focus your questions on how the Christian faith has been communicated within his or her home culture. Explain the idea of "indigenization" to the student, and try to determine if knowledge of the gospel came by way of "home-grown" communication vehicles or "imported" ones. You may need to do some book research about his or her culture to gain fuller understanding.
3. Play cross-cultural simulations in class. This suggestion is aimed mainly at your instructor, but you might help get the ball rolling. Look for organizations such as Simulation Training Systems, 11760-J Sorrento Valley Rd., San Diego, California, 92121, and request their list of simulation games for cross-cultural experiences. STS sells the games "Where Do You Draw the Line?" (regarding cross-cultural ethics), "Star Power" (about power, its use, abuse, and how it is communicated in culture), and Bafa Bafa (about intercultural communication, culture shock, and cultural norms). After playing a game, analyze your experience by using ideas in this chapter as well as intercultural communication textbooks. This analysis may take the form of a thorough debriefing after the simulation (led by your instructor) or a paper written by you.

NOTES

1. See Carol Werner and Pat Parmalee, "Similarity of Activity Preferences Among Friends: Those Who Play Together Stay Together," *Social Psychology Quarterly*, Vol. 42, 1979, pp. 62-66 and Denise B. Kandel, "Similarity in Real-Life Adoles-

cent Friendship Pairs," *Journal of Personality and Social Psychology*, Vol. 36, 1978, pp. 302-312.

2. Marvin K. Mayers, *Christianity confronts culture*, Zondervan Publishing House, Grand Rapids, MI, 1987, pp. 247-249.
3. Mayers, p. 241.
4. Mayers, pp. 248-249.
5. Sherwood Lingenfelter, *Transforming culture: A challenge for Christian mission*, Baker Book House, Grand Rapids, MI, 1992, pp. 17-18.
6. Lingenfelter, p. 23.
7. Quoted in John Stott and Robert Coote, *Gospel and culture*. William Carey Library, Pasadena, CA, 1979, p. 97.
8. See, for example, the work of Henri Tajfel and Michael Billig, "Familiarity and Categorization in Intergroup Behavior," *Journal of Experimental Social Psychology*, Vol. 10, 1974, pp. 159-170 and Henri Tajfel, "Social Psychology of Intergroup Relations," *Annual Review of Psychology*, Vol. 33, 1982, pp. 1-39.
9. David G. Myers, *Social psychology*, Third Edition, McGraw-Hill Publishing, New York, NY, 1990, p. 345.
10. See Y. Amir, "Contact Hypothesis in Ethnic Relations," *Psychological Bulletin*, Vol. 71, 1969, 319-342.
11. Of note, the work of Christian missions in India has had the strongest impact on two groups: the high caste Brahmans and the untouchable Harijans. Christian missionaries, largely from wealthy countries of the United States and Britain, have related well to the socially elite Brahmans. What explains outcast conversion to Christianity is the Christian doctrine of "no caste in Christ." Harijans have, therefore, identified with the "spiritual status" of missionaries who do not claim to be superior on a spiritual ladder of caste.
12. Murray Moerman, "Ethnic Communities are 'Bridges of God' to Spread the Gospel," *Christian Info News*, May 1996, p. 6.
13. See John Seamands, *Tell it well: Communicating the gospel across cultures*, Beacon Hill Press of Kansas City, Kansas City, MO, 1981.
14. Amir, pp. 319-342.
15. Donald K. Smith, *Make haste slowly: Developing effective cross-cultural communication*, Institute for International Christian Communication, Portland, OR, 1984, Chapter 6. See also his textbook, Donald K. Smith, *Creating understanding: A handbook for Christian communication across cultural landscapes*, Zondervan Publishing House, Grand Rapids, MI, 1992, pp. 23-40.
16. See for example Young Y. Kim, "Communication Patterns of Foreign Immigrants in the Process of Acculturation," *Human Communication Research*, Vol. 4, 1977, pp. 66-77.
17. See Huston Smith, *The religions of man*, Perennial Library, Harper and Row, Publishers, New York, 1958. Also, John T. Seamands' book, *Tell it Well*, has four excellent chapters that address how to share the gospel with Hindus, Buddhists, Animists, and Muslims. (See above for full citation)
18. A missionary friend of mine to Indonesia described Indonesian as a "perfect language" because it holds consistently to its rules for spelling, pronunciation, and grammar.
19. Eugene A. Nida, *Message and mission: The communication of the Christian faith* (Revised Edition), William Carey Library, Pasadena, CA, 1990, p. 28.

20. Reference to Jones made by Seamands, p. 109.

21. Mayers, p. 116.

22. Smith, *Make haste slowly*, Chapter 14 "Structure Determines Strategy."

23. Nida, p. 139.

24. This is the observation on which the work of Abraham Maslow's theory of hierarchical needs is based. He suggests that all people experience the need for physical well-being, safety, a sense of belonging, self-esteem or self-respect, and self-actualization. See A. H. Maslow, *Motivation and personality*, 2nd ed., Harper & Row, New York, NY, 1970.

25. Nida, p. 18, is critical of Christians who promote a "common ground" approach to communicating the gospel. He writes "We insist upon a "point of contact" approach rather than a "common ground" orientation because it is impossible to take any element of belief out of its context and still have the same belief. Religions are systems, and the individual beliefs have meaning only in terms of the system to which they belong.

26. Don Richardson, *Eternity in their hearts*, Regal Books, Ventura, CA, 1981.

27. Key works by the three authors not referred to yet in this chapter include: Donald McGavran, *The clash between Christianity and cultures*, Canon Press, Washington, D.C., 1974; Alan R. Tippet, *Verdict theology in missionary theory*, 2nd edition, William Carey, South Pasadena, CA, 1973; Paul Hiebert, *Anthropological insights for missionaries*, Baker Book House, Grand Rapids, MI, 1985.

28. This is Seamand's term and quotation, p. 75.

29. Seamands, p. 78.

30. Nida, p. 131.

31. Seamands, pp. 54-56.

CHAPTER 9

Electronically (Dis-)Connected
Arguments Against the Media

*Do not love the world or anything in the world. If
anyone loves the world, the love of the Father is
not in him. For everything in the world — the
cravings of sinful man, the lust of his eyes, and the
boasting of what he has and does — comes not from
the Father but from the world. The world and its
desires pass away but the man who does the will of
God lives forever.*

I John 2:15-17

It was like most days in speech class. Five students were prepared to convince their classmates to begin thinking or behaving in a new fashion. Four
topics that day elude me just now. One will stick with me for a long time.

The student who gave the speech, Ben Ridley, was new to our program.[1]
What I knew of Ben was that he enjoyed sports and hoped to be a sports
journalist someday. I got the sense he valued his hook-up to ESPN and
Canada's equivalent, TSN (The Sports Network). He had written sport
shorts for his hometown paper during high school, and now wrote the same
for the university's paper. For classmates who knew Ben, I suppose they
were expecting a topic such as "You should consider sports journalism as a
career," or "Ken Griffey — a man of integrity." Our expectations were off.

Ben went to the front of the class and said, "For years we've been hearing about all the bad stuff television does to us. We hear that it attacks our
values and makes us do things we normally wouldn't. Well I'm an avid TV
watcher, and I'm here today to convince you that TV isn't harmful."

In a university environment, and a Christian university environment,
you might imagine the muffled shock to such a proposal. Students here are
keen at analyzing the impact of the media on culture, and the professors in

169

our department who address this issue suggest a more mixed response, especially toward television. No harmful effects?

What Ben presented that day were observations from his own experience with television. Although he loved to watch murder mysteries, he never felt the urge to murder anyone. Despite TV's brash commercialism, he claimed he had his purchase behavior in check. Even though he watched many a fight break out during hockey games, he never turned to punch out his friend.

Ben's experience with television is a starting point for the next two chapters. Few of us escape the presence of media technology and media messages. In one day alone you are likely to wake up to music on a clock radio, read a newspaper over breakfast, watch an instructional video in class, watch an evening newscast, and surf the Internet to research a paper. Since many good texts can help you understand the media industry complex, it is my desire to address how Christians have responded to media content and technology. Observing their response — and reasons for their response — will help us understand guys like Ben and believers quite unlike him as well.

To that end, the next two chapters are built around a model of Christian responses to the media (see Figure 9.1). This chapter introduces all five responses, and then addresses the first one at length. Chapter 10 will address two other responses that most believers enact. Let's begin with the model.

Christian Responses to Media: Reject, Accept, Critique

Through the centuries, believers have responded to popular culture in a variety of ways based on their understanding of what it means to be in the world but not of it (see John 17:14-16).[2] Their responses have ranged from resolute rejection to welcomed acceptance, and both with biblical rationales. Between these extremes are Christians who accept technologies with caution and critique their messages with godly mindfulness to discover what is beneficial.

Figure 9.1 attempts to grid these responses along two axes. One axis represents the range of responses to media technologies. The questions we have about purchasing the latest in virtual reality headset games are the same ones believers at the turn of the century asked about radio. Is this technology good, evil, or neutral? Should we bring them into our homes? The other axis concerns our response to media content. Do we give thanks for the NBC Nightly News but shy from the news of *People Magazine*? What criteria do we use to evaluate television shows and movies? Should we embrace *Touched by an Angel*, but avoid *All My Children*?

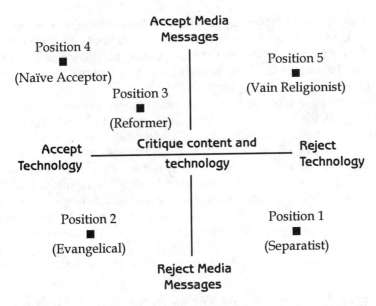

Figure 9.1.   A Grid for Understanding People's Responses to Media Technology and Media Content

It may be a bit simple, but my experience with students suggests that Christians respond to both technologies and their content with acceptance, rejection, and/or mindful criticism. By acceptance I mean watch, listen to, enjoy, identify with, learn from, and find God's truth in. By rejection I mean avoid and judge negatively. By mindful criticism I mean observe actively and judge holistically in order to find the wheat amidst the chaff. The model could be viewed from the center outward, that is, criticism first and acceptance or rejection second. For example, after evaluating some new virtual reality technology or a software game for a VR headset, you may then arrive at a thumbs up or thumbs down resolve. For the sake of simplicity though, we will address each response as a pure type.

POSITION 1: REJECT MEDIA TECHNOLOGIES AND MEDIA CONTENT

If you saw the movie *The Witness*, you saw this view at work in the life of the Amish. Some Christians, including the Amish, certain Mennonite groups, and Hutterites, refuse to bring communication technologies into their homes in the first place. They believe that being in the world but not of it means to live a simple lifestyle and work and worship communally. "To the Amish, worldliness denotes specific behaviors and lifestyles. High school, cars, cameras, tape recorders, television, films, showy houses, certain farm machinery and bicycles, all tagged *worldly*, are censured."[3] The

Amish do not use telephones, for example, because telephones mock the separatist call to find one's place in Amish community and not relate to outsiders. Also, the Amish value for contextual, family interaction as opposed to the decontextualized messages sent by telephone, help us understand why they don't have phones in their homes.[4]

You don't have to be Amish to respect their response or admit that you've responded similarly. Any time we refuse to clutter our lives with one more media toy or rightly judge media content as dishonoring to God, we're living the spirit of a Position 1 stance. To understand why some Christians ban or censor the ugliest of media content from their own consumption, we'll look at their arguments in the second half of this chapter.

Position 1 Christians may avoid the negative effects of media — such as impersonalization and questionable values. In their media-less environment they enjoy the intensity of community in which they find identity and accountability. What they lack, however, is any basis for changing the media industry or enjoying God's general revelation these media may offer.

POSITION 2: ACCEPT MEDIA TECHNOLOGIES, BUT AVOID OR REPLACE QUESTIONABLE CONTENT

If you came to Christ in what is termed an evangelical tradition, there's a good possibility that you hold a Position 2 response to the media. Evangelicals may spurn some of modernity's technological advances, but many consider media technologies as gifts from God sprung from human innovation. Evangelicals are apt to say that technologies are benign; what might kill you is their content. The evangelical community is particularly concerned with mediated depictions of sex, violence, profanity and the occult. Avoiding such programming and choosing wholesome or family-values material is a strategy they use to cope in the media environment. Evangelicals are likely to praise the media for their educational and informational role in alerting us to the material and spiritual needs of others (e.g., World Vision television specials). They are also prone to consider media channels as gifts from God so we might assist him in drawing others to himself. Christ's great commission (see Matthew 28) compels these believers to embrace radio, television, and the Internet as one more "available means" by which Christians can proclaim the Good News of Christ.

You are likely in the Position 2 camp if you approve of Chuck Colson's use of radio for *Breakpoint,* or Billy and Franklin Graham's use of television to broadcast crusades. If you own a raft of Christian CDs and subscribe to *CCM (Contemporary Christian Music)* Magazine or enjoy clicking on ministry Internet cites for resources, then it's evident you accept the medium but selectively choose your content.

Position 2 Christians might condemn the media's most obvious ills, but overlook less overt woes such as *Wheel of Fortune's* materialism and *Princess Bride's* belittling of the church. Some Position 2 Christians are also accustomed to the sub-professional standards that certain Christian media producers settle for in order to get the Word out. Even still, these Christians usually avoid the ugliest and most demeaning of media fare because they choose to avoid it. We'll look more deeply at their arguments for accepting media technology in Chapter 10.

POSITION 3: CRITIQUE MEDIA TECHNOLOGIES AND MESSAGES FROM A CHRISTIAN PERSPECTIVE

If you came to know God in what is termed a reformed tradition of the church, there's a chance that you hold a Position 3 response to media. Reform theologians underline that God not only gave us a great commission to assist him in reaching those he has chosen, but also a cultural mandate to redeem cultural institutions, including the media. By redemption they mean the process of finding the moral good that already exists in culture, and attempting to transform cultural institutions (whether school systems, governments, or the media industry) to the glory of God. They take Philippians 4:8 seriously when it encourages us to think upon whatever is true, noble, right, pure, lovely, admirable, excellent or praiseworthy, whether it originates from scripture or not. Reformers reject the split between "sacred things" and "secular things" that some Christians believe define God's world. Rather, if all truth is God's truth, and if even the media can convey truth, then we can search and use the media to advance God's kingdom.

You exercise Position 3 when you genuinely search for faith-affirming interpretations of family life among the Taylors on *Home Improvement,* or grasp the pain and despondency of people through *General Hospital.* Reformers define holiness as not the avoidance of sin or its depiction, but our response to sin when we encounter it.[5] You also exercise a transformer response when you ask "How does the structure of a medium, like TV, send its own message, separate from the programming?" Realizing that television delivers a sedentary lifestyle is one such insight.

Christians who hold a Position 3 response to media sometimes walk a fine line between being in, understanding, and attempting to change the world, but not succumbing to the mold of the world. Some of these Christians may fool themselves when they believe that they are able to rise above non-redeemable media content and walk away better people. Sometimes, they gain a fuller understanding of sin at the price of their own moral sensitivity and spiritual walk. We will look more fully at Position 3 in the following chapter.

POSITION 4: ACCEPT MEDIA TECHNOLOGIES AND CONTENT UNCRITICALLY BASED ON A NAIVE "NO INFLUENCE" BELIEF

Ben Ridley represents a group of Christians who have a carefree attitude about media. They likely prize their multi-media center, and like Ben, spend significant time on TV-room cushions. Their response is justified by at least three ways of reasoning. One is to believe, like the reformers, that God's message is available to us through cultural expressions, including the media. His grace might hide in the shadows of garbage, but it's there for our interpreting. The second is the belief that we, as God's image-bearers, are plenty able to defend ourselves against messages antithetical to the faith. We are not sponges, but Spirit-filled critics. The third, and perhaps the only questionable one, is that God is more concerned with behavior than attitudes or intentions. As long as Ben doesn't haul off and punch his brother as they watch *World Wrestling Federation*, God has few qualms with animal mentality. These assumptions free the Position 4 believer to relish in drama, film, music, and television with the calm assurance that tucked away therein is an expression of God's good to us. If they fail to find it, and cross the line, God's grace abounds.

However, while some believers may manage to please God plopped in front of the tube with a highly discerning spirit, there's an equal or greater likelihood that they experience self-deception. Or at least they're not thinking logically. Consider the results of a study by Karen Foss and Alison Alexander who interviewed twenty people who watch at least six hours of television per day. The researchers discovered that heavy viewers tend to see their TV watching as motivated by outside forces rather than personal choice, believe that TV watching has negative effects on people generally but not them specifically, and say that TV viewing is *not* important to them.[6] A person who blames their environment, excludes themselves from being like most people, and suggests that a 6-hour-a-day activity is not important to them hardly sounds like the mindful critic noted in Position 3.

Contrary to the "no effect" hypothesis that Position 4 believers hold, much evidence suggests that high exposure to television, in particular, is associated with a host of attitudes and beliefs with which Christians should be concerned. People who believe that TV's destructive potential applies to everyone but themselves seem to be victims of the master deceiver.

POSITION 5: REJECT MEDIA TECHNOLOGIES BUT ACCEPT NEGATIVE MEDIA VALUES

I'm not sure I've ever met a Position 5 believer, but it's possible to imagine someone who has refused to purchase a television or VCR on ideological grounds, but who lives out media values anyway. Now when I say

"Am I mindful when I watch TV? Sure I am. Touch my TV and you'll see how much I mind."

"lives out media values anyway," what does that mean? It could mean a quiet, pastoral life like *The Waltons* who struggled humbly with depression-times poverty, or it could mean a life of violence like that on *Millenium* or *Tales From the Crypt*. What makes me think it's more macabre than pastoral is the fact that you've got to have strong reasons, and perhaps some anger too, to denounce media and take off for the woods. That's what Ted Kaczynski did.

Theodore John Kaczynski is the infamous Unabomber who took to the Montana wilderness to write a 35,000-word anti-technology manifesto and mail letter bombs to high-tech industry CEOs. The "hit list" that FBI agents found tacked to his shack wall targeted the airline industry, the computer industry, and geneticists. From his wooded seclusion he mailed death packages to the likes of Thomas Mosser, a New Jersey advertising executive and Gilbert Murray, a timber-industry lobbyist. Both died.

The sad consistency of Kaczynski's behavior is that his rejection of technology mirrored his rejection of human community. Unlike the Amish whose community is the defining feature of their world view, Theodore Kaczynski defined himself more along the lines of the rugged *Marlboro* man, a favorite media image. Although he denounced technology, he used it to blow away those he believed were ruining society.

The point here is that rejecting technology generally or media toys specifically is no guarantee of godliness. Four thousand years of human history before the dawn of the printing press and microchip is evidence enough to prove that true.

The label "vain religionist" comes from my reading of James 1, where the apostle says that people who consider themselves religious but who can't control their tongues practice a worthless faith (1:26). By parallel, believers who claim God's sovereignty in their lives but show no controlled discretion in their media consumption may only be fooling themselves.

It may go without saying that Position 4 and Position 5 believers stand on uncertain ground. My reading of scripture indicates that our walk should be mindful of what we take in, and full of charity in what we dish out.

Other readers may feel that the evangelical and reformer positions represent the only realistic options. Since the media complex is here to stay, they may reason, we had best figure out how to work within it, not around it.

But for some believers the best option is still avoidance. For some that means not owning a television set; for others it means being highly selective in what they read and view. Behind both responses is the belief that despite our made-in-God's-image likeness, we are still frail people who succumb to banal and base media content. If there's anything to this belief, then it's worth considering the type of media content concerned Christians attempt to avoid.

The Case Against the Media
(Or, Could the Amish be Right?)

Position 1 is based on the belief that consuming media content and becoming dependent on technology inhibit community, holy living, and service to others. Position 1 believers value enmeshment in other people's lives and dependence on God more than entanglement in celluloid imagery and reliance on CBS. What are the arguments in favor of this view? What evidence suggests that the media do little to enhance our relationship with God, and are better off avoided? We will consider four of their arguments.

THE VALUES ARGUMENT

Values are what we consider of ultimate worth and attention. The argument that separatists and evangelicals use here is fairly basic. Christians are better off avoiding much of what the media dish up because those messages often run contrary to kingdom values. Christian values such as selfless love, service to others, deferred gratification, and devotion to God in the person of Christ find little airtime in popular media. Let's consider four media values that conflict with the call of Christ.

Media value #1: you deserve a comfortable life. In an average year, American advertisers churn out 12 billion display ads, 2.5 million radio commercials, and 300,000 television commercials. If you watch television for three hours straight, including the ads, you'll see about 36 minutes of advertisements, or 45-60 ads depending on how many are 30 seconds or 60 seconds. And their message is uniform: *we are what we buy, and only when we have bought enough will we accomplish the American dream and be content.* While McDonalds convinces us that we deserve a break today and Silver Wing Holidays suggests we need a vacation, we know that Jesus had no place to lay his head and left as his only possession a bloodied robe at the time of his crucifixion.

If the ads are the worst, programming is a close second. One critic has suggested that the world of prime time television looks and feels like it does because it reflects the comfortable lifestyles of producers and actors — the rich and famous of Los Angeles, California.[7] From *Bay Watch* to free stuff on the Web, it's tough to shake the notion that what counts is our comfort.

Does this message really affect us? Can we rise above it? One television study on adolescent perceptions of work suggests "no." The researcher found that "heavy viewing adolescents were more likely [than low viewers] to want high-status jobs that would give them a chance to earn a lot of money but also wanted jobs to be relatively easy with long vacations and time to do other things."[8] Even if these heavy viewers grow up with a disposition for a life of ease, it is likely that their watching the tube only strengthens this value. Position 4 Christians would like to think otherwise, but this evidence suggests that increased exposure to the posh and privileged makes us devalue a lifestyle like the Son of Man's.

Media value #2: you deserve an exciting life. You probably recall the series of Claratin advertisements starring the James Bond type guy. In one scenario he's maneuvering his sports car with insolent skill around slower drivers and road obstacles in an attempt to dodge the bullets being rifled at him by a gorgeous would-be assassin who follows in a convertible. The Claratin man coolly adjusts his glasses and looks up to see a rope-ladder dangling from an out-of-no-where friendly helicopter. He grasps a rung and rises to a glorious meeting in the air. (Remember, they're selling an allergy medication here!)

Similar fare is served up on action-packed dramas such as *FX: The Series*, and suspense footage on shows like *Real TV*. I watched the 1997 fall debut of *Real TV* to witness: a shark's jaw clamping onto an unsuspecting fisherman's hand; the rescue and resuscitation of a child caught in a fire;

the successful dislodging of a stuck landing gear on a small plane in flight by a man being carried by a speeding car. Did the show keep me glued to my seat? Sort of. Do I now believe that God or the government owes me a life of thrill? Maybe. The question is whether or not I can choose to rise above this message again and again, or if somewhere it gets under my skin and into my soul.

A soul need for excitement is akin to what Elizabeth Perse examined. She believes that some people are naturally wired to require a Claratin life. She calls such people "high sensation seekers," and she examined how they meet their need for a stimulating life. She found that high sensation seekers (HSS) attend more horror films, like horror films more, watch horror films for the gore and thrills, prefer rock music, consume more X-rated magazines, books, and movies, express more willingness to watch erotic films, and spend more time watching action movies in experimental conditions than low sensation seekers.[9] Although Perse treats HSS as a personality trait that influences media choices, you can see how the material chosen is largely questionable and only confirms and strengthens the value for excitement. In the case of serial killer Ted Bundy, exposure to absorbing material increased his threshold for what produced a kick. Eventually he acted out those images of rape and torture as a means to get the same degree of stimulation provided earlier by pornography.[10]

Media value #3: you deserve a happy life, now! Tony Campolo cites the work of Cornel West, head of the black studies program at Harvard University, as evidence to prove that television is demonic. "...West points out that television has become a primary force in generating a sense of *nihilism* among black teenagers. Television, he says, has communicated to young people a lifestyle that allows them to believe that the seeking of pleasure and the acquiring of possessions is what life is all about. From the ads to the videos played on MTV, the message is the same: The meaning of life is the immediate gratification of desires."[11]

Although few media sources preach nihilism explicitly (the doctrine that nothing exists or can be known) they can be faulted for rarely affirming God's existence or the possibility of knowing him personally. If you don't believe that God exists and has expectations of us, then the immediate pleasure-seeking messages the media give us make a lot of sense. Why devote yourself to committed relationships or generational ministry if tomorrow we die and turn back to dust? The media's call to happiness *now* because we deserve it contrasts with God's call to holiness over a lifetime. Holy living, some suggest, results in joy and peace that outlives the happy high from a media fix.

Media value #4: you acquire friends through things. Please get this straight. The media depict a healthy value on the power of friendship. A telephone company's ad to "reach out and touch someone" is similarly reflected in the friendships among characters in situation comedies and daytime soaps. The concern is not with having friends but with how you acquire them.

Advertisers convey the myth that we make and keep friends by wearing the right cologne (please be obsessed with me), driving the right car (hey babes, look at me), having athletic prowess (I can dunk; aren't I cool?) and drinking the right beer (it don't get no better than this). Of particular concern is the myth propagated by the 100,000 beer ads we see by age eighteen. These ads show the party crowd drinkers relishing in fellowship, but experiencing no addiction, impaired driving, vomiting, or idiotic behavior toward each other. Over and over the message is: drink this beer and you'll be a social magnet.

Another concern is that the media depict a fallen view of friendship. Christian media critic Quentin Schultze casts relationships on soap operas in Darwinian terms. He says soaps reflect "an evolutionary naturalism in which human society is a collection of animalistic individuals battling for survival. There is no God and no place for transcendent values from a god."[12] Producers of television, rock videos, and R-rated movies are too willing to portray self-centered, back-stabbing, and sex-based friendships as the norm and chalk it up to survival of the fittest.

We should not be surprised with this list of media values. Media producers are businesspeople, bent on selling us goods—whether programs or perfume. To gain our attention, they sell us an attractive bill of goods: comfort, excitement, happiness, and friends. They do not want relationship with us; they want our income through advertising. They care less about truth and more about making us feel good. They do not care about community among us; they want us to sit quietly and individually, drinking in their human answers to meet our needs.

THE TIME USE ARGUMENT

A second argument Position 1 believers advance for avoiding the media is that media use is a waste of time if our larger goal is to glorify God. God does not call us to mission work every waking hour, but they believe he has called us to redeem everything, including our use of time.

How much time does a typical individual spend with media sources? One study indicated that high school students spend an average of thirty-two (32) hours per week watching TV, listening to the radio, going to movies, and reading newspapers and magazines.[13] Other studies indicate that younger children and the elderly often spend thirty-two (32) hours per week watching television alone.

The same statistics hold for people who call themselves Christians. In regard to the blue box, Quentin Schultze writes that "Christians on average view the same amount of television as non-Christians; moreover, they tend to watch the same programs, except that believers tend to watch more religious broadcasts."[14] Even Christians who have historically held a position of avoidance are watching a good share of TV. Diane Umble found that over half of Mennonite Church members watched between seven and twenty-one hours of TV per week.[15] Finally, according to one Barna Research Group poll, Generation X believers were more likely to report that they watched MTV during the past week (42 percent) than their non-Christian counterparts (33 percent).[16] If you add to these TV figures the time spent with other media, the average number of hours could easily climb to forty hours per week, or over 5.5 hours per day.

Why do people spend time with media sources in the first place? McQuail, Blumler and Brown suggest that we use the media to gratify important needs. "People wanting *information* may tune in *The MacNeil/Lehrer News Hours* on public television; individuals seeking to clarify their *personal identity* may watch *Donahue*; viewers searching for clues about *social interaction* may turn on *All My Children*; and people looking for *entertainment* may select *Wheel of Fortune*."[17] The concern of Position 1 believers is that even if these motives are genuine, media may not be the best source for meeting these needs. If *Home Improvement* entertains me for 30 minutes after a hectic day at work, I'm probably a saner individual. But if five hours of television per day distracts me from time with my wife and children, I'm digging a relational grave. Similarly, if I turn to Tom Cruise as a role model for my male identity, I may end up defining myself as homely and incompetent and, therefore, unlovable.

In Paul's exhortation to the believers at Ephesus, he encourages them to "be careful then, how you live — not as unwise but as wise, making the most of every opportunity, because the days are evil" (5:15-16). Some believers question whether it is wise to spend as much time with media sources as one would at a part-time job. Does it glorify God? Position 1 Christians answer "no," and make attempts to redeem their time with activity that better pleases him.

THE SPOILED SEXUALITY ARGUMENT

The third argument against the media is one that separatist and evangelical Christians make often and make clear. It asserts that media producers are far too willing to depict spoiled versions of our sexuality in media content, and that these images pain the heart of God. The orthodox Christian view of sexuality is that God gave erotic love for pleasure and procreation within a loving, committed marriage relationship. Through our sexuality, we consummate the mystery of two becoming one and show each other agape love. Eros love, or physical love, is of God, but fallen people abuse eros for personal gain and perverted pleasure. For single individuals, sexuality is an area for practicing God's grace and self-control. People of faith are perhaps most concerned with the pervasiveness of spoiled eros and the twisted messages these depictions convey.

The pervasiveness of sexual material in the media. Your own experience will likely affirm that sex is a common theme in the media. The amount we consume depends, in part, on our choices. Other times, we are exposed to this material without warning. The sheer quantity of sexual content in media often makes it impossible to avoid.

Take television as a case in point. "One study revealed that there are some 14,000 sexual references on TV annually and only 165 of these references deal with sex education, contraception, abortion, or sexually-transmitted diseases."[18] The bulk of these references include sexual innuendoes, sexual advances, people making out, people making love, and sexual crimes.

How do these sexual references add up in the life of one person? Based on research in Cassatta and Skill's *Life on Daytime TV* and Greenberg's *Life on Television,* we can estimate that a person who watches one hour of soaps and one hour of prime-time drama per day will, conservatively, consume 21 physically suggestive behaviors per week, 16 aggressive touching sexual behaviors per week, and 39 verbally suggestive sexual behaviors or comments per week.[19] These figures total to approximately 3940 sexual references in one year.

Moreover, when TV characters make love, they are far more likely to do so outside of marriage than within marriage. In soap operas that adolescents say they watch most often, the ratio of unmarried-to-married sex is 2-to-1.[20] In prime time shows young people like to watch, the ratio is 6-to-1.[21] In a sample of thirty R-rated movies which teenagers said they prefer to watch, the ratio rockets to 32-to-1.[22]

Although prime time television continues to dominate the mediated image environment in North America, other media are equally guilty of propagating a spoiled view of our sexuality. Explicit sexual material abounds in MTV rock videos, R-rated and X-rated movies, erotica Internet sites, pornographic magazines and rock music lyrics. For example, in the same sample of the thirty R-rated movies noted above, all films included nudity, with female nudity exceeding male nudity 4 to 1. In a major study involving 178 high school and 609 college students, researchers got a tab on just what percent of them consume sexual media material.[23] Their results appear in Figure 9.2. While some of this exposure is by chance, a good portion of it is by choice.

What cumulative effect this content has on people is hard to tell since we certainly learn a lot about sexuality from our parents and friends as well. Even still, some effects are measurable, and we turn to those now.

Impact of sexual material. If the impact of this material ended with increased heart rates and sweaty palms, perhaps fewer Christians would be in a huff about its prevalence. But the effects go beyond mere physical arousal. Sexual themes influence how we think, feel, and treat people around us.

A number of studies confirm what many media people and Position 4 Christians do not want to admit: sexual material—especially explicit material (that is, pornography)—negatively affects our attitudes and values about our real-life partners and our behavior in the real world. Richard Harris reports these tendencies in his chapter "The Impact of Sexually Explicit Material."

1. Viewing sexually explicit materials even once can lower your value of your sex partner. In three different studies, male subjects were shown videotapes of attractive nude models in various types of sexual activity. Soon after they rated their own partners as being less physically endowed, reported loving their own partners less, and were more likely to proposition a female interviewer during the debriefing period than were guys who were shown a control (non-sexually explicit) video. This study calls into question the use of pornography to enhance one's own sex life. Soaking in

---

68% listen to explicitly sexual music lyrics

46% read explicitly sexual books

39% read "soft pornographic" male magazines

37% rent X-rated films

30% read detective magazines

14% watch X-rated films at movie theaters

14% read "soft pornographic" female magazines

15% use a variety of other hardcore materials

12% rent hardcore pornographic materials from "adult" bookstores

5% order mail-order pornography

Figure 9.2. Box Score on Explicit Sex Consumption by American College Youth

From Nancy L. Buerkel-Rothfuss, and others, "Adolescents' and Young Adults' Exposure to Sexually Explicit Media" in Bradley S. Greenberg, and others, *Media, Sex and the Adolescent,* Hampton Press, Inc., Cresskill, New Jersey, 1993, p. 112. Used by permission.

filmed or glossy magazine images of erotica diminishes one's pleasure with a partner.

2. Viewing sexual material over an extended period influences numerous interpersonal perceptions and values. Researchers Zillmann and Bryant had male and female subjects watch pornographic videos weekly for several weeks. They found that:

> respondents seeing the explicit films reported, relative to a control group, less satisfaction with the affection, physical appearance, sexual curiosity, and sexual performance of their real-life partners. They also saw sex without emotional involvement as being relatively more important than the control group did. They showed greater acceptance of premarital and extramarital sex and a lesser evaluation of marriage and monogamy. They also showed less desire to have children and greater acceptance of male dominance and female submission. Results generally did not differ for males versus females or college students versus nonstudents.[24]

The reason for this result is due to the nature of pornographic material. Gorgeous models entwine in nontraditional positions and experience nirvanic ecstasy in a childless, relationship-free vacuum. Few real life friends and lovers measure down to this spoiled, but highly idealized view of sex.

3. Consuming explicit sexual messages over time tends to encourage similar behavior in real life, whether good or bad. Some people hold to the catharsis argument — the belief that exposure to sexual material serves as an emotional release and thereby substitutes for the real thing. Richard Harris counters this view with the evidence of copycat activity, disinhibition, and sex crime research. Numerous examples suggest that some people copy activity they find in sexual media. Sometimes their behavior is positive, as in imitating sexual techniques taught from an educational video; other times their behavior is heinous, for example, sexual torture and rape as depicted in porn magazines. Disinhibition refers to lessening your resistance to act immorally because you have seen material that shows other people acting immorally. If they can do it, the logic goes, why can't I?

Although it is difficult to find a direct causal relationship between availability of sexual material and rape, Harris cites evidence that at least a correlation may exist. In a study by Baron and Straus, the correlation between rape and the circulation of eight sex magazines, was +.64 in 50 states (where 0.0 means no correlation and +1.00 shows perfect correlation). The effect was particularly strong in states where magazines depicted sexual violence.[25]

Sexual messages in the media today have seemed to go schizophrenic. On one hand, entertainment programming preaches that sexual involvement is natural, necessary, common, and free from responsibility. Consenting partners meet and hop into bed at their earliest convenience. On the other hand, health and government authorities advocate responsible sexual involvement in their "safe sex" campaigns, and women's groups lead the charge against sexual abuse. The first group preaches freedom, the latter responsibility and self-control.

The statistics, however, suggest that the entertainment industry is winning, and the fall-out is not just increased promiscuity, but increased social ills as well. "By age 20, 70 percent of girls and 80 percent of boys in the U.S. have had sexual intercourse and 1 in 7 of these has contracted a sexually transmitted disease, in some cases AIDS. The United States has the highest rate of teen pregnancies in the industrialized world and is the only such nation where these rates are still rising; currently, 25% of pregnancies occur to mothers under 20 years of age."[26]

The sexuality argument alone is sufficient for some people of faith to cancel their cable, restrict their movie choices, and buy a copy of Net Nanny. Others do the same because of media violence.

THE VIOLENCE ARGUMENT

The fourth argument against the media that separatists and evangelicals muster is that media producers are far too willing to depict violent behavior between people. They follow the lead of George Gerbner, noted media violence researcher, who comments, "We are awash in a tide of violent representations such as the world has never known, and the consequences are very troubling."[27] Just how deep is this tide, and what is the basis for some Christians' call to beach our involvement with it?

Prevalence and nature of violent material. If you are a regular TV watcher, you will likely witness around 120,000 depictions of violent actions, including 18,000 violent deaths, before you enter university. This is about 27 violent acts per day from age 5 to 18, and includes acts such as slaps across the face to shootings, fist fights, car crashes and exploding buildings. In real life, FBI estimates indicate "that in any 1 year less than 1% of people in the United States are victims of criminal violence."[28] People who watch TV four hours or more per day tend to be more fearful and suspicious of people in society than are low TV viewers. Gerbner claims that symbolic violence cultivates our minds toward fear and distrust of neighbors, and dubs this the "mean world syndrome."[29]

It is easy to see how TV's numbers add up. Over 65% of major TV characters are involved in violence each week, and seven out of ten prime time

"Don't worry kids, that's not __real__ blood."

shows (those shown between 7 and 10 p.m.) contain violence. Regular entertainment programs average 150 acts of violence and 15 murders per week.

Who pulls the trigger and who gets the bullet is equally disturbing. The victims of TV murders are more likely to be blacks, Hispanics or Asians than whites. And, while white males are the most likely to perpetrate these evils, they are also the least likely to pay for them in punishment or restitution with their victims.[30]

For parents of teenagers, a primary concern is not television violence but representations in song lyrics and rock art. Compared to two decades ago, the prevalence of songs glorifying rape, sadomasochism, incest, the occult, and suicide appear to be on the increase. Even liberal writer Ellen Goodman comments: "The outrageous edge of rock and roll has shifted its focus from Elvis's pelvis to the saw protruding from Blackie Lawless's codpiece on a WASP album. Rock lyrics have turned from 'I can't get no satisfaction' to 'I am going to force you at gunpoint to eat me alive.'"[31]

Similar themes are common in slasher movies such as the popular series *Halloween, Friday the Thirteenth,* and *Nightmare on Elm Street* and less known but equally violent films such as *Flesh Feast, Alien Prey,* and *Make Them Die Slowly.* "*Alien Prey* shows a blood-stained vampire sucking out a dead woman's entrails through a hole in her stomach. *Flesh Feast* treats us to maggots consuming live human beings, starting with the face and working down. *Make Them Die Slowly* promises '24 scenes of barbaric torture,' such as a man slicing a woman in half."[32] Do people really watch this stuff?

Two-thirds of U.S. college students report that they regularly watch or rent slasher films.[33]

Finally, the emerging technology of CD-ROM interactive computer games has also capitalized on violent material to attract buyers. *Urban Decay* allows players to enact close-range murders, including cop-killing. *Harvester* includes scenes of gruesome deaths and cannibalism. *Crusader* shows humans catching fire and screaming until they disintegrate. And *Expect No Mercy* promises "blood, visual nightmares and uncensored violence." The concern of psychologists and communication scholars is that this sort of participatory violence will erase the line between virtual reality and reality. Some Christians join them when they examine preliminary evidence that suggests that this line is already fading.

Impact of violent content. Barrie Gunter reviews the types of responses people have to mediated violence. They include catharsis, arousal, disinhibition, imitation, and desensitization. *Catharsis* is an emotional release mechanism which some people experience. Rather than making people aggressive, mediated violence sometimes keeps people from being aggressive because they work out their pent-up emotions with a video thriller. Although Gunter strongly criticizes the research that supports the catharsis hypothesis, he admits that it may occur among people with well-developed imaginations. For others, however, the effect does not hold.[34] Catharsis is the only positive effect of media violence that scholars propose. All other effects are negative or potentially so.

Arousal is the stirring up of emotions such as anger, hatred, revenge and the like. After arousal, a person is susceptible to emotional cues in his or her environment. For example, a guy who returns home after watching *Die Hard with a Vengeance* and finds a wife or girlfriend doing something that upsets him, is likely to respond aggressively toward her. The smallest thing can cue people to violence. In one study, second- and third-grade boys watched a violent video in which perpetrators used walkie-talkies as part of their equipment. Later, these boys were much more aggressive while playing floor hockey in a room where adult supervisors were using walkie-talkies ostensibly to do "sports interviews." The kids who saw a non-violent video (where no walkie-talkies were shown), played hockey less aggressively.[35]

Disinhibition, as already noted, is the process by which you become less inhibited to act aggressively because of exposure to mediated aggression. For example, a 10-year longitudinal study indicated that the amount of TV violence consumed by 8-year-old boys was a strong predictor of their aggressiveness as 18-year-old men. The more they watched as kids, the more aggressive they were as young adults.[36] Repeated images of violence appear to develop a set of values and response options that make real-life aggression acceptable.

Imitation is the simple copycat behavior in which some people engage after viewing violent material. Although children are most susceptible to this kind of immediate social learning, there are gruesome cases of adults doing similar things. After MTV's Beavis and Butthead lit aerosol can contents, some viewers tried the same with terrifying results. In Moraine, Ohio a 2-year-old girl died in a fire when her 5-year-old brother mimicked B&B. In Sydney, Australia, an entire apartment complex burned down when a group of teens followed suit.

Desensitization is the lessening of one's emotional response to violent content and the increase of one's acceptance of violence in real life. A poignant example, again, is the testimony of serial killer Ted Bundy. In his final interview with family activist James Dobson, Bundy admitted that he required more and more violent material to get the same emotional kick. Violent pornography and alcohol dulled Bundy's emotional response to heinous acts. He eventually murdered twenty-six young girls and women.

Since many of the effects noted here are behavioral, some Christians might believe that they would "never go so far" as to act aggressively or destructively towards others. Like Ben Ridley who argues for "no effect," they use this reasoning to explain their innocent reading of *Playboy* and viewing slice-and-dice movies the odd weekend. Many separatist and evangelical believers bemoan such a libertarian philosophy that proposes people have the right to watch or do anything they please as long as it doesn't hurt others. It also conveys an ill-conceived view of purity and godliness that equates only external behavior with what God is interested in. Students like Ben may forget that the God whose eyes are so pure he refuses to look on evil (see Habakkuk 1:13) requires his children to exercise self-control and be holy like himself (see 1 Peter 1:13-16).

A typical comeback by Position 3 and 4 believers to avoidance arguments is that the conservative arm of the church focuses largely on media woes. The media also inform, educate, and provide acceptable entertainment if you look for it. Transformers also point out that God also said "to the pure all things are pure" (Titus 1:15). What they mean is that God has not made us machines who respond in hard-wired, cause and effect ways to all the ills of media and their content. Rather, there is much to say about how our frame of reference, and Spirit-led interpretations of media faire weaken its negative impact and at times loudly proclaims God's truth. The media offer benefits and channels for influence enjoyed by millions, including Christians. We will look at these positions in Chapter 10. For now it is sufficient to acknowledge what separatists and evangelicals have in their favor to argue avoidance of media technology and selected content.

Summary

1. Media sources, as a whole, do not uphold Christian values. They espouse a life of excitement brought on by material comfort, immediate gratification, and artificially induced community. Sorely lacking are strong messages of altruism, sacrificial love, long-term commitment in relationships, and peace which is derived from God, not from one's circumstance.

2. Media sources, as a whole, are not a wise use of time. While we may learn about the world around us and receive affirmation that people are badly in need of support and salvation, the blunt facts are that people spend more free time sitting idly with entertainment media than with needy others.

3. Media sources, as a whole, shed more lust than light about the way in which we ought to think and behave as sexual creatures. The treatment of women especially as mere objects for personal gratification thwarts God's sacred view of sexuality.

4. Media sources, as a whole, confirm that we are like Cain — sinners prone to violence — but at the expense of creating more Cains. Exposure to mediated violence is more likely to result in negative arousal, disinhibition, imitation, and desensitization than healthy catharsis. Planted Cain raises Cain.

For all the clout these four concerns pack, this chapter has not mentioned others perhaps equally disturbing. These include the effect of depreciated reading skills among heavy TV viewers and the biased flow of world information from the likes of CNN. Other individuals claim that the subtle messages of racism, ethnocentrism, and blind nationalism are more insidious than overt sex and violence. These concerns also weigh into the equation against the media.

Worth the Talk

1. What position on the response-to-media grid represents your leaning? What is your attitude about technology? Is it good, bad, neutral? What about media content generally? Do you think it influences you positively, negatively, not at all?

2. Is a separatist's call for media abstinence a viable one? Specifically, what actions would you need to take in order to live in a media-less environment? Is it possible or desirable with regard to print media? Is it possible or desirable with regard to electronic media?

3. How valid is the evangelical position? Can Christians tiptoe around objectionable content? Should Christians tiptoe around objectionable content?

4. Position 3, the reformed view, suggests that we can redeem (find the good) in media messages and redeem (change for the good) the media industry. Do you agree with these views? Why or why not?

5. Ben Ridley's Position 4 is based, in part, on the belief that the media provide harmless fun. Another assumption is that, within reason, a life of entertainment is okay in God's eyes. What do you think?

6. Do you know anyone like Ted Kaczynski who appears to reject technology on ideological grounds but who simultaneously accepts negative media values?

Consider the Walk

1. Survey and interview students at your college as to their views on what a Christian response to media ought to be. See if their responses fit the model presented in Figure 9.1 or if some other model works better.

2. Pick up copies of *Seventeen, Mademoiselle* or other women's magazines and analyze their photographs and articles for sexual messages. What myths does this material convey? What truths? Try to determine if these messages convey redeeming insights (for example, beauty is of God, beauty is good, inner character determines the beauty of a person, and the like).

3. Write a paper that compares violence in R-rated movies with violence in the Bible. See what scholars say on both issues and use ample examples. Try to grasp how violence in each is similar and different. Determine the purpose of each.

NOTES

1. The name "Ben Ridley" is fictional, but this illustration is not.

2. The challenge of living in the world as members of God's kingdom has fascinated Christian writers through the centuries. A significant work, to which I am indebted, is Richard Niebuhr's book, *Christ and Culture*, Harper & Row, Publishers, New York, NY, 1951.

3. Donald Kraybill, *The riddle of Amish culture*, The Johns Hopkins University Press, Baltimore, MD, 1989, p. 38

4. Kraybill, pp. 144-145.

5. For an insightful and readable reformer's view on culture and how evangelicals might respond, see John Fischer's *What on earth are we doing? Finding our place as Christians in the world*, Servant Publications, Ann Arbor, MI, 1996. Fischer gives examples of finding God's message in cultural expressions as diverse as rock music lyrics and baseball games.

6. Karen A. Foss and Alison F. Alexander, "Exploring the Margins of Television Viewing, *Communication reports*, Vol. 9, 1996, pp. 61-68.

7. Ben Stein, *The view from Sunset Boulevard: America as brought to you by the people who make television*, Basic Books, New York, NY, 1979.

8. N. Signorelli, *Television's contribution to adolescents' perceptions about work*. Paper presented at the annual conference of the Speech Communication Association, Chicago, November, 1990.

9. Elizabeth M. Perse. Sensation seeking and the use of television for arousal, *Communication Reports*, Vol. 9, Winter 1996, pp. 37-48.

10. Serial killer Ted Bundy acknowledged the role that pornography played in increasing his need for greater stimulation. See *Fatal addiction: Ted Bundy's interview with Dr. James Dobson*, Focus on the Family Films, 1989.

11. Tony Campolo, *Is Jesus a Republican or a Democrat?* Word Publishing, Dallas, TX, 1995, p. 94. See chapter nine, "Is Television Demonic?"

12. Quentin Schultze, *Television: Manna from Hollywood?* Zondervan Publishing House, Grand Rapids, MI, 1986, p. 47.

13. From Michael W. Gamble and Teri Kwal Gamble, *Introducing mass communication*, 2nd ed., McGraw-Hill Book Company, New York, NY, 1989, p. 13.

14. Schultze, p. 12.

15. Diane Zimmerman Umble, "Mennonites and Television: Applications of Cultivation Analysis to a Religious Subculture, in Nancy Signorelli and Michael Morgan, *Cultivation analysis: New directions in media effects research*, Sage, Newbury Park, CA, 1990, pp. 141-157.

16. Reported by Bob DeMoss in "Do You Know What Your Kids are Watching?" *Focus on the Family Magazine*, August, 1994, p. 2.

17. This quotation is taken from Em Griffin, *A first look at communication theory*, 2nd ed., McGraw-Hill, Inc., New York, NY, 1994, p. 330. For a full description of the "uses and gratification" model see D. McQuail, J. G. Blumler, & J. R. Brown. *The television audience: A revised perspective*, in D. McQuail (Ed.), *Sociology of mass communications*, Penguin, Middlesex, England, 1972, pp. 135-165.

18. John Davies, "Growing Up On the Media," *Connect*, Summer 1994, No. 7, p. 9.

19. Mary B. Cassatta and Thomas Skill, *Life on daytime television: Tuning in American serial drama*, Ablex Publishing Corp., Norwood, NJ, 1983, and Bradley S. Greenberg, *Life on television: Content analysis of U.S. TV drama*. Ablex Publishing Corporation, Norwood, NJ, 1980.

20. Bradley S. Greenberg, Cynthia Stanley, Michelle Siemicki, Carrie Heeter, Anne Soderman and Renato Linsangan, "Sex Content on Soaps and Prime-time Television Series Most Viewed by Adolescents," p. 35 in Bradley S. Greenberg, Jane D. Brown, and Nancy L. Buerkel-Rothfuss, *Media, sex and the adolescent*, Hampton Press, Inc., Cresskill, NJ, 1993, pp. 29-44.

21. Bradley S. Greenberg, Cynthia Stanley, Micelle Siemicki, Carrie Heeter, Anne Soderman and Renato Linsangan, "Sex Content on Soaps and Prime-time Television Series Most Viewed by Adolescents," p. 39 in Bradley S. Greenberg, and others, *Media, sex and the adolescent*, pp. 29-44.

22. Bradley S. Greenberg, Michelle Siemicki, Sandra Dorfman, Carrie Heeter, Cynthia Stanley, Anne Soderman, and Renato Linsangan, "Sex Content in R-Rated Films Viewed by Adolescents," p. 49, in Bradley S. Greenberg, Jane D. Brown, and Nancy L. Buerkel-Rothfuss, *Media, sex and the adolescent*, Hampton Press, Inc., Cresskill, NJ, 1993, pp. 45-58.

23. Nancy L. Buerkel-Rothfuss, Jeremiah S. Strouse, Gary Pettey & Milton Shatzer, "Adolescent' and Young Adults' Exposure to Sexually Oriented and Sexually

Explicit Media," p. 112 in Bradley S. Greenberg, and others, *Media, sex and the adolescent*, pp. 99-113.

24. Richard Jackson Harris, *The impact of sexually explicit media*, in Jennings Bryant and Dolf Zillmann (Eds.), *Media effects: Advances in theory and research*, Lawrence Erlbaum Associates, Publishers, Hillsdale, NJ, 1994, pp. 247-272.

25. Harris, p. 256.

26. Harris, p. 247

27. George Gerbner as quoted in the Media Education Foundation's *Video Resources for the 21st Century 1996 Catalogue*, p. 8.

28. George Gerbner, L. Gross, M. Morgan, & N. Signorelli. *Growing up with television: The cultivation perspective*, p. 29, in Bryant and Zillmann, (Eds.), pp. 17-41.

29. See George Gerbner and Larry Gross, "The Scary World of TV's Heavy Viewer," *Psychology Today*, April 1976, pp. 41-45, 89.

30. The Media Education Foundation's *Video Resources for the 21st Century 1996 Catalogue*, p. 9.

31. As quoted in the statement of the Parents Music Resource Center to the U.S. Senate, 99th Congress, 1st Session. Committee on Commerce, Science, and Transportation. Record Labeling. Hearing, September 19, 1985. Washington, D.C.: Government Printing Office. (S. Hrg. 99/529).

32. Harris, p. 261, based on his review of "Child's Play: Violent videos lure the young," 1987, June 1, *Time*, p. 31.

33. Bradley S. Greenberg, J. D. Brown, and N. L. Buerkel-Rothfuss. *Media, sex, and the adolescent*. Cresskill, NJ: Hampton Press, 1993, p. 295.

34. B. Gunter. "The Cathartic Potential of Television Drama," *Bulletin of the British Psychological Society*, Vol. 33, 1980, pp. 448-450.

35. W. Josephson, "Television Violence and Children's Aggression: Testing the Priming, Social Script, and Disinhibition Predictions," *Journal of Personality and Social Psychology*, Vol. 53, 1987, pp. 882-890 as cited in Eunkyung, Jo and Leonard Berkowitz, "A Priming Effect Analysis of Media Influences: An Update," in J. Bryant and D. Zillmann (Eds.), *Media effects: Advances in theory and research* Lawrence Erlbaum Associates, Publishers, Hillsdale, NJ, 1994, pp. 43-60.

36. L. D. Eron, L. R. Huesmann, M. M. Lefdowitz, and L. O. Walder. "Does Television Violence Cause Aggression?" *American Psychologist*, Vol. 27, 1972, pp. 253-263, and L. R. Huesmann and L. D. Eron (Eds.) *Television and the aggressive child: A cross-national comparison*. Lawrence Erlbaum Associates, Publishers, Hillsdale, NJ, as cited in Gunter, 1993, p. 174.

CHAPTER 10

Electronically (Re-)Connected:
Arguments For the Media

He who seeks good finds good will, but evil comes to him who searches for it.

Proverbs 11:27

To the pure, all things are pure, but to those who are corrupted and do not believe, nothing is pure.

Titus 1:15

Suzie is a communications major at my school, and last summer she found herself in a pickle. Suzie needed to land a job back in California, but she also needed more course credits. After she explained her predicament to me, we arranged with the dean for her to take an independent study course with me from 800 miles away. Suzie went home, found a job, and began writing the first of three lengthy papers about children and the media. We connected by electronic means. Suzie phoned six times for our required discussion sessions, faxed me her papers, and e-mailed me progress reports. I responded by commenting on papers and faxing them back to her, and once I e-mailed lengthy comments and suggestions. It was slick.

Half-way through paper number three Suzie called me. "I am so frustrated with my local library! It has so few magazines and books about instructional media. Do you mind if I get most of my sources from the Internet?" There was a pause and then we both laughed as I responded — "Yes, it should be okay to use the medium that is revolutionizing our children's education to discuss instructional media!" Eventually five of her six sources referred to Internet sites.

Suzie's experience is probably like your own—it's increasingly difficult to accomplish school and life goals *without* media dependence. My guess is that most believers today assume that technological advances since the 1450 Gutenberg press have all but erased the Amish option response. Suzie and

I didn't lament the intrusion of information technologies in our lives, we welcomed them, even needed them.

This chapter looks at the rationale behind Positions 2 and 3, the evangelical and reformed responses to media, as described in Chapter 9. How is it that most North American Christians adopt media gadgets and gizmos with hardly a blink of an eye? On what basis do many believers watch the same television shows and rent the same movies as unbelievers?

Position 2 Revisited: Buy All the Media Toys You Like, Just Consume Christian Content and Avoid Worldly Garbage

Even though few Christians may practice this position right down to the last video rental, the pattern and thinking is common to a good segment of the Christian population. On what is it based? I think there are at least three reasons.

BECAUSE TECHNOLOGY IS NEUTRAL

Neutral? In what way? Most believers in this position mean technology is morally neutral; TVs and VCRs are soulless, therefore neither sinful or redeemed. Lynn White claims that this idea took root when Christian views of nature replaced animistic views of nature during medieval times.[1] The Greeks and Romans believed that spirits existed in trees, rivers, and hills, and that messing with nature was to mess with the gods. Christians believed otherwise, and read the scriptures to say that God created the earth but he did not emanate within the earth. With no fear that God would be distressed, Christians felt free to investigate the earth's resources and develop new technologies.

One and a half millennia later you can still find scholars who affirm this way of thinking. As one writes, "Technology in itself is neutral and should not be labeled 'good' or 'bad.' It is the uses to which we put new scientific developments that enhance or degrade personal well-being and prosperity."[2] Another writes that technology is "essentially amoral, a thing apart from values, an instrument which can be used for good or ill."[3] This was Suzie's and my view as we used faxes, the Internet, and telephones to connect last summer. We saw these channels as mere conduits for the papers and notes we exchanged.

BECAUSE TECHNOLOGY MAKES LIFE AND CULTURE BETTER

Position 2 Christians adopt media technology readily because they believe such devices improve life. Some would note that just as medical discoveries have staved off diseases from reaching epidemic proportions, so too media sources have curtailed widespread global ignorance through news and educational programming. Similarly, just as nutritional insights have lengthened our life span, so too media sources have enriched that life through arts and entertainment. Quentin Schultze calls this "technological optimism," and makes comment on Americans and televangelists in particular.

> The national imagination [of Americans] has always linked technological development with human progress. As a result, Americans, including televangelists, have generally been technological optimists. In the case of television, cable channels, remote controls, satellite transmitters and receivers, VCRs, large screens, and enhanced audio all become symbols of what most people believe are better and more pleasant ways of life."[4]

An article in a missions magazine I receive bears this out. The writer described a common situation: Joe Missionary senses that Jenny Seeker is close to making a decision to trust God for salvation. Joe wants to mobilize believers to pray, but time is short. Joe's task is made easy, however, thanks to his new Internet hook-up; Joe e-mails a prayer request to one of his support churches in Long Beach, California. The pastors photocopy the request for all the midweek group leaders, and within two days 400 believers are praying for Joe and Jenny.[5] Position 2 Christians applaud speed, efficiency, choice and convenience because these qualities appear to make the work of the church more effective.[6]

BECAUSE GOD KEEPS ON GIVING US THIS STUFF

Finally, many Christians use media technologies freely because they consider them signs of God's progressive revelation.[7] This way of thinking also began in medieval times when the Christian linear view of history replaced pre-Christian Greek and Roman cyclical views. Augustine read the scriptures to mean that we are not spinning our wheels historically or culturally, but that we are actors in God's drama—creation, fall, Christ's intervention, and kingdom consummation. All along the way God speaks with us and reveals himself to us. Part of that revelation is the garden of scientific knowledge and the produce of technology.

What this means today is that many Christians view technological advances as gifts from God and proof of his grace. For example, in writing about the Internet, one Christian media scholar wrote, "*There comes a time when the church of Jesus Christ has to be bold enough to lay claim to a new medium. As I like to put it, new technologies are part of the unfolding of God's*

Creation. We don't own these technologies; God does." [8] Many ministers, youth leaders, missionaries, and professors would agree.

Responsible ambivalence. Although many Position 2 believers view media inventions as morally neutral, others feel uneasy about lumping TVs and VCRs in with non-media machines. Isn't there a fundamental difference between a VHS cassette and the Salk vaccine for polio? Between a CD boom box and a Volkswagen Jetta? The difference, some might suggest, is that the second ones were developed with narrowly defined beneficial ends: the vaccine to eradicate polio and the car to ease transportation. While it's true that the narrow end of media technology is to help us communicate efficiently with millions, some people believe that the benefit of efficiency can be undercut by the less-than-beneficial *content* of what is communicated.

This ambivalence (a mix of love and disdain) toward media technologies goes deep in Christian thought, and was especially strong in the 1920s and 30s. In those days many believers and bullet theorists cast the newly invented medium of radio as a powerful force that molded its pliable, unsuspecting listeners at will. Hitler's success at transforming Germans' beliefs with radio spots and film clips fueled this model through the 1940s. In 1946, the founder of a large missionary radio station in Quito, Ecuador expressed concern about radio's potential. No doubt viewing radio through "bullet" eyes he wrote,

> The phenomenal speed and size of the growth of radio…indicate[s] vast potential for future good or evil. Whether mankind is to be blessed

or blighted by this scientific marvel…is chiefly a moral and spiritual question for which individual Christians and the Church of Christ do well to assume a responsible attitude.[9]

This trend continues today in popular culture, especially in the wake of the Heaven's Gate ordeal where cult members used the Internet to attract converts. In fact, the followers of Herff Applewhite were more than casual users of the Internet; they were employed as web site *designers*. When not at work designing sites, they logged hour upon hour searching cyberspace for testimony of alien life, UFOs, and the paranormal in addition to promoting their own theology of the "Level Above Human." In "Blaming the Web" (*Newsweek,* April 7, 1997), Steven Levy captures the anxiety many hold toward this newest medium — a sentiment that echoes feelings toward radio fifty years ago.

> If there are lessons to be learned for the Net from this sad story, they are the same ones that cyberspace has already been grappling with since its recent emergence as a major force. The Internet is simply a medium that boosts the reach of all speakers, benevolent and otherwise. Those on the receiving end should use caution — and parents, of course, should convey this to children.[10]

Benevolent (that is, kindhearted) and malevolent (that is, malicious) content on the same medium result in Position 2 ambivalence toward media generally.

BECAUSE THERE'S SO MUCH CHRISTIAN MATERIAL TO CHOOSE FROM

The belief that God gave us technology to redeem others to himself goes deep for many Christians. Driven by this understanding, thousands have built TV networks, published magazines, launched Internet ministries, and invested in film. The result today is that believers and non-believers alike can avail themselves to Christian comic books, CD-ROMs, TV talk shows, Internet chat lines, call-in radio programs and magazines galore. What follows is a brief description of their successes — and failures — to create material for Christian living. By God's grace, and for God's glory, this is their song of achievement.

Magazines: choices galore. Although you may not recognize it from the magazines available at your Superstore check-out counter, one could fill a yacht-sized magazine rack with the variety of Christian publications available today. One way to categorize all magazines is by function: entertainment and escape, news and information, and advocacy and opinions. Christian publishers offer all three types, but are stacked in the direction of information and advocacy.

Denominational magazines, such as the *Catholic International* and the Evangelical Free Church's *Pulse* magazine, nurture group identity through reports and articles linked to the denomination's activities, personnel, and doctrine. Even with denominational ties becoming less important to most church attendees, we will likely see a continuation of these types of publications.

Scholarly journals such as the *Journal of Biblical Literature, Christianity and Literature*, and *Theology and Sexuality* offer venues for scholars to debate matters of biblical interpretation and life ethics. Seminary and college professors often raise issues here before going public in the popular press. You probably have a good variety of these in your college's library.

Professional ministry magazines such as *Leadership* and *Youth Worker*, resource full-time ministers, teachers, and administrators with sermon outlines, counsel on tough body-life questions and reflections by nationally recognized leaders. People who lead need ample ideas to remain innovative and in touch, and these magazines deliver those kinds of ideas.

Family improvement magazines provide articles on parenting, marriage, budgeting, school concerns, and health. *Marriage Partnership, Today's Christian Woman*, and Promise Keepers' *New Man* are prime examples in a crowded field. Finally, *Christian trade magazines* appeal to a broad yet targeted readership as in the cases of *Christianity Today, Campus Life, Contemporary Christian Music Magazine*, and one of the most recent, *Computing Today* (subtitled *A Christian Guide to Software, Internet, Online and Multimedia Resources*). Much like *Psychology Today* or *Newsweek*, these magazines appeal to a wide readership. They also gain their revenues by selling advertising space for everything from pews to a college education.

The pattern here reflects the magazine medium generally: publishers search out niche markets and develop specific magazines to meet the needs of readers. No matter what you are looking for, you are bound to find it eventually.

Radio: sound success. Few media historians would squabble over the claim that the invention of radio was simultaneously the birth of religious radio. It is reported that Samuel Morse's first telegraph message in 1837 was "What hath God wrought?"[11] and Reginald Aubrey Fessenden's first wireless voice transmission in 1906 was a Christmas eve service consisting of a reading of Luke's Gospel, a singing of Handel's *Largo*, and a violin solo of "O Holy Night."[12] Religious broadcasters haven't looked back since.

Pulpit and podium radio programs were common among liberal and conservative Christians alike who jumped on the radio bandwagon in the 1920s and 1930s. The ease with which broadcasters transmitted a minister's sermon or lecture probably explains why this format endures today. Dr. Walter Maier's "The Lutheran Hour," Bishop Fulton Sheen's "The Catholic Hour," and Charles E. Fuller's "The Old Fashioned Revival Hour" are mirrored today in the preaching ministries of Chuck Swindoll's "Insight for Living" and Woodrow Kroll's "Back to the Bible."

Talk shows and *call-in talk shows* are arguably the most engaging radio fare. Family advocate James Dobson's "Focus on the Family" talk show and apologist Hank Hanegraaff's "The Bible Answer Man" call-in show tackle questions head-on with no-nonsense conservatism and the help of research staff, guest experts, and facts on cults and culture. While radio programs serve as the flagship medium of these and similar Christian ministries, most have an equally impressive literature distribution service available to listeners.

Christian music programming probably fills more time than talk shows or preaching ministries, though you'll find all three on Christian radio stations. This pattern is unlike non-religious commercial radio that tends to be all-talk or all-music (what the industry calls *format radio*). Christian stations have typically conformed to *program radio* (a mix of programs, i.e., talk shows, preaching ministries, news, and music). Traditional music is featured at stations such as WMBI of Moody Bible Institute in Chicago, IL, while contemporary Christian music and alternative / fringe moods typify Christian commercial and college radio stations.

Finally, *missionary radio* has been developed abroad by evangelical groups who praise its ability to transcend geographic and political borders. Today Trans World Radio, Far East Broadcasting Company, and HCJB World Radio Missionary Fellowship — the three major networks — broadcast biblical teaching and music in over 150 languages to within reach of most the earth's population. Some have developed Internet sites to encourage listeners to make contact, and to develop community among believers.[13]

Christians' use of radio will likely not die out soon. Its relatively low cost, personal feel, and omnipresence in kitchens, cars and offices of the world's urban centers and remote jungles make it an appealing medium for people with a message.

Film: mixed reviews. If there were a medium that many of faith love to hate, yet admit using, it is film. Diatribes against the cinema from fundamental and moderate Christians dot the historical landscape, including Stephen Paine's classic piece *The Christian and the Movies*. In no uncertain terms he writes, "We [Christians] don't attend movies....Even if it were possible for you to attend the movies without personal detriment, ...you would still be an accomplice to an industry that is causing untold crime and moral degradation among the young people of our country."[14] He penned those words in 1957.

This kind of condemnation may sound foreign to most of us who grew up on television and crossed the stream to movie-going and video-renting with no wet feet. However, Paine's sentiment may explain why filmmakers have been slow to depict religion in movies, why Christian filmmakers entered the industry late in the game, and why Christian film critics seesaw in their praise and disgust for Hollywood's cultural myths. This love-hate relationship with film probably explains why you can find three quite different types of religious films today: the biblical epic film, the universal thematic film, and the explicit evangelistic film.

Only your largest and best video stores will stock what is termed *biblical epic* films. These date back to the oldie goldies when D. W. Griffiths and Cecil B. DeMille were new masters with a new medium. Griffith's *Intolerance* and DeMille's *The Ten Commandments*, *King of Kings*, *The Sign of the Cross*, and *Samson and Delilah* led the way for other biblical drama such as *David and Bathsheba*, *The Robe*, *Ben Hur*, *Barabbas*, *Sodom and Gomorrah*, *The Silver Chalice*, *The Greatest Story Ever Told*, and *Jesus of Nazareth*. As with most movies based on true life, these films are criticized for falling short in authenticity, playing heavily on sentimentality, and brandishing the sensational. Even still, these films create a scriptural presence in film history.

More common to your viewing, perhaps, are thematic films that portray Protestant and Catholic Christians in dramatic relief. For example, *A Man Called Peter* retells the life story of Methodist minister Peter Marshall in a most positive light. In more recent years, *Tender Mercies* depicts character Mac Sledge who finds religion among members of a Baptist church choir and experiences the first pains of new birth. In *The Trip to Bountiful* lead character Carrie Watts is a devout Christian woman who longs to return to her childhood hometown of Bountiful only to discover that life moves forward, not backward. Finally, in *Dead Man Walking* Susan Sarandon plays a Catholic sister who shows unreturned love to a convicted murderer played by Sean Penn. The sister's strong testimony of God's love leads the convict to eleventh-hour repentance. Unlike many pictures put out by Christian studios, these feature films depict characters who struggle in their search for God, and who find him without the help of a sermon. They are more *show* and less *tell* about a life with God.

Gospel Films and Billy Graham's World Wide Pictures account for a good percent of the *evangelistic films* produced. (WWP has produced 125 since the 1950s.) These producers use drama, documentary, and biography to convey God's life-changing message that Christ in us is our strength for today and our hope for glory. While many of these films are intended for general viewing, most find their way into churches and youth group halls where religious leaders use them to affirm the faith and challenge the unchurched visitor. World Wide Pictures has attempted to broaden viewership by showing films such as *Cry from the Mountain*, *The Hiding Place*, and *Joni* in cinemas.[15]

One billion viewers of *Jesus* make this movie the most watched in world history. Campus Crusade for Christ based the film entirely on the life of Christ as described in the gospel of Luke, and uses scripture for its script. Paul Eshleman, director of the *Jesus* film project, comments that this has made it a draw among many mission agencies:

> The power of the film is not in the cinematography, the presentation or even in the actors, but the power is in the Word of God. Because it stays close to the Scripture, it can be used like the Bible and that is why mission organizations want to use it. It presents Christ in such a powerful way.[16]

The *Jesus* film project coordinators report that 56 million individuals have indicated their decision to trust Christ for salvation after a viewing of the film. A commitment by local believers to follow-up new believers is required before *Jesus* is shown.

Like any medium, film has its own biases: it feeds human stardom, but often starves images of God; it tugs at emotions, but avoids tough intellectual questions; it can capture goodness and the gospel, but often depicts debauchery (as noted in the previous chapter). This may explain why many believers give the cinema one thumb up and one thumb down as an avenue for redemptive art.

Television: famine or feast. For some people, the only two things that come to mind regarding a Christian presence on television are televangelist scandals and the query "what presence?" Without doubt, televangelism takes up a good portion of what is Christian on the tube, and one would be naive to assume that Americans aren't skeptical of TV ministries after the confessions of Jim Bakker and Jimmy Swaggart. However, to typify Christian use of television as solely televangelistic or to label all TV ministers as frauds would be simplistic and unfair. What some believers lament even more is that you can hardly find Christian views and values in prime time programming. This is especially irksome when the media elite claim they reflect reality in their programming, but then marginalize religious content in news and entertainment. How scant is religion's exposure on the little blue box, and is it favorable?

In their 1995 study of religion on television, the staff at the conservative watchdog Media Research Center (MRC) reported that "total network news coverage of religion in 1995 remained numerically insignificant; out of more than 18,000 evening news stories in 1995, religion drew only 249; out of more than 26,000 morning news segments, religion drew only 224."[17] These figures represent a less than one-percent exposure rate for religion in what the major networks consider news for millions of viewers. And the tenor of those stories is largely negative. Catholic dissidents, abortion clinic violence and the "extreme religious right" drew more stories than church-affirming ones. Reporters and anchors reflect the general attitude that Catholic and Protestant beliefs systems are outdated forms of morality that constrain the human spirit.

These famine-like conditions are repeated in prime time entertainment programming. MRC's research determined that in almost 1,800 hours of programming, religion of any sort was portrayed only 287 times, or about once every sixteen hours. The ray of hope was that 38 percent of these portrayals were positive while 28 percent were negative, 7 mixed, and 27 neutral.[18] These are sobering statistics.

Not only is it difficult to find religious depictions on television, but the slant producers give them squeeze them into the medium's mold. For example, the creators of The X-Files surprised many viewers with an affirming portrayal of Catholicism in one episode when Scully, an FBI agent, returns to her childhood faith. What motivated Scully was her discovery that numerous murder victims appeared to have stigmata — bodily wounds similar to the ones Christ received in the passion and crucifixion and miraculously impressed on certain people as a token of divine favor. While the show affirmed Catholic belief, The X-Files producers pushed a controversial button by focusing on what some believers consider the controversial doctrine of stigmata. But it made great television.

Other producers are willing to risk an entire series, as in CBS's Touched by an Angel. Week after week its three celestial emissaries love and guide down-trodden mortals in God's ways. The high ratings Touched receives may indicate that Americans and Canadians are ready for overtly Christian themes if cast dramatically and professionally. Certainly North Americans' renewed interest in spirituality and alternative religions make religious drama more salable.

Some believers may take these signs at the major networks as reason to produce overtly Christian programs for prime time viewing. While this appeals in theory, one has to admit that such a call is a tremendous financial and artistic challenge. Mounting a successful prime-time sitcom or drama is a 1-in-3000 proposition given the number of new shows pitched every year in Hollywood where, again, network executives tend to shun religious programs.[19]

Some Christians respond to all this in classic Position 2 repose: why not produce our own programs and buy time on the major networks? Hey, why not build our own network? And a handful have. As William F. Fore notes in Television and Religion, Christian leaders who broadcast religious programs represent at least five "generations" of styles and strategies over the past fifty years.[20]

In the 1950s Billy Graham used television to cover his rallies, but the rallies themselves remained unchanged despite the camera's presence. He maintains this approach today for his (or his son Franklin's) televised specials. In that same era, Oral Roberts typified a *participative* style in that he offered to heal viewers if they would place their hands on their TV sets and provided viewers with telephone numbers for calling in to his ministry headquarters. Roberts understood the importance of *feedback*. Next, Rex Humbard and Robert Schuller represent the *production* generation in that they built churches expressly for producing television-ready services. What happens at the Crystal Cathedral on Sunday morning is as much for the television audience as it is for the attendees, if not more so.

The fourth strategy, the *host-show program*, is embodied in Pat Robertson's "The 700 Club." It looks and feels much like *The Late Show with David Letterman* as Robertson banters with co-hosts, cuts to commercials for various ministries, and engages in dialogue with his studio audience. Finally, the *genuine TV network* has emerged as a Christian presence in the cable network system. Most notably is Robertson's *The Family Channel* (originally the *Christian Broadcasting Network*) that plays golden age re-runs such as *Father Knows Best, Gunsmoke* and *Name That Tune* in addition to Christian soap operas and *The 700 Club* talk show.

Critics of these five strategies point out what research bears true: programs such as Robert Schuller's *The Hour of Power* (the most widely viewed of all TV ministers) attract at best two million households per week, and those largely Christian viewers.[21] In effect, any salt these programs attempt to spread falls back into the shaker.

Just where religious TV programming will go in the future is hard to predict. *The X-Files* and *Millennium* may signal a move to religious themes to fill the spiritual hunger of the continent. Similarly, organized churches appear to have gained a second wind following the steep scandal hills of the 1980s. What is probably a given is that the number of choices available to viewers will increase. Viewer choice will determine feast or fast.

The Internet: cyberspace sanctuary? Unlike print, radio, and television that we *receive*, the Internet is something we *do*. And by now you have probably traveled your way to various corners of this newest medium, sometimes in awe of its speed, other times frustrated by a million "hits." Whatever your disposition, one fact is clear: the Internet is fast-becoming the number one challenger of information dissemination worldwide, crossing geopolitical and real-time boundaries as easily as you cross the street. And Christian groups are in the thick of it.

When the author of "Finding God on the World Wide Web" (*Time*, December 1996) searched cyberspace for references to "Bill Gates," "God," and "Christ," the deity duo won hands down. While the search engine Alta Vista found 25,000 references to Gates, it found 410,000 to God, and 146,000 to Christ. Six months later my own search with Alta Vista turned up 123,414 hits for any kind of Gates (1,187,747 for any type of Bill), but 2,116,298 for

God and 645,624 for Christ. Do it today and who knows how many sites you will find.

Behind this exponential growth in Christian sites ("Christian" yielded 991,090 hits) is a strong Position 2 mentality. As Jason Baker, author of *Christian Cyberspace Companion* writes, ". . . the machine is neither inherently good nor evil; it is simply a tool to further the ideology of the person using it. [T]he Internet can be employed to build God's kingdom or assault it."[22] So how are Christians using it for God's glory?

One way to find out is to visit **http://www.crosssearch.com** or **http://www.gospelcom.net.** From either site you'll be able to link with institutions and individuals involved in Christian ministry, education, media development, missions, relief work, and more. Here's a taste of who you'll find online: Christianity Today, Inc., Inter Varsity Christian Fellowship, Evangelical Lutheran Church in America, Wycliffe Bible Translators, Gospel Films, Southern Baptist Convention Foreign Mission Board, Food for the Hungry and the Bible Gateway (the Bible in multiple languages and translations that you can search).

Besides resources, the Internet delivers services that ten years ago took more effort or were not available at all. Consider this list which Quentin Schultze lists on the back of his book, *Internet for Christians:*[23]

communicate quickly and inexpensively with other believers (i.e., E-mail)
conduct theological and Bible study free of charge
access free daily devotionals for all ages and spiritual levels
keep up on Christian periodicals for little or no cost
meet new friends, colleagues and believers around the globe
search for jobs posted by churches and Christian organizations
follow concerts and activities of many Christian artists
select and purchase online Christian videos, Bible software and rent Christian films

What makes the Internet so inviting is that you don't have to be wealthy or well known to create your own home page. A standard desk-top or laptop personal computer and the right software plus an Internet service provider (through your telephone line) get you going for under $4,000. Many times these things are provided at school or at work for free.

Luring elsewhere in cyberspace are sites that Christians need to handle with care or avoid entirely. And this, of course, is the drawback of the Net: *almost anyone with any world view can set up shop, and this seems to be the case.* However to reject the Internet's potential for God's kingdom based on a few bad apples would be short sighted. We need prudence and responsible wills if we want to redeem others and the Net. Responsible, critical use of all media is what we called Position 3 in the preceding chapter. We consider it now as the last of three realistic responses Christians might take toward media use.

Position 3 Revisited: Buy Media Technologies at Will, and Consume Most Anything, But Be Willing to Critique Both Medium and Message for What's Beneficial

Christians who hold a Position 3 response to media (I called them transformers) differ in significant ways from those holding Position 2. First off, they aren't convinced that technology is value-free; they say it is *value laden*. Second, they have more faith in the human spirit; they believe that critical thinking and a pure heart help us understand and benefit from even "questionable" material. And third, while they affirm the production of overtly Christian content, they suggest that believers diversify their strategies in order to redeem media and their audiences. Let's take each in turn.

BECAUSE TECHNOLOGY IS NOT VALUE FREE

Like their Amish brothers and sisters, transformers are skeptical that technology is value-free; rather, they suggest that technology is inherently *value-laden*, that is, it represents and nurtures the inventor's values. Take computers for example; they didn't just happen, they were developed by sensing, valuing, religious (in some way) people, such as Bill Gates, who had a goal in mind: to crunch numbers efficiently, send messages quickly, and connect the world in community. Efficiency, speed, and connection are the values that embody your PC. Marshall McLuhan would say that they are the "message" of the computer medium.[24] Sounds innocent so far.

The dark-side message of the PC is evident in the behaviors of some computer programmers. At least one study has shown that computer compulsives (that is, heavy-weight programmers) think and act differently toward people than most of us. "In their interaction with spouses, family, and acquaintances, they are often terse, preferring yes-no responses. They are impatient with open-ended conversations and are uncomfortable with individuals who are reflective or meditative. Computer compulsives demand brevity and view social discourse in instrumental terms, interacting with others as a means of collecting and exchanging useful information."[25]

"But the *computer* isn't rude or terse," a Position 2 person might counter. No, but Position 3 Christians liken that response to the argument that "guns don't kill people, people kill people" or to put it more obviously, "Atom bombs don't kill people, people kill people." Their point is that you cannot separate human intention from metal and microchips. All technology is created for some human need—some noble, others ignoble. Even if the designers of the computer did not intend for hackers to become robot-like communicators, the fact is many have.

What this means for us is that we need to learn how to critique each medium by asking at least two key questions: What values are inherent in this medium (my TV, PC, and CD)? What impact does using this medium have on my relationship with others and with God?

Let's look at the inherent biases of television as an example. For good or for bad, television values images over words, and biases us to think that *seeing is believing* more than *reading or hearing is believing*. Television values the 7-second dramatic cut and the two-second advertising cut over a long-term event like a date or worship service. Television values interruption (or what Neil Postman has called the "now this..." phenomena[26]) over the continuity you find in a Bach symphony or through quiet reflection on the end of a pier. Television biases you toward physical inactivity as you watch a PBS version of *Swan Lake* and discourages your immediate effort to practice ballet. Finally, television images are made to attract your attention to itself rather than to a friend. (Have you ever heard someone say, "Hush! I can't hear the television"?)

Note how all of these comparisons are intrinsic to the *structure* of TV's manner, not its content. That is, no matter if you are watching *Swan Lake* or *Good Morning America*, the images, audio, rhythm, and purpose of television is to keep you seated and sedated. But even to this analysis transformer Christians shout, "Rise above it: don't let the medium control you; you control and critique the medium!" That means choosing to attend to your friend when she enters the room and cutting an evening short so there's time to workout. It means recognizing that a 20-second news bite can take on odd meaning when out of context or when placed between two contrasting stories. Acknowledging the structural biases of a medium depends significantly on your mindfulness as you use it.

BECAUSE PEOPLE ARE MINDFUL AGENTS, NOT PASSIVE SPONGES

This chapter began with two verses that embody this point. The writer of Proverbs says, "He who seeks good finds good will, but evil comes to him who searches for it" (Proverbs 11:27), and Paul writes, "To the pure, all things are pure, but to those who are corrupted and do not believe, nothing is pure" (Titus 1:15). Transformers take these teachings seriously and suggest that what we bring to media will determine what we get from them. If we expect evil, we'll find it; if we look for the good, it will light on our shoulder.

So while Position 1 and 2 believers feel that an evil ace is an evil ace and there's no way around it, transformers are not so sure. In regard to movie-going, Lloyd Billingsley notes, "To assume that everyone will imitate [in belief and behavior] what they see [in a movie theater] is practically to deny free will, spiritual discernment, or moral courage."[27] He believes, rather, that we can engage in beneficial meaning-making from most media sources so long as we are armed with a godly heart and a critical mind. The same holds for critiquing a medium. If we approach it mindfully, we should be able to discern its beneficial features. In short, we need to be *media literate* by the Spirit's empowering.

Media literacy is the training of our mind and heart to discern what is morally beneficial in media programming and technology. Or as some media educators define it: "Media literacy is the ability to choose, to understand, to question, to evaluate, to create and/or produce and to respond thoughtfully to the media we consume. It is mindful viewing, reflective judgment . . . an ongoing process. . . ."[28] This means that we are committed to being TV viewers, not mere watchers, and music appreciators, not mere head-bangers.

Media literacy is largely about asking questions that lead to understanding and a balanced evaluation of a media product. Questions such as:

who produced this product, and what is his or her world view?
what messages — overt and covert — does this program or medium promote?
is God's natural world depicted in its glory or is it ignored and marginalized?
is this material artistically well done or is it imitative and plastic?
what is predictable about this message? what is unique and refreshing?
does this material mirror real world history or is it history-less?
is the church present? affirmed? absent? attacked?
what value for people and God does this message depict?
are dramatic characters believable or are they simplistic and static?
are people depicted as accountable, moral agents or do they "get away with murder"?

Position 3 believers don't use critical thinking as a license for consuming garbage however. Few would suggest that you rent *I Spit on Your Grave* or cruise Internet porn sites to eke out some moral revelation (as in "the world's in rough shape"). They understand that God calls us to be transformed by a renewed *mind* (Romans 12:2), and that some material is not redeemable.

BECAUSE WE ARE CALLED TO REDEEM CULTURE AS WELL AS PEOPLE

Transformers want to do more than redeem people with the gospel message. Many feel called to what they term the cultural mandate. They see all of God's creation under his lordship — every person, animal, city, vocation, technology, and cultural product. Our job is to be co-regents with God in managing, nurturing and stewarding earth and society so both experience God's goodness and grace (undeserved favor).

So, when transformers speak of "redeeming" the media, they mean activity such as improving the laws that regulate media, lessening the profit-motive of commercial media, advancing programs with moral themes, and creating material that shows respect for human life. As one Position 3 writer comments, "I use the word *redemptiveness* to refer to the apparent goodness or value of a human creation in the eyes of God."[29] Here are some practical ways you can redeem the media.

Work in the "secular" industry. Transformers don't even like the phrase "secular industry." They see the whole world under God's sovereignty. Just as the heart of the king is in the hand of the Lord (Proverbs 21:1), so too the media industry is ultimately claimed by God. No vocation is beyond Christ's lordship; we can offer up every job to God as a sweet smelling sacrifice.

That doesn't mean media industries brim with godly virtue. What it does mean is that you can be a Christian in the thick of the media complex. The media business might stand for ideals quite opposed to Christian ones, but it will likely not change its ideals without a moral option.

The producers of *Batman Forever* had a moral option when looking for screenwriters. Eventually they hired Lee and Janet Scott Batchler, who explain why: "Warner Brothers asked us to work on *Batman Forever* because they knew that we could write an exciting film without a lot of blood and gore."[30] The Batchlers, who are also deacons at Bel-Air Presbyterian Church near Hollywood, now have opportunity to work on a forthcoming Disney film about missionary David Livingstone. Lee and Janet's professional record plus their conservative values landed them the *Batman* contract and more. Their willingness to be God's people in Hollywood provided a redemptive option for filmmakers.

Create pre-evangelistic cultural products. Another strategy Position 3 believers encourage is the creation of pre-evangelistic material. If you have ever walked out of a movie theater deep in thought about the big questions of life (such as, Why are we here? How did we get here? Where are we headed?, etc.), you may have viewed a pre-evangelistic film. Such material does not present Christ; they prepare the way for Christ. Like John the Baptist in the desert, it goes before, nurturing, prodding, hinting, and prophesying that life without God is hollow and eternity without God is hell. In short, pre-evangelistic content encourages people to ask the important questions *that lead up to* their search for a Savior.

A documentary about Elizabeth Kübler-Ross and children facing death might make viewers ponder their own mortality or what it means to love hurting kids unconditionally. Similarly, an episode about the cosmos on David Suzuki's *The Nature of Things* may cue people to the possibility that God was the mastermind behind such intricacy and balance. Or consider a news story I saw the other night about the treatment that wheel-chaired citizens receive from inconsiderate taxi cab drivers. I felt righteous indignation toward the taxi drivers when I heard one woman comment that she felt more like cargo than a person. No matter what medium you work in, consider how it may help people see the world as God sees it. Promote human good-will and hint at God's will as much as you can.

Promote media literacy in your school, church, and home. Transformers also encourage Christians to stop complaining about media content and start promoting new ways of encountering it. For example, rather than throw a video party and then quietly mumble disapproval of this scene and that four-letter word, a reformer will suggest that you host a "video club gathering." Like the book club, video clubs come together for the express purpose of viewing and analyzing films. You don't want the gathering to bog down with too much theory and criticism, but your members should be as committed to discussion as they are to popcorn. If you want to spice things up, you might invite your favorite media professor.

Along the same lines, a transformer might teach a class at church titled "The Christian and the Media." Even if you're not an expert, you can get parents talking with their kids, invite special guests, and critique movie clips for their redemptive value. Or you may choose to invest in a media literacy kit to guide you through issues and around land mines. The Catholic Communications Campaign publishes a set of books and videos for this purpose and comes highly recommended by the Center for Media Literacy.[31]

Teaching younger siblings and cousins to consume less media and converse more about media is tough but rewarding. The role I like to play with my young sons is "media commentator." Like a sports commentator who frames what we see through commentary, so I like to frame my children's understanding of media (especially television). It's my goal to help my boys rise above the medium and its message to cast it in Christian and human perspective. I might ask "Do you think everyone who smokes is as happy as this lady in this magazine picture?" (Answer: No. Some people who smoke get very sick and are unhappy.) "What is this beer ad telling us about the beer itself?" (Answer: Nothing.) "About people who drink beer?" (They are always riding horses and smiling a lot!) "Does drinking beer make you happy? (Answer: Maybe for a while, but it can also make you throw up.) Of course I've needed to prime them on the answers, but they are becoming more adept at seeing past the glitz to what lies beneath it.

Keep your pencil sharp and your invention skills active. A fourth and final suggestion Position 3 advocates often make is that we provide feedback to media producers and take a stab at being producers too. When you've seen a program you like or read an article that inspired you, you might write or e-mail the people responsible and affirm their redemptive work. We all know how much more we respond to strokes than to swift backhands.

You can keep your creative juices flowing by finding ways to create your own redeeming material. I recall a drama student at my institution who came to our department to take Introduction to Film. The professor who taught the course had lived in Hollywood and produced hundreds of ads and several short films. He challenged his students, and this one in particular, by saying, "No one from Christian colleges will make a difference with film unless they *make films.*" Today this student produces a Christian entertainment video package for use in a nightclub once a month in Vancouver. He also dreams of making a feature film some day.

Finally, the spirit of the transformer is seen in the likes of Tim Collings, a professor of engineering and believer who invented the V-Chip (Violence Chip). Tim became concerned with media violence in 1989 after it was reported that the man who massacred sixteen women in Montreal, Canada viewed a steady diet of violent videos. He understood that the videos were just one of the contributing factors to the murderer's action, but he figured there must be some way to alert consumers to a show's content before it is too late. As Collings says, "The point is not censorship, but to give people information and the means to decide whether or not they want to watch something."[32] Choice for the people—that's a redemptive move for television viewers.

Summary

While Chapter 9 presented arguments against the media, this one has presented arguments for the media. Those arguments are divided along two camps. The Position 2 view contends that media technologies are neutral conduits through which morally charged messages are sent. The Position 3 view suggests that technologies are value-laden, and critiquing them and their content requires a pure heart and active mind.

Position 2 Christians see technology as gifts from God and are keenly optimistic that they improve life and help save the lost. This has motivated many to use magazines, radio, film, television, and the Internet to convey the clear message of Jesus Christ's gospel to people worldwide, though sometimes with mixed results. While confident that media channels are amoral, Position 2 Christians are often ambivalent toward new media because they know, that like any tool, they may be used to affirm or attack God's kingdom. In order to tip the moral balance to God's end, these believers value the production of material deemed unquestionably Christian for the purpose of ministry and missions.

Position 3 believers also regard media technology as blessings from God, but they contend such technologies are not morally neutral. They hold that technology embodies the values and goals of sinful and sometimes sanctified human beings who often pursue a profit. Transformers believe that we can rise above media content to interpret it redemptively and analyze its impact. Doing so requires a pure and faithful heart lest material become a stumbling block (see Romans 14:23). Finally, they suggest numerous strategies for how believers can redeem the media, including a career dedicated to creating morally uplifting and pre-evangelistic programs, education in critical thinking about the media, and active feedback-giving to media producers.

Worth the Talk

1. Some critics might say that the evangelical call to avoid objectionable media content is wishful thinking or evidence of an undeveloped faith. That is, they suggest that it's impossible to avoid objectionable content

(e.g., the news of a mass murderer on the six o'clock news, or an advertisement for a violence-loaded film), or that one's faith is weak if you can't handle such material. What do you think of these charges?

2. Other critics suggest that the transformer's freedom to interpret even objectionable media content for God's general revelation truth is license for consuming most anything, and that the worst of this material is not beneficial to believers. They might ask, "What's beneficial from R-rated sex-n-gore films or profane stand-up comedy skits?" What do you think?

3. Which do you think is better — a television program that makes explicit reference to God and how he works with people (e.g., *Touched by an Angel*, Robert Schuller's *The Hour of Power*), or a program that depicts presumably non-Christian people living relatively moral lives (e.g., *Home Improvement*)? What criteria are you using to judge one "better"?

Consider the Walk

1. Evaluate the best in Christian broadcasting, publishing, or computing and try to determine what makes their messages successful. For example, you might use *Christianity Today* magazine as a case example and describe its format, features, departments, editorial policy, and audience.

2. Try your hand at television or film criticism in the manner of a reformed approach. Select a show or movie and then analyze it for all the good it contains from God's perspective. Criteria you might use include the ones noted under the "People are mindful agents" section above or these:
   a. Are characters depicted as moral agents? As responsible agents?
   b. Is God's creation represented in magnificence and beauty?
   c. Does the program reflect history or reflect real events?
   d. Are the church and spiritual realm acknowledged? Respected?

3. Write a proposal for a radio program, television show, film, or Internet Web site that you think would be pre-evangelistic. Write as if you were pitching your idea to a producer who wants to produce moral content but is cautious about overtly religious material. Your proposal should address issues such as:
   a. Format: Will it be a drama, talk-show, information resource, comedy?
   b. Moral questions: What tough questions will be characteristic of your product? Will it consider the after-life? Ethics in the work place? Origins of the world?
   c. How will you convince an audience that your product is worth watching/listening to/ buying? That is, why do you think today's culture is ready for your program?

Notes

1. Lynn White, Jr., "The Historical Roots of Our Ecological Crisis," *Science*, Vol. 155, 1967, pp. 1203-1207 as quoted in Stephen V. Monsma, (Ed.), *Responsible technology: A Christian perspective*. William B. Eerdmans Publishing Company, Grand Rapids, MI, 1986, p. 41.
2. Richard R. Landers, *Man's place in the dybosphere*, Prentice-Hall, Englewood Cliffs, NJ, 1966, p. 207 as quoted in Monsma, (Ed.) p. 24.
3. R. A. Buchanan, *Technology and social progress*. Pergamon Press, Oxford, England, 1965, p. 163 as quoted in Monsma, (Ed.), p. 24
4. Quentin Schultze, *Televangelism and American culture*. Baker Book House, Grand Rapids, MI, 1991, p. 49.
5. Dennis E. Callaway, "Missions in cyberspace," *CBInternational Impact*, Fall 1995, pp. 8-9.
6. This view imitates the apostle Paul's report that he used all possible means to save people (1 Cor. 9:22). See, for example, Marvin Mardock, (Ed.), *By all means: Trends in world evangelism today*. Bethany Fellowship, Inc., Minneapolis, MN, 1969. Murdock includes the 1 Corinthians 9:22 passage opposite the book's title page. Chapters cover twelve means: aviation, television, laity involvement, international students, athletics, translation, mass rallies, relief work, literature, anthropology, medicine, and radio.
7. See Lynn. White, Jr., "The Historical Roots of Our Ecological Crisis," *Science*, Vol. 155, 1967, pp. 1203-1207 as quoted in Monsma, (Ed.), p. 41.
8. Quentin J. Schultze, *Internet for Christians*, Gospel Films Publications, Muskegon, MI, 1996, p. 11.
9. Clarence W. Jones, *Radio: The new missionary*, Moody Press, Chicago, IL, 1946, p. 7.
10. Steven Levy, "Blaming the Web," *Newsweek*, April 7, 1997, p.47.
11. Hal Erickson, *Religious radio and television in the United States, 1921-1991*. McFarland & Company, Inc., Publishers, Jefferson, NC, 1992, p. 1.
12. J. Harold Ellens, *Models of religious broadcasting*, William B. Eerdmans Publishing Company, Grand Rapids, MI, 1974, p. 14.
13. For example, you will find Trans World Radio at <www.twr.org> and Far Eastern Broadcasting Company at <www.febc.org>.
14. Stephen Paine, *The Christian and the movies*, Eerdmans, Grand Rapids, MI, 1957, p. 5 & 70 as quoted in Lloyd Billingsley, *The seductive image: A Christian critique of the world of film*, Crossway Books, Winchester, IL, 1989, p. 17. William Orr represents this position as well when he writes, "I have absolutely nothing to say against the invention of moving pictures. . . . . But what I want to mention particularly is the [Hollywood] *amusement* industry. For this industry I have only the severest condemnation. . . . These companies have become monsters, rich, unprincipled, and corrupt. And the commercial pictures of today are dramatized and produced by sinful, wicked people, and their influence is a vile curse upon our land," in William Orr, *The Christian and amusements*. Moody Press, Chicago, IL, 1960, p. 93.
15. You can check out films by both groups online at www.gospelcom.net/gf/ and www.wwp.org.

16. See "The *Jesus* Film Project Takes on the World," *Mission Frontiers: Bulletin of the U.S. Center for World Mission*, Vol. 19, November-December 1997, pp. 7-12.

17. Media Research Center, *Faith in a box: Television and religion*, 1995, p. 2.

18. *Faith in a box*, pp. 2 & 4.

19. The 1-in-3,000 figure comes from Todd Gitlin, *Inside prime time*, Pantheon Books, New York, 1985, p. 21.

20. William F. Fore, *Television and religion: The shaping of faith, values, and culture.* Augsburg Publishing House, Minneapolis, MN, 1987, pp. 82-83.

21. In the mid 1980s Robert Schuller's program attracted 1.27 million households. See Fore, 1987, p. 84.

22. Jason Baker, *Christian cyberspace companion 2nd Edition*, Baker Book House, Publishers, Grand Rapid, MI, 1997, pp. 23-24.

23. Quentin J. Schultze, *Internet for Christians*, Gospel Films, Inc., Muskegon, MI, 1996, back cover. I highly recommend this book or Jason Baker's book (see preceding endnote) whether you are a new or experienced Internet surfer.

24. McLuhan captured this idea in his now famous line, "the medium is the message." See Marshall McLuhan, *Understanding media*, McGraw-Hill, New York, NY, 1964.

25. Jeremy Rifkin, *Time wars: The primary conflict in human history*, Henry Holt and Company, New York, 1987, p. 17.

26. Neil Postman, *Amusing ourselves to death: Public discourse in an age of show business*, Viking, New York, NY, 1985, Chapter 7, pp. 99-113.

27. Lloyd Billingsley, p 21.

28. *Curriculum Report*, Vol. 26, No. 4, March 1997, National Association of Secondary School Principles, Reston, VA.

29. Quentin Schultze, *Redeeming television*, InterVarsity Press, Downers Grove, IL, 1992, p. 121.

30. Dave Geisler, "Christians Get Hollywood's Attention," *Charisma*, September 1995, p. 34.

31. To receive a copy of the *Catholic Connections to Media Literacy* Workshop Kit™, write the Center for Media Literacy, 4727 Wilshire Blvd., Suite 403, Los Angeles, CA, 90010 or call 1-800-226-9494.

32. David Dawes, "V-chip Inventor Offers Parents Control Over TV Viewing." *Christian Info News*, May 1996, p. 3.

PART 3

Talk for Students of Communication

CHAPTER 11

Searching for Truth in a Postmodern Age

*Buy the truth and do not sell it; get wisdom,
discipline and understanding.*

Proverbs 23:23

In a recent faculty meeting, our school's director for enrollment reviewed some research for what motivated Christian high school students to attend college or university. Number one on the list was "to get a better job" (77%), number two was "to learn about X" (74%) and number three was "to make better money" (72%).[1] My faculty colleagues and I sighed a breath of relief, for we saw that sandwiched between the pragmatic drive for a promising career and earning a healthy income was students' desire to learn. In a more local survey, our school found that the top two concerns of entering freshmen were whether or not they could make it academically (that is, could they make the "truth curve") and whether or not they would make friends. These findings confirm what we already know: people juggle a bundle of motivations and dreams. We are not just rational robots pursuing truth; we are moral agents who need the affection of others and a vocation to put food on the table.

Curiously though, a lot of university students enter the academy with a low view of truth, at least what has been termed "absolute truth." A recent study showed that 72 percent of Americans age eighteen to twenty-five believe "there is no such thing as absolute truth." The figure is 66 percent for Americans generally.[2] "Moreover, the study goes on to show that 53 percent of those who call themselves evangelical Christians believe there are no absolutes."[3]

Many suggest that after we deny any sense of absolute truth, our only alternative is relativism—the belief that what is true is relative to one's culture, time, and experience. What is true for you may not be true for me.

They suggest that the obligation of educators, therefore, is not to teach truth, but to empower students with critical thinking skills so they may sift through and arrange information into personal package form. Since we are simply rearranging information as we see it, no one has a moral right to impose their interpretation on others. We are called to tolerate everybody's experience and their description of reality.

My sense is that the postmodern cry for tolerance has made sloppy our methods for looking into truth. Why get hung up on method if we can't lay claim to finding a shareable truth? The catch is that not all communication instructors have bought into postmodern thought, and they will be expecting you to show proof for what you believe in papers and projects. Other instructors may be more sympathetic to postmodern views. Still others may have high value on the scriptures and require biblical explanations for communication. Since you are the one caught in the middle, it may be helpful for us to discuss three views on truth.

THREE UMPIRES: VIEWS ON WHAT IS TRUE

Before we look at the umps though, we need to distinguish between God, reality, and truth. In Christian thought (and in much Western cultural thought), we understand *God* to be an all-knowing, all-powerful spirit who caused the origin of the cosmos and who superintends it. *Reality* often refers to everything that exists, whether that be God or his creation, the spiritual, social, and physical realms. Angels are real spirits, and the earth, animals and people are real creations God spoke into existence. *Truth* is not the same as reality, but is found in our attempts to describe that reality. (And believers would add that complete knowledge of reality is found in Jesus Christ.) We make truth claims in light of evidence or facts as in, "Speakers of English use no more than fifty-two phonemes/sounds" (the claim) because, "Professor Jones' study of standard English shows fifty-two, not less or more" (the evidence). We assume that Jones looked into the matter deeply, counted all the sounds used in standard English, and sought corroboration from other scholars. If so, we say the claim is true—faithful to fact or reality. If someone else claimed, "Speakers of English use twenty-nine phonemes" we would have a basis to say, "No, that's not *true*." Again, the point is that truth is not synonymous with reality. Many say that truth is the quality of our truth claims when they reflect or hook up with spiritual, social and physical reality.[4]

These differences between God, reality, and truth are important to understand as we look at the amusing yet enlightening conversation among three baseball umpires. The first says "There's balls and there's strikes, and I calls 'em the way they are." The second responds, "There's balls and there's strikes, and I calls 'em how I see 'em." The third umpire chimes, "There's balls and there's strikes, but they ain't nothin' until I calls 'em."[5] It is simplistic but helpful to label the first an *objectivist*, the second a *subjectivist*, and the third a *constructivist*.

Umpire #1: the objectivist. Ump #1 believes in an external reality that his senses can tap into with no slippage. What he sees (hears, tastes etc.) is what he gets, objectively. He believes that language is the vehicle by which we convey to others what we get. Words may get in the way, occasionally, but by in large they deliver the reality we take in around us. Ump #1 is a staunch *foundationalist*. He believes, as do many even today, that "knowledge is the reflection of truth and that we can discover a stable foundation for it in God, History or Reason."[6] Some people of faith are objectivists. Bathed in the scriptures and blessed with common sense, they believe that God reveals himself and his creation to us through his physical, spiritual, and social world.

Ump #1's view also represents the modernist perspective — the idea that what is true about reality is knowable through reason and the scientific method. This way of thinking began as early as Plato and Socrates but gained momentum in the Renaissance (1300-1500 AD in Italy, and Europe thereafter) and the Enlightenment. During the Enlightenment (the 1700s) scholars and scientists began to rely less on religious texts and traditions and more on human understanding and science for determining what was true.

French philosopher René Descarte's dictum "I think, therefore I am" epitomized the elevation of human self and experience above a God-centered view of life. Secular (without God) humanism increasingly replaced a Christian appreciation of human accomplishment. At the same time, Isaac Newton and other modernist scientists conceived the physical world as a mechanism fit for human investigation and use. Science drove the industrial revolution (the application of scientific truths to technology) and provided a framework and rationale to introduce *social* science. Social scientists, communication scientists included, thought they could discover social laws as readily as physical scientists could discover natural laws. The goal for both was improvement of the human condition. In the 1900s, reliance on the scriptures and the church's traditions to determine what was true was all but abandoned as science gave us media technology and voyages to the moon. The spirit of modernism continues today in many circles and is captured well in the ethos of *Star Trek* (the original series) where scientific optimism and Spockian individualism led the charge to "explore new life and new civilizations, to boldly go where no man has gone before."[7]

While some believers embrace the modernist spirit of knowing truth for sure, they are less accepting of the view that we can grasp all truth through pure reason or the scientific method. Somewhere God's Word needs to be introduced, and not just through his creation. Christian objectivists generally assume that the Bible is clear about the important truths for life: to love God and enjoy him forever, beginning with love for my neighbor and relying on God for salvation.

Umpire #2: the subjectivist. In contrast to ump #1, ump #2 believes that his limited senses and flawed reasoning keep him from seeing reality as it is. He'd like to be a realist, but must resign himself to the label of critical realist, because to him the pursuit of truth is a subjective affair. What he *perceives* (rather than *receives*) is what he gets, but his perceptions are influenced by vice (like selfishness), pre-set expectations, and an outright shortage of brain power (Whoa! I can't process all that!).

Communication subjectivists support this view of truth with studies from social perception—the study of how we perceive other people. For example, in one classic study a group of subjects were shown a picture, for a few seconds, of an incident on a New York subway. The picture showed two men: one white and one black; one wearing a business suit and one in blue-collar clothes; one holding an open razor in a threatening manner, the other showing fear in response. Later, many of the white subjects "recalled" that a black laborer was robbing a white executive. In fact, it was the white man in denims who held the razor to the black man in the business suit.[8] Although all subjects were shown the same picture, some people's expectations (or stereotypes) influenced their instant reply. Somewhere along the way, the truth got edited.

Some Christians consider themselves subjectivists. In faith they believe that the entire creation is a certain way (and is known by God as a certain way), but in humility they acknowledge that humans still see through a glass darkly (1 Corinthians 13:12). Even with regard to the scriptures, believing subjectivists think Christians can know its mysteries in only a limited sense. They recognize the role of the Holy Spirit to lead them into all truth, yet exactly what that looks like in everyday life and their state of mind is difficult to grasp.

Umpire #3: the constructivist. Finally there's ump #3. He claims that balls and strikes don't even exist until he declares them so. Ump #3 represents today's postmodernist view of truth. Constructivists can hardly ignore that there's a physical reality, so they focus mainly on what we called social reality in Chapter 1. Social reality is what exists because humans have made it so. The social fact that Richard Duvall starred in *A Family Thing* is quite unlike the physical fact that Mt. Everest exists. (But the fact that Mt. Everest is said to be 29,000 feet above sea level is a social fact, because humans determined what a foot length is and scientists agreed that sea level is a good starting point for measuring mountains.) Like ump #3, postmodern constructivists question whether an objective reality exists (such as real balls and strikes, or real virtue and vice). They also question whether language can represent the way things really are. They say we should not ask how things really are, rather how we might make things be. Since *how we make things be* is largely determined by our language and social group, they suggest that our obligation is only to promote these views for our group's good. Forcing your group's view on others, however, is viewed as a terrible modernist activity.

Postmodernist writer Walter Truett Anderson, author of *Reality Isn't What It Used To Be*, summarizes the constructivist view.

> The constructivists...say that we do not have a "God's eye" view of nonhuman reality, never had, never will. They say we live in a symbolic world, a social reality that many people construct together and yet experience as the objective "real world." And they also tell us the earth is not a *single* symbolic world, but rather a vast universe of "multiple realities," because different groups of people construct different stories, and because different languages embody different ways of experiencing life.[9]

You probably see the implications for communication studies and for people of faith. Language is no longer considered God's gift for revealing truth; rather language becomes a "prison house" for concealing truth (that is, it keeps us from understanding how others think). Language may stake out coordinates for what we sense is an objective reality, but it's only a local reality. They say that even if we think we have a *metanarrative* (an overarching story that explains the way the world really is, such as Christianity), we only fool ourselves because we huddle with God-believers and create a secret code called Christianese. In brief, we are not simply making honest mistakes as we perceive the same "out there" world (like ump #2 believes), but we have created entirely different worlds. Christians are symbolically constructing Jupiter, other groups some other planet.

The spirit of postmodernism shows up in *Star Trek's* sequel *Star Trek: The Next Generation*. The new *Enterprise* crew is more diverse than the old crew (representing the validity of every group's view), and the Enterprise often encounters beings more highly advanced than humans (which displaces humans as the pinnacle of modernist evolution or divine imaging). The character Data is a lot like Spock, but believes he is incomplete because he lacks human qualities such as emotion and humor (reflecting the postmodern value on experience over truth). The crew relies on the intuitive and emotional to solve problems, not just rugged rationalism.[10]

Believers who have wrestled with the propositions of postmodernism give it mixed reviews. Of most concern are its claims that there exists no metanarrative—no overarching story—to explain human experience, and that we have no hope to know anything objectively. Believers beg to differ on both counts. What Christians can respect in postmodernism is its cri-

"So let me get this straight, ump. You're tellin' me that because the strike zone is a human creation, you can make it as big as you like?"

tique of modernism. Christians agree with postmodernists when they lament that modernist individualism, driven by pure rationalism, gave us science, and a quest for knowledge, at the price of community, wisdom, and a search for God.[11]

Even if you do not believe in ultimate truth, your role as a student will require you to ponder questions such as, What is truth?, What is good?, and What is beautiful? Each year millions of students sign up for university and college courses in pursuit of what I call *truth that is true enough.* Every semester thousands of students debate policies and values they consider *good that is good enough.* And every day classmates evaluate television shows, theater productions and even Web sites for *beauty that is beautiful enough.* These kinds of activities hint at the existence of a standard for truth, goodness and beauty outside of those studying it and arguing for it. Many Christians point to the person of Christ as the *logos* of the universe who existed before all things and in whom all things hold together.[12] In him, they suggest, we understand why knowledge, morality and elegance are worth pursuing in our communication.

Special and General Revelation[13]

Some of you will be frustrated with the 3-umps discussion. Why pay so much attention to postmodernists in the first place? Why not side with the more traditional modernist view? Why not ignore them both and opt to read the scriptures alone for our understanding of communication?

These are important questions. They represent what Christians have struggled with since the first century after Christ. Certainly the claims of Christ should guide our behavior and our inquiry into what is true, yet on this side of heaven we are still cultural, finite creatures who live in an imperfect world that demands our attention. Do we respond like the Amish by circling the wagons to fight off every idea that comes from outside of scripture? Or do we stop the wagon train and dialogue with unbelievers to discover God's truth to them by his grace? The first ten chapters of this book assume the latter view as they join scientific studies and the ideas of learned scholars along with biblical insights and scriptural references. I believe that truth is God's truth whether it originates in the scriptures or in our humble attempt to find it in the world around us. Theologians call the first *special revelation*, the second *general revelation*. Together they form an integrated view of God's truth.

SPECIAL REVELATION: BECOMING WISE FROM SCRIPTURE AND GOD'S SPIRIT

We call the Bible "special revelation" because it is a historical, readable, and explicit text. We understand that men wrote the scriptures, but by faith we believe that God spoke through them. In the words of Timothy, "All scripture is God-breathed and is useful for teaching, rebuking, correcting and training in righteousness, so that the man of God may be thoroughly equipped for every good work" (2 Timothy 3:16, 17). Note that this training is for right living and service, not for grade-point-average boosting.

We also rely on his Holy Spirit as we seek to know him and discover truth. Paul's prayer for the Ephesians is that "the God of our Lord Jesus Christ, the glorious Father, may give you the Spirit of wisdom and revelation, so that you may know him better. I pray also that the eyes of your heart may be enlightened in order that you may know the hope to which he has called you . . . ." (Ephesians 1:17b-18a). Notice that the focus of this truth is Jesus and the hope he offers us. The naturalistic modernist may laugh at the idea of a spirit communicating with someone (for the naturalist assumes there is no spirit world), while the postmodernist may applaud communication with the spirits (because angelic constructions may give inner peace). Christians are instructed to test (discern among) the spirits when listening for God's voice. Conservative Christians suggest that we return to revealed scriptures as a plumb line for orthodox belief and communication practice.

What the Bible says about communication may come to us in the form of prescriptive commands or descriptive insights. For example, commands such as "Don't lie" (Exodus 20:16) and "Speak the truth in love" (Ephesians 4:15) are there for our moral good, and we take these as "gospel." Descriptive insights are the reporting of facts, as in how the mob stoned Stephen after his speech (Acts 6:54-59), or how Paul addressed the Greek philosophers of the Aeropagus (see Acts 17:16-34). The temptation is to make descriptions into prescriptions—recorded facts into rules for all. But just because Stephen's speech began with a review of his audience's shortcomings and concluded with a scathing attack ("You stiff-necked people…You always resist the Holy Spirit!"), we don't "blister our audience" as a universal rule. Even Paul's strategy of beginning his speech with reference to his group's religious views is not to be taken as a hard-and-fast rule. Knowing our audience (like he did) seems to be the wiser rule.

NATURAL OR GENERAL REVELATION: LEARNING FROM THE EARTH, OUR CONSCIENCE, AND PEOPLE AROUND US

In addition to special revelation, God chooses to communicate to us in his natural creation (see Romans 1:18-23) and our moral conscience (see Romans 2:14-15). Theologians call this the doctrine of common grace, because it asserts that you don't have to be a Christian to know the truth that God exists, as evidenced in the universe, and that right and wrong exist, as evidenced in the "still small voice" of our conscience. As one author puts it, "common grace endows all people, believers and unbelievers alike, with a capacity for truth, goodness, beauty, and creativity."[14] God, in his mercy, stems the full brunt of sin's consequences, and gives to all people the capacity to discover truth.

This is why your professors ask you to consider material from a wide variety of sources to understand human and mediated communication. Not everything written in the *Journal of Communication* or *Adbusters* is true, but it's often a good start or all we have on a topic. Some believers make a big distinction between "big T" Truth and "little t" truth—the first being biblical truth and the latter being everything else. Others believe, as I do, that truth is truth, no matter where it is found, and it all originates with God.

A word of caution though. As James Sire has said, "All truth is God's truth, but not all claims to truth are true."[15] I agree, and hasten to add that knowing the difference is not always easy. Do we side with a film reviewer whose insights are eye-openers but whose lifestyle merits concern? Do we listen to a social scientist whose factual study seems to undermine a tenet of the faith? In these cases it is wise not only to search God's Word again, but also understand the philosophy or world view that under girds the film reviewer's or scientist's truth claim. How you figure out that bedrock matter is what we turn to now.

Putting Truth Claims to a World View Test

A world view can be defined as *the way a group of people look at reality.* "It consists of basic assumptions and images that provide a more or less sensible, though not necessarily accurate, way of thinking about the world."[16] The subjectivist and the constructivist would say that these assumptions and images largely determine how much validity (truth value) we attach to someone's truth claim. For example, in a culture where people value informal communication networks on paths to the rice paddy, the claim "A media blitz is the only way to reach people" rings hollow. But how do we figure out the world view of a paddy-goer, film reviewer, scientist, or classmate?

James Sire suggests a way in his book *Discipleship of the Mind.* He recommends that you ask people questions about their view of reality, being human, the after-life, knowledge, right and wrong, and history. If at all possible, he suggests you ask him or her these questions.

1. What is prime reality—the really real?
2. What is the nature of external reality, that is, the world around us?
3. What is a human being?
4. What happens to a person at death?
5. Why is it possible to know anything at all?
6. How do we know what is right and wrong?
7. What is the meaning of human history?[17]

Although I risk being criticized as simplistic or generalizing, I feel it's worth taking a stab at what many people of faith believe in regard to these questions. 1) God and his creation are the really real, not the mere constructions we make of them in our heads. 2) The external world is spiritual, social and material and is sustained by God through Jesus Christ. It is dynamic and known by God. 3) People are creatures made in God's image, unique and unlike animals in important ways, including our symbol-using capacity, as noted in Chapter 1. 4) People enter heaven or hell to experience eternal communion with God or eternal separation from him; they do not cycle back through reincarnation or become one with the universe. 5) People are created by God with the capacity to sense, reason, test, and exercise faith so that through Jesus Christ, the *logos*, we may know God's revelation to us. 6) People can discern right from wrong because they have a conscience (Romans 2:14-15) and because we can know God's standard for right living in the example of Jesus Christ and through his Word. And 7) Human history is about our creation, fall, redemption, and ultimate judgment; it is the metanarrative of God's communication with people.[18]

Believers will disagree in good faith with some of my observations. You may disagree. But these answers at least offer a starting point for dialogue with people who make truth claims that seem invalid. For example, people like ump #3, who contend that language is a "prison house," may be better understood if we ask them about their view of human nature. If they assume that we are not made in God's image, and that language is human-made, not God-given, then we might grasp why they call humans "social nodes" trapped in "webs of significance." We may not agree with them, but understanding their beliefs about human nature helps us dialogue.

In an ideal world, we would be able to pose these questions in person. But that's usually not the case with film reviewers and social scientists. In fact, all we may have is their film review or their article in *Human Communication Research*. How might we test their text for it's underlying assumptions?

Again James Sire provides insight. We test for assumptions by examining what a scholar studies (reality), how the scholar studies it (method), what truth claim the scholar makes (theory or facts), what terms make those claims reasonable (truth value) and what assumptions under gird all of it (world view). (See figure 11.1)

The double-headed arrow reflects what Sire says is the push and pull between our object of study and our world view. "Any given scholarly theory or perspective or way of studying a subject matter of any discipline is rooted in a specific world view. On the other hand, what one does in the laboratory or library affects the world view undergirding one's efforts."[19]

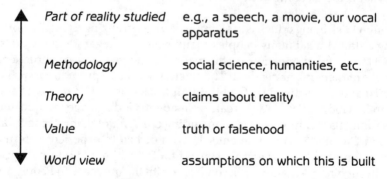

Part of reality studied	e.g., a speech, a movie, our vocal apparatus
Methodology	social science, humanities, etc.
Theory	claims about reality
Value	truth or falsehood
World view	assumptions on which this is built

Figure 11.1. The Relationship Between World View and Scholarly Inquiry.

Let's take the naturalistic, modernist world view as an example. If one begins with the assumption that there is no God, like they do, then it makes sense that they are trying to explain human speech without God in the picture. A naturalist who compares human speech with chimpanzee speech will likely ask the obvious evolutionary question, "How did we get from chimp to Chip?" Once that question has been answered sufficiently on an evolutionary assumption, it's just a matter of time before other questions and methods are asked and enacted that exclude supernatural explanations (see Figure 11.2).

With this said, let us acknowledge that many scientists try very hard to keep their personal convictions out of the lab. All they want to do, for example, is to describe how tongue and teeth, brain and body work together to produce human speech. Some critics might say these folks in white lab coats only fool themselves — for they have already asked a question of physics (i.e., how does the speech machine tick?), not metaphysics (i.e., how might we see God in our speech ability?). More sympathetic critics would suggest that the examination of God's creation (our bodies) is one way he reveals his truth to us, and to understand physics is to appreciate God's handiwork.

Once again you can see the utility of seeing God's truth as whole and unified. Whole truth doesn't cower when expressed in different ways. Two explanations for the same thing (such as our speech ability) do not necessarily undercut each other. David Myers, a psychologist at Hope College, addresses this issue in *The Human Puzzle*. "If we are to understand why scientific and religious explanations need not be considered mutually ex-

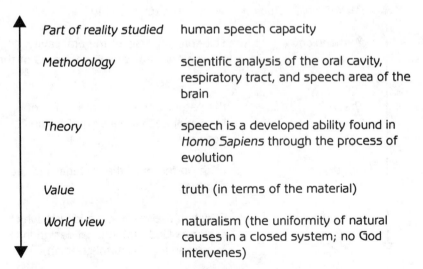

Figure 11.2. Naturalism and an explanation for human speech.

clusive, we must recognize that there are a variety of possible ways by which one might explain a given event, all of which are simultaneously true in their own terms."[20] Em Griffin, a Christian communication professor, affirms the same view in his text on communication theory: "Don't assume that one [theory] has to be true and the others false. Rather, they all help explain communication behavior."[21]

Myers and Griffin suggest that we can study human speech (or media criticism, or intercultural communication) at various "levels" (naturalistic, artistic, theistic) without the paralyzing fear that explanations at one level cancel explanations at the others. For example, the best naturalistic description of human speech is evidence for a quite different truth claim for many believers. (See figure 11.3)

Some readers may consider this a soft example, claiming that it is easy for natural scientists to describe our speech capacity and then blithely quip "and God designed it so." But what about truth claims made by social scientists or humanities scholars? Are they not more susceptible to human error since their objects of study are more elusive, namely, people's behavior and cultural products? How should we respond to theorists who claim to understand human communication but acknowledge no world view assumptions held by believers? How do we grapple with a critic's claims about a film or play who makes thin reference to any moral framework? In short, how much faith should people of faith put in human scholarship?

What these questions point to is a need to understand the methods by which thinkers arrive at their truth claims. In communication studies, those

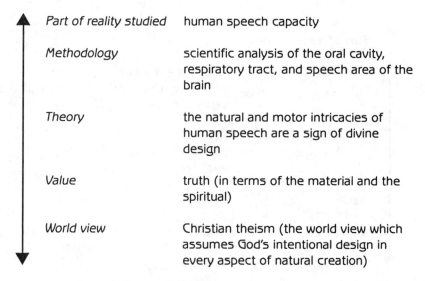

Part of reality studied	human speech capacity
Methodology	scientific analysis of the oral cavity, respiratory tract, and speech area of the brain
Theory	the natural and motor intricacies of human speech are a sign of divine design
Value	truth (in terms of the material and the spiritual)
World view	Christian theism (the world view which assumes God's intentional design in every aspect of natural creation)

Figure 11.3.   Christian Theism and an Explanation for Human Speech.

methods differ considerably. Depending on their type, they reflect different assumptions about reality, being human, and the purpose of theory-making. We turn to these methods for a closer look in chapters twelve and thirteen.

Summary

Remember the three umpires? We can only imagine their responses to doing a world view test, but they do well to summarize our ideas about truth. The objectivist ump #1 might retort, "No world view influences *my* read on reality; I just claim true what I see as true; you other guys just need to rely on common sense, a little science, and the clear Word of God." The subjectivist ump #2 might respond, "Of course we are influenced by some world view, but thank God that our fallen, finite condition does not obliterate all hope to know God and to understand communication in meaningful terms. In humility though, I feel it is my responsibility to qualify many of my truth claims." The constructivist ump #3 might say "Things aren't so simple. Not just our world views, but our language and social groups also cause us to construct what we take as true about God and communication. What is real is like a cloud, and human words condense it into local drinking water." Perhaps you can determine where you side in the truth debate.

Worth the Talk

1. What is your response to the idea that "All truth is God's truth wherever it is found?" On what basis do you agree? Disagree?
2. Which of the three umpires do you think has the truth on truth? Where do you see yourself aligning with the ideas of the objectivist, subjectivist, or constructivist? Can you explain why?
3. Who has shaped your views of truth and reality? What reasons or evidence did that person give you to persuade you to this view?

Consider the Walk

1. Take a topic such as deception, or a tougher one like virtual reality technology, and try to make a case for how Christians ought to think about these issues using only the Bible and biblical commentaries as your sources. Near the end of your analysis you might consider whether you gained or lost much insight by constraining your analysis to the biblical record.
2. Take two theories that explain the same communication activity and show how each does so in its own terms. Consider whether these two explanations conflict or invalidate each other.

3. For an advanced analysis, take a theory of your choice and put it to a world view test. Describe what the theorist hopes to explain (i.e., the reality examined), how he or she collected data to test the theory (i.e., the methodology used), what the theorist's major claim is, what terms determine its truth value, and what assumptions undergird it all.

Notes

1. This research was performed by the Coalition for Christian Colleges and Universities, Washington, D.C. in 1996, and reported on by Ron Kuehl, Vice President for Enrollment Management at Trinity Western University, Langley, British Columbia, Canada, March 1997.
2. George Barna, *The Barna report: What Americans believe*, Regal Books, Ventura, CA, 1991, pp. 83-85, as cited in Gene Edward Veith, *Postmodern times: A Christian guide to contemporary thought and culture*, Crossway Books, Wheaton, IL, 1994, p. 16.
3. Gene Veith, p. 16, citing Barna's report.
4. Students of philosophy will recognize this definition of truth as reflecting the correspondence theory of truth. Statements are true when they correspond or mirror objective, factual reality. As the next section shows, however, this notion of truth as been largely discredited by postmodernist truth theorist. I use it here because of it ringing true with what many Christians believe about truth and as a point of comparison for what follows. For a discussion of the correspondence theory of truth see Michael Devitt, *Realism and truth*, Princeton University Press, Princeton, New Jersey, 1984, pp. 25-28.
5. This example and a full discussion of these world views may be found in Walter Truett Anderson, *Reality isn't what it used to be*, Harper & Row, San Francisco, 1990.
6. Patricia Waugh, ed., *Postmodernism: A reader*, Edward Arnold, London, 1992, p.5, as quoted by Veith, *Postmodern times*, p. 50.
7. See Stanley J. Grenz, *A primer on postmodernism*. Wm. B. Eerdmans Publishing Co., Grand Rapids, MI, 1996, especially chapter one: "Star Trek *and the postmodern generation.*"
8. Gordon W. Allport and Leo F. Postman, "The Basic Psychology of Rumor," *Transactions of the New York Academy of Sciences*, Series 2, 8, 1945, pp. 61-81 as cited in Em Griffin, *Making friends (& making them count)*, InterVarsity Press, Downers Grove, IL, 1987, p. 81.
9. Walter Truett Anderson, p. 6.
10. Grenz, pp. 8-9.
11. See Grenz, Chapter 7: "The Gospel and the Postmodern Context," pp. 161-174.
12. See Colossians 1:15-20 for scripture that describes the supremacy of Christ in Christian faith.
13. See Bruce Milne's *Know the truth: A handbook of Christian belief*, InterVarsity Press, Downers Grove, IL 1982, pp. 19-27 for a full explanation of special and general revelation.

14. Leland Ryken, *Culture in Christian perspective: A door to understanding & enjoying the arts*, Multnomah Press, Portland, OR, 1986, p. 13.
15. James W. Sire, *Discipleship of the mind*, InterVarsity Press, Downers Grove, IL, 1990, p. 142.
16. Michael Kearney, *World view*, Chandler & Sharp Publishers, Inc., Novato, CA, 1984, p. 41.
17. Sire, pp. 30-31.
18. These answers are based on my understanding of our faith and on Sire's answers to each question in his book.
19. Sire p. 149.
20. David G. Myers, *The human puzzle: Psychological research & Christian belief*, Harper & Row Publishers, New York, 1978, p. 11 and following.
21. Em Griffin, *A first look at communication theory* (2nd ed.), McGraw-Hill, Inc., New York, 1994, p. 5.

CHAPTER 12

Looking at the Social Sciences in Christian Perspective

Yet for us there is but one God, the Father, from whom things came and for whom we live; and there is but one Lord, Jesus Christ, through whom all things came and through whom we live.
1 Corinthians 8:6

A couple years ago our campus was privileged to host Tony Campolo—professor of sociology from Eastern College, and well-known social activist. Some 1400 students, faculty, administrators, staff, and off-campus guests crammed into our modest gymnasium to hear a man wrapped in the purposes of God and capable of articulating them. Perhaps you have had opportunity to hear him speak or read one of his numerous books.

Dr. Campolo's speaking serves as a basis for examining how scholars study communication. One might assume that even unchurched people would agree that Tony's speaking ability represents above average accomplishment. Who's to know how many listeners have changed their beliefs and motivations due to Campolo's speeches? Social scientists might suggest that Tony excels because he is credible in the eyes of his audience, uses two-sided arguments with skeptical crowds, and uses plenty of relevant material that people can grasp. All three have been shown to increase speaker persuasiveness in social scientific research.[1]

Humanities scholars might suggest that Tony surpasses rhetorical mediocrity because he interprets scripture well, appeals to our logic and emotions, practices what he preaches, and exhibits an articulate command of English. These factors, more than a scientific cause-effect model, explain his speaking success.[2]

Finally, communication practitioners, while not ignoring these other interpretations, would likely add, "And what a delivery!" He not only has a fine command of English, but he breathes life into his message with passionate volume, pitch, pacing, pausing, body posture, and gestures.[3]

This chapter and the two that follow examine the social science, humanities, and performance approaches to our field from a Christian perspective. They are intended to help you understand how scholars in communication studies arrive at defendable truth claims. To do so, we will look at their methods for marshaling proof and their assumptions about reality and truth. My hope is that you will develop a discerning eye for your own research as you sift through books, articles, and Web sites during your college years and beyond. Let's look at the social scientific approach now.

The Scientific Method

Even though a good number of communication scholars wave the flag of postmodernism, another set remain walled within the fortress of modern science. By now you have heard or read of investigations reported in this manner: "According to a study done at State University, researchers discovered facts XYZ that seem to support theory Q about human communication." Communication scientists believe that people interact in patterned, generalizable ways, and their goal is to discover and measure variables that predict a communication outcome. To do so, they ask questions, observe communication activity, and answer their questions the best they can. In more expanded form, the process they follow includes five steps. (See Figure 12.1).

Perhaps you have heard about the "sleeper effect" in your public speaking class. It is the finding that, over time, audience members forget *who* said something but not *what* they said. In other words, people may forget that it was Tony Campolo who said this or that, but they are less likely to forget a theme or key point he made. (As anecdotal proof, consider the times you've said, "I forget who said this, but..." and then go on to state the point you recall.) This means that a well-argued speech from a low-credibility speaker may be almost as convincing as the same speech from a high-credibility source *two weeks later*. Let's apply the scientific model to see how Carl Hovland and Walter Weiss came up with such a finding during the early years of credibility research.[4] In step form, it probably looked like this:

> *Step 1: Look Into It.* These researchers wondered how differences in a speaker's credibility were related to persuasion over time. They read previous studies on credibility and persuasion to discover that no one had examined this specific question before.

Step 1. Look Into It. Researchers review existing books, articles, and communication activity around them to determine a question that others have not answered.

Step 2. Form A Hunch. From their reading and casual observations, researchers form an hypothesis or hunch about that aspect of communication.

Step 3. Observe Others Systematically. They set up a study that employs a standard method to gather data/information (for example, a questionnaire, experiment, or interview process).

Step 4. Interpret the Data. They interpret the information gathered in light of an existing theory or a new theory they want to propose.

Step 5. Discuss Importance of Results. Researchers suggest implications of their findings for future research and theorizing.

Figure 12.1.   Overview of the Scientific Method

Step 2: Form A Hunch. In light of what they read, they formed the hypothesis that over time, people tend to forget who said what, and this may lead to a delayed, greater acceptance of messages proposed by low-credibility sources.

Step 3: Observe Others Systematically. They did studies to prove or disprove their hypothesis. They had two groups of people listen to the same message, with one group believing that the speaker had high credibility, and the other believing that the speaker had low credibility. They measured each group's attitude change on a standard paper-pencil scale immediately after they had received the message and again several weeks later.

Step 4: Interpret the Data. They took their results and analyzed them statistically to see if there had been a significant change in either group's attitudes over time. They discovered that both groups believed the message more over time, but the low-credibility group had increased its favorable attitudes substantially more than had the other group.

Step 5: Discuss Importance of Results. They explained their findings by asserting that people tend to disassociate the speaker from the message over time, thus allowing the "sleeper effect" to occur. The major implication: there's hope for speakers who may not have the favor of high credibility in the eyes of their audience as long as their speeches are well-reasoned and relevant.

ASSUMPTIONS SOCIAL SCIENTISTS HOLD

The description of the scientific method hints at the way social scientists see the world. Like umpire #1 in Chapter 11, they are more likely to assume that reality is a certain way and that our senses and method can help us discover it. At the same time, even some social scientists assume, like umpire #2, that the scientific method suffers from human flaws that render our knowledge incomplete. So, while you may find social science profs who sit firmly in the *objectivism* camp or the *subjectivism* camp, you will also find a good number waxing philosophic somewhere in between. Regardless of these differences, most communication scientists hold some basic assumptions about reality and our understanding of it.

Social scientists assume some form of objectivism. That is, they assume that a method for collecting information can be free from human bias, and that the data they collect with that method is pure information about the world. *Objective realism* is the idea that the social, physical and spiritual world is a certain way regardless of how we try to express it. Our truth claims about reality might be cloudy, but reality remains rock solid. *Objective methodism* is the idea that we can use scientific methods to examine reality without bias — to remove ourselves from what we study. Objectivity in method assumes that even if you are an avid fan of Tony Campolo, your results are true because you went by the book, not by your bias. Scientists work hard to distance themselves from whom and what they study, in an attempt to get "just the facts and nothing but the facts." Of course they admit that interpreting and evaluating these facts (or data) is a human activity, but even then they attempt to offer a balanced reading.

Social scientists assume a stable and discoverable reality. That is, they assume that a phenomena, such as credibility, is always at work in human interaction and that you can tap into that dynamic pattern with some method. They aren't saying that someone's credibility never changes, rather, they assume that the variable of credibility won't go away, and that it always contributes to the outcome. What we need, they suggest, are tools, such as a credibility scale, to discover whether a speaker enjoys high or low worth with a particular audience.

A research tool or method is considered an empirical way to tap into the law-like relationship variables display. Empirical means "of the senses" and is quite unlike intuition (that is, I know because it feels right) or Spirit revelation (that is, I know because God told me). For scientists, empirical also means "guided by evidence obtained in systematic and controlled scientific research."[5] The battery of methods scientists use to gather information systematically include experiments, surveys, interviews and observation. We will examine these later in this chapter.

Social scientists assume a generalizable and replicable reality. If what's true for Tony Campolo generalizes to other public speakers, then other scientists should be able to replicate (that is, repeat) this finding in their own studies. If what holds for Campolo's rhetorical success does not generalize to other public speakers, we have a poor base for writing public speaking textbooks or requiring students to take a course in public address. Scientists who desire to replicate earlier findings are required to use the same method as the original researcher. This would include using the same type of subjects, the same scales for credibility and attitude change, and the same statistical analysis for examining the data. If the results are consistent, we deem them replicable.

Social scientists assume distinct criteria for communication theory. Theories are not reality; they are maps or pictures of reality. The goal of scientists is to chart that map with the skill of a cartographer while still acknowledging that social reality is not as easy to draw as hills and dales. Em Griffin explains in *A First Look at Communication Theory* the criteria scientists use to guide their theorizing.[6] (See Figure 12.2)

Good theories explain data. Scientists suggest that if we can't make heads or tails of our data with an existing theory, then it's time to throw it out and

---

1. Explanation of the Data. A good scientific theory explains an event or behavior.

2. Prediction of Future Events. A good scientific theory predicts what will happen.

3. Hypotheses That Can Be Tested. A good scientific theory is testable.

4. Relative Simplicity. A good scientific theory is as simple as possible.

5. Practical Utility. A good scientific theory is useful.

Figure 12.2. Scientific Standards For What Makes A Good Social Science Theory

start fresh. This goes for prediction as well. If variable A brings about or is often found to correlate with variable B, we should be able to predict "If A, then B." But if the presence of A is rarely or incidentally related to B, then we should chuck the theory "If A, then B."

When we say a theory is testable we mean it can be proved or disproved. Some theories are so complex or vague they defy support or challenge. Suppose a theory suggested that Tony Campolo (or any good speaker) excels because he exhibits qualities A, B, C, D, E, F, G, H, I, and J. The theory may be comprehensive, but there's hardly a time when one of these variables isn't working (to which the theorist might say, "See, I was right!"), and hardly a time when all of them are working simultaneously (to which the theorist might say, "Well only half of the variables need to be active.") The question is, which half? And will this half be the same set tomorrow? This criterion hints at the goal of simplicity. If two theories explain the same communication activity, but one makes sense with three variables and another with ten, most scientists regard the simpler one as better.

For some, however, the litmus test for truth is whether you can use a theory in everyday life. If you're pressed for time and need to prepare a speech for later this week, you don't want advice from a theorist who hasn't "been there" or whose theory hasn't "done that." Eloquent speeches are crafted on the foundation of sound theory, and any theory that cannot impute practical advice is less valued than the one that can.

GATHERING DATA IN THE SOCIAL SCIENCES

Hovland and Weiss used an experimental method for gathering evidence to answer their question about speaker credibility. Other methods available include survey research, interview research, and observation research. Understanding these methods might help you do your own research for various projects.

The experimental method. Social scientists use experiments to manipulate variables to see how they influence other variables. For example, if you wanted to measure the effect of high and low credibility on speaker persuasiveness, your job would be to control these variables with two groups of subjects. You might do so by telling one group that the speaker was an expert in her field, and tell the other group that she was a hobbyist in the field. By creating a "high credibility" group and a "low credibility" group, you would be able to see the effect these perceptions have on how each group responded to her speech.

The variable you control (that is, vary) is called the *independent variable*, and you assume it has influence on the *dependent variable(s)*. (An easy way to remember these types is to say that the value of the dependent variable is *dependent* on the value of the independent one.) In the above example, a speaker's perceived credibility (the independent variable) is manipulated high or low to see its influence on long-term attitude change (the dependent variable). We call the *low credibility* and *high credibility* subjects "*treatment groups*" because they were exposed to (that is, treated with) different degrees of the independent variable. Occasionally a researcher will include a *control group* — a set of subjects who receive *no information* about the independent variable. A control group gives a researcher a base line for comparing the effect of the manipulated independent variable on the dependent ones.

Experimental studies are often considered the most scientifically rigorous because they allow the researcher to set up situations that weed out other variables as potential explanations for communication outcomes. However because they are set up, experiments are sometimes criticized for being artificial and not generalizable to the real world. Doing experimental research requires ample planning, organizing, training (of lab assistants for example), and patience in loading data onto a computer. You will probably not be required to perform an experiment in your undergraduate experience, but you will likely read the results of many such studies before your graduation day.

The survey method. Whereas experimenters manipulate variables in a laboratory setting, survey researchers often use questionnaires to measure variables as they exist already in communicators. Survey research is particularly helpful in understanding the relative incidence, distribution, and interrelations of demographic information and communication practice. For example, opinion polls concerning a politician's credibility or popularity after a televised speech, is done by telephone survey. A survey researcher can measure a thousand people's impressions of a leader's credibility two days before the speech, and then measure their attitudes about the speech after it's delivered. This allows the researcher to avoid unethical application of certain independent variables. For example, it would be highly questionable for a researcher to stand at the door where Campolo was to speak and hand out false information about his credibility just to measure people's attitudes toward him and his topic. However it would be fine to assess people's impressions of Campolo's credibility before he speaks. The survey researcher could still "manipulate" the credibility factor later by placing Campolo-admirers in one set and Campolo-critics in another set on the computer before analyzing how each group responded to his speech.

Although constructing valid questionnaires is a time consuming and mindful chore, the resulting data is often ripe for understanding communication. It is common for communication students to use existing questionnaires to tap into the local student body's communication habits. It is also common for professors to ask students to develop their own surveys for some new or unique question.

The interview method. The interview method is a cousin to the survey method except that you, as researcher, are the one asking the questions orally and recording the answers on the form. Interviews are conducted door-to-door, by telephone, and by appointment. How structured these questions are, and what freedom you have to deviate from them, varies according to your study's purpose. The *standardized interview* "consists of a set of prepared questions from which the interviewer is not allowed to deviate"[7] whereas the *unstandardized interview* "allows the interviewer as well as the respondent considerable latitude."[8] Standardized interviews are commonly used among market researchers who want to determine people's buying habits and intentions (e.g., "Which of the following brands of television have you heard of? ___ Panasonic ___ Zenith ___ Sanyo ___ JVC ___ other: please specify." "Which of these brands would you intend to purchase the next time you shop for a television?").

The astute interviewer is aware of two categories of questions. *Closed questions* require the respondent to answer with a brief response, such as "yes" or "no," "Panasonic" or "Sanyo." "How many televisions are in your home" is a closed question because it is answerable with one word. *Open questions* allow the respondent to answer in a lengthy, unspecified way. "What is your opinion about the newly developed violence chip for television monitoring?" is an open question because the person answering might go on at length with praise or criticism. Obviously, answers to open questions are more difficult to record because of their length.

Interviewing requires a capable researcher who is able to listen actively and record accurately the stream of material interviewees provide. Interviewers must also guard against biasing the respondent to answer a certain way and be aware of respondents who prefer to answer the socially expected way rather than genuinely. Even with these potential drawbacks, interviewing provides a robust method for discovering people's attitudes, fears, intentions and peculiarities regarding communication. Journalism students may be accustomed to interviewing one or two individuals to write a story; social scientists will likely interview 30-300 individuals to grasp broad patterns of communication truth.[9] If five students in your class interviewed ten students apiece as to their views of Campolo's speech, you would be on your way to a solid research project.

The observation method. Suppose you wanted to determine people's attitudes toward Tony Campolo's speech from their behaviors, not their reported attitudes. As an observation researcher you might videotape the chapel crowd inconspicuously as they listened to Tony, and then go back and review the tape to read their nonverbal responses. You might use some of the classic research on facial expressions to count and categorize the smiles, frowns, laughter, ho-hum gazes, and the like. Then you would infer from these behavioral observations how the subjects really felt toward Tony.

Observation is, therefore, a "direct" approach to measuring behavior. Some think it is superior to interview research because it does not depend on people's memory to recall what they did, nor on their honesty to say what they think. From this example you can see that observation research "gathers data through systematic watching, studying, or interpreting the source of the data."[10] Observation research is at work under a variety of different labels including case studies, content analysis, interaction analysis, relational analysis, network analysis, and naturalistic inquiry. What holds all of these methods together, however, is that each attempts to describe the status quo (that is, how communication is), and each uses observation.[11]

The limitation of observational research is that the same behavior could be categorized in quite different ways. (Was that an *unfriendly frown* or a *sympathetic smirk*?) To lessen this drawback, a researcher will train a team of coders for consistency. Coders are people who review videotapes of Campolo watchers or whomever you are examining. Coders become familiar and accurate with the coding scheme, in this case the types of facial expressions, by doing dry runs on sample taped material. The research director then compares the coders' work, determines how reliable their use of the scheme has been, and then provides feedback to the coders so they can improve consistency. This consistency is often expressed as a statistic called the inter-coder reliability index, and good studies strive for 85-90% overlap among coded results.

You may have already done some sort of observational research.

Observational research is therefore different from casual observation. It assumes you have a way to capture data for review (on video or audio tape), a scheme for coding the data, and trained coders who can recognize the variables of interest. The Media Research Center uses observation research (called content analysis) each year to determine the types of themes TV news and dramatic programs depict (see Chapter 10).

Christian Responses to Social Scientific Scholarship

By now you have evaluated the social science enterprise for yourself. You might be drawn to its penchant for objectivity and the crunching of statistics to discover "out there" laws of communication. Others of you may feel uneasy, noting that so much science smells of determinism. Where does our free will fit into all this? Your response mirrors how other believers respond to this modernist project. What follows is an attempt to show how Christians have responded to the social scientific enterprise is a bit like they've responded to media. Some pay little attention to it; some see it as harmless; others see it as a direct line to God's general revelation.

REJECTION OR IGNORING OF SOCIAL SCIENTIFIC SCHOLARSHIP

For believers who place preeminent worth on special revelation, human science may be regarded at odds with the faith. Such individuals first point to the adjective *social* in social science and lament that its focus is on people, not God. They insist that the modernist agenda, with its promise to solve human problems through social research, has given us few answers and false hope. If we are made in God's image, they assert, then let us begin our study of humans by studying God and our relationship to him.

Others note that the social sciences gave us the notion of "cultural relativity" and they find this a cancerous concept for absolute truth.[12] Cultural relativity is the postmodern idea that what is true or right for one culture is best understood relative to its world view and assumptions. Although social scientists intended cultural relativity to be an antidote to ethnocentrism, conservative Christians attack it for undermining any sense of universal truth. As one critic writes, "To make cultural relativism an absolute is precisely to destroy objective truth and normative values," and "either there is a 'transcultural' common truth which is intelligible to 'all the nations,' or the Great commission is impossible of implementation."[13]

Another reason why some believers are wary of social science is because of its link with determinism. *Determinism* is the school of thought that suggests that we do not have free will, but only react to forces around us. For example, some Christians may suggest that if a communication ill, such as verbal abuse, can be explained by the abuser's environment, then it's all too easy to excuse the abuser.[14] They feel that abdicating our responsibility for sinful habits may be worse than the habits themselves.

Other Christians are not antagonistic towards social science research; they simply pay little attention to it. Three communication books written from a scriptural and humanities perspective include Grant Howard's *The Trauma of Transparency: A Biblical Approach to Inter-Personal Communication* (Multnomah, 1979), Howard Hendrick's *Say it with Love: The Art and Joy of Telling the Good News* (Victor Books, 1972) and Calvin Miller's *The Empowered Communicator* (Broadman & Holman, 1994). These authors cite few, if any, scientific studies as they suggest guidelines for communicating with friends, strangers, and audiences. They use scripture references, personal examples, anecdotes, poems, and rhetorical concepts to paint a lively and engaging picture of the communication process. It's likely that these books probably reflect the authors' fondness for words more than any disdain for the social sciences.

SUBJUGATION OF SOCIAL SCIENTIFIC SCHOLARSHIP TO CHRISTIAN TEACHING

Other believers welcome insights from the social sciences but with one proviso: God's Word still trumps science. As some Christian sociologists have written, "The Christian's main concern with any model is whether or not the model squares realistically with Christian conceptions of human nature and needs."[15] And another writes:

> Any approach to sociology [or we could just as well say communication] that ignores the biblical account of the origin of humans and its implications, as well as the effects of the fall and the potential of redemption, will always come short of the full truth. An understanding of the scriptural view of human nature is essential for a valid sociology [or, study in communication].[16]

With this said, we should note that conservative Christians seem to be more concerned with the world view and resulting interpretations scholars bring to communication data, than with the data alone. For example, a study on lying indicates that people deceive others for a variety of reasons, including: to gain personal needs (such as money), to increase desired relationships, to protect self-esteem, and to gain some personal satisfaction.[17] These are facts that believers will admit describe why people lie. However, any attempt to interpret these facts to suggest that lying is justified or natural is deemed a non-Christian perspective.

ACCEPTANCE OF SOCIAL SCIENTIFIC SCHOLARSHIP AS GENERAL REVELATION

Another group of believers suggests that good science is one more means by which God reveals himself and his creation to us. They echo the scripture verse that begins this chapter. If *"there is but one God, the Father, from whom things came"* and *"one Lord, Jesus Christ, through whom all things came,"* then discovering the structure of everything is entirely about finding God's revelation to us. As Richard Bube writes, "Christian science is good science. And good science is science that is faithful to the structure of reality."[18] David Myers resounds this view when he writes, "To do science means to remain open to reality and not to force upon it prior conclusions from any source."[19] These believers are optimistic that science can deliver God's truth. But they are not so boorish as to place science above scripture. They are not even willing to place scripture above science. Of one thing they are sure: our sinfulness and our limited brainpower inhibit our ability to make definitive truth claims about God or humans. In classic reform theological manner Myers and co-author Malcolm Jeeves write:

> If God has written the book of nature [including human communication nature], it becomes our calling to read it as clearly as we can, remembering that we are humble stewards of the creation, answerable to the giver of all data for the accuracy of our observations. Indeed, it is precisely because all our ideas are vulnerable to error and bias — including our biblical and theological interpretations as well as our scientific concepts — that we must be wary of absolutizing any of our theological or scientific ideas.[20]

These writers suggest that the scriptures may all be true, but all the truth God has for us is not restricted to the scriptures. This means that knowing God's truth is not an either (scripture), or (science) proposition. These faithful scientists are bent on knowing both/and truth.

These responses to the social sciences bring us back to the ideas in the preceding chapter. Social science, like any human scholarship, is not a perfect method for inquiry. Moreover, we have to admit that it is a method based on a modernist view of the earth and its inhabitants. Finally, we have to acknowledge that even "the facts" are subject to interpretation given one's world view.

A World View Test on Social Science Research

Before we end this chapter, I thought it would be useful to provide an application of James Sire's world view analysis to a scientific theory. (We

did one of these in the preceding chapter with regard to our speech ability).
My hope is that you will make a habit of using this kind of test to discern
what researchers assume about the human condition, the function of language, the purpose of relationships and the like, as you read their studies.

The theory I have chosen is John Thibaut and Harold Kelley's social exchange theory. I will assume you have access to a full description of this
theory elsewhere.[21] In its basic form, social exchange theory claims that
our primary motivation, in interdependent relationships, is to maximize
our personal rewards and minimize our costs. Interdependence is the idea
that our communicative behavior is linked to how others might respond.
Before we say or do something, we tally up the perks and penalties that
may result. With terms such as "rewards" and "payoff," it is no surprise
that some supporters of this theory dub it the "theory of economic behavior."

Let's suppose now that Thibaut and Kelley are asked to explain why it is
that people communicate help and support to others they find attractive or
whose approval they desire.[22] How would a theory of economic give-and-take interpret this fact? Figure 12.3 offers one possible analysis.

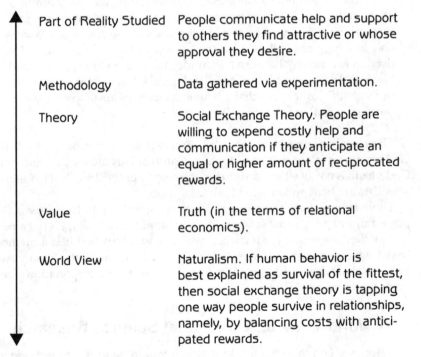

Part of Reality Studied   People communicate help and support
                           to others they find attractive or whose
                           approval they desire.

Methodology   Data gathered via experimentation.

Theory   Social Exchange Theory. People are
                           willing to expend costly help and
                           communication if they anticipate an
                           equal or higher amount of reciprocated
                           rewards.

Value   Truth (in the terms of relational
                           economics).

World View   Naturalism. If human behavior is
                           best explained as survival of the fittest,
                           then social exchange theory is tapping
                           one way people survive in relationships,
                           namely, by balancing costs with antici-
                           pated rewards.

Fig. 12.3. A Naturalistic Interpretation of the Social Exchange Model for
Communicating Help to Others

Social exchange theorists would explain kind behavior by suggesting that the caregiver expects an equal or greater reward. But as one critic has asked, "Do individuals respond so selfishly that they always opt to do what they calculate is in their own best interest?"[23] This question suggests two things. One is that Thibaut and Kelley's model doesn't hold true somewhere in the world. Somewhere, a person akin to Mother Teresa exercises unconditional care. The other point is that if, in fact, people act selfishly even through helping behavior, then maybe people are less like stockbrokers and more like thieves. Stockbrokers buy and sell stock for their clients' benefit. Thieves rob for their own pleasure. If this is the case, then the critic's comments hint at a view of human nature that is darker than the term "relational economics" implies. Figure 12.4 represents a biblical analysis of the care-giving study that re-interprets the deeper truth.

What we can learn from even this simple comparison is that we would be wise to dig below the levels of "reality studied," "methodology," and "theory" when reading social science research. What a researcher claims as true often makes most sense if we can unearth the assumptions beneath it. You will get better at recognizing different world views as you continue your college or university education. You will encounter Marxist thought (the belief that communication is primarily about the use and abuse of power) and feminist thought (the assumption that women's voices have been stifled through various cultural biases). Seeing the connection between world views and social science data is not an easy task, but the effort returns a flood of understanding.

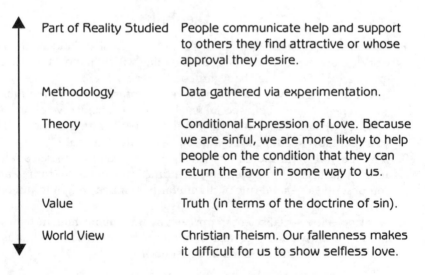

Figure 12.4. A Christian Interpretation of the Social Exchange Model for Communicating Help to Others

Summary

For some Christians, the idea of discovering God's truth about communication scientifically is very attractive. For them, the belief that God knows things *as they really are,* is their motivation for discovering an objective, stable reality. These people relish in being able to say "Campolo is a great speaker, and I've got the facts to prove it!" Well-meaning professors of sound and humble faith work entire lifetimes in departments of communication and other human science disciplines to examine human interaction scientifically. I think most of them would agree with these summary statements about social science and Christian faith.

1. Social scientists endeavor to describe law-like relationships among communication variables at work in people by using standard methods of data gathering, analysis, and interpretation.
2. Social scientists assume objectivity of reality and objectivity of method. Even still, most social scientists admit that the interpretation of their data is a subjective human affair. Christians attribute this inability to know reality definitively to our sinfulness and finiteness.
3. Christian responses to the social science enterprise range from rejection to acceptance. The moderate view is that social science is one more means to discover general truth, but with the qualifier that all research is inherently linked to a particular world view which should be acknowledged and articulated.

Worth the Talk

1. Do you agree with the assumptions that social scientists hold about the world? How can they be regarded as aligning with what we know from scripture? How can they be regarded as not aligning?
2. David Myers believes that if God revealed himself to us in the Bible and in creation, then both special revelation and general revelation are "divine" (that is, "of God"). How is this view liberating to the social scientist? How should such optimism be qualified, if at all?
3. What do you think should be the balance between a Christian's reliance on the scientific method and scriptural approaches to truth? Can you describe a general rule of thumb for how much weight to put on each?
4. What does the social science approach assume about human nature and particularly about free will? What implications arise from this assumption? How should Christians respond?

Consider the Walk

1. Take a theory about communication that is rooted in the social science approach, and analyze it at the levels described by James Sire. These include the unit of reality studied (i.e., some aspect of communication), the method used to gather data, the theory itself, the truth value (and in what terms), and the governing world view. As an extension of your analysis, or as a completely different study, consider the same unit or reality from a Christian perspective.

2. Interview a social science professor in your department. Ask him or her about views on special revelation and general revelation and how the social sciences fit in. Also ask about how our view of human nature can (or should) influence the way social science research is performed.

Notes

1. Bert Bradley summarizes these findings in *Fundamentals of speech communication: The credibility of ideas* (6th ed.), Wm. C. Brown Publishers, Dubuque, Iowa, 1991, Chapter 19.

2. The practice of interpreting scripture is known as hermeneutics, and the theory that we persuade others by appealing to logic, emotions, and our credibility goes back to Aristotle four centuries before Christ.

3. The study of speech delivery as a high art form reached its peak during the British rhetorical era (1700-1880 AD), most notably among the elocutionists. Their efforts arose out of a frustration that Greek, Roman, French, and Italian scholars had written much on creating speech material, organization, and wording, but little on delivery. See "The Elocutionary Movement," Chapter 8 in James Golden, Goodwin Berquist & William Coleman, *The rhetoric of western thought*, 4th edition, Kendall / Hunt Publishers, Dubuque, Iowa, 1989.

4. Carl Hovland and Walter Weiss, "The Influence of Source Credibility on Communication Effectiveness," *Public Opinion Quarterly*, Vol. 15, 1951, pp. 635-650.

5. Fred N. Kerlinger, *Behavioral research: A conceptual approach*. Holt, Rinehart and Winston, New York, NY, 1979, p.14.

6. Em Griffin, *A first look at communication theory*, (3rd ed.) McGraw-Hill, Inc., New York, NY, 1997, p 34-38.

7. Stewart L. Tubbs and Sylvia Moss, *Human communication* (7th ed.), McGraw-Hill, Inc., New York, 1994, p. 244.

8. Tubbs and Moss, p. 244.

9. The small group research on which Robert Wuthnow's book *Sharing the Journey* is based (see Chapter 6) was based on interviews with approximately 2,000 people, half of whom were members of ongoing groups and half of whom were not. This kind of interviewing requires a well-trained team of interviewers to guarantee consistency, and ample funding to pay the interviewers.

10. Raymond K. Tucker, Richard L. Weaver, II, and Cynthia Berryman-Fink, *Research in speech communication*, Prentice-Hall, Inc., Englewood Cliffs, NJ, 1981, p. 109.
11. Tucker, Weaver, and Berryman-Fink, p. 110.
12. See Charles E. Garrison, *Two different worlds: Christian absolutes and the relativism of social science*, University of Delaware Press, Newark, DE, 1988.
13. Joe Carson Smith, "Contextualization or Christ? *Christian Standard*, Vol. 114, 1979, p. 427 as quoted in Garrison, p. 19.
14. In John T.D. Keyes' article "Serial Batterers: What Turns Boys into Brutes?," *Homemakers Magazine*, April 1996, pp. 54-61, he cites Don Dutton, professor of forensic psychology at the University of British Columbia who testified at the O.J. Simpson trial who suggests that Simpson's upbringing mirrored three traumatizing factors that often lead to abusive tendencies as an adult: "a shaming or disparaging father who regularly humiliates the boy, often in public; an insecure attachment to the mother figure, ...and experiencing or witnessing an abusive home environment," p. 57.
15. Charles P. DeSanto and others, *A reader in sociology: Christian perspectives*. Herald Press, Scottsdale, PA, 1980, p. 14 as quoted in Garrison, pp. 142-143.
16. Stephen A. Grunlan, "Sociology and the Christian," in Stephen A. Grunlan and Milton Reimer, (Eds.), *Christian perspectives on sociology*, Zondervan Publishing House, Grand Rapids, MI, 1982, pp. 411-412 as quoted in Garrison, pp. 147-148.
17. Carl Camden, Michael T. Motley, and Ann Wilson, "White Lies in Interpersonal Communication: A Taxonomy and Preliminary Investigation of Social Motivations," *Western Journal of Speech Communication*, Vol. 48, 1984, pp. 309-325.
18. Richard Bube, "Editorial," *Journal of the American Scientific Affiliation*, Vol. 23, 1971, pp. 1-4, as quoted by Myers in *The Human Puzzle*, p. 10.
19. Myers, p. 25.
20. David G. Myers and Malcolm A. Jeeves , *Psychology through the eyes of faith*, Harper, San Francisco, CA, 1987, p. 15.
21. A succinct and readable discussion of social exchange theory can be found in Em Griffin's *A first look at communication theory* (2nd. ed.), McGraw-Hill, Inc., New York, 1994, Chapter 16.
22. See, for example, D. Krebs, "Altruism — An Examination of the Concept and a Review of the Literature. *Psychological Bulletin*, Vol. 73, 1970, pp. 258-302.
23. Griffin, p. 205.

CHAPTER 13

Looking at the Humanities in Christian Perspective

When he was at the table with them, he took bread, gave thanks, broke it and began to give it to them. Then their eyes were opened and they recognized him, and he disappeared from their sight. They asked each other, "Were not our hearts burning within us while he talked with us on the road and opened the Scriptures to us?"

Luke 24:30-32

For some of you, the cool, calculated methods of social science strike a particularly inhuman chord. You may feel fine with measuring an audience's shift in attitude after hearing Tony Campolo speak, or even approve of interviewing people about their motivations for showing kindness. But something doesn't sit right when a data-crunching professor proposes that social science can plumb the meaning of Martin Luther King, Jr.'s *I Have a Dream* speech or the love expressed in a wooden 3rd Century crucifix. Making sense of King and crucifix requires human involvement, not statistical significance.

If that's your sentiment, then you'll probably do well with the following riddle. The question is, What do a

- *Runner's World* poster,
- a jewelry store billboard
- an episode of *Unsolved Mysteries*,
- the movie *Dead Man Walking*, and
- the Taj Mahal in Agra, India

have in common? Up until the Taj Mahal, you could say they are all media products, and you would be right. The category that envelops them all is a

249

bit broader, and I propose it is this: they are all intentional, human, symbolic expressions. By *intentional* I mean each one required forethought and planning. A *Runner's World* editorial committee probably mused over the poster design; twenty-thousand Uttar Pradeshi Indians toiled twenty years to construct the 200-foot tall mausoleum. By *human* I mean not made by nature. Humans create culture (as noted in Chapter 8), by taking what is natural and reshaping it for their use and expression. By *symbolic expression* I mean the crafting of words, images and stone to create messages that signify emotion, represent other objects, or allude to abstract ideas. Like the breaking of bread by Jesus that signaled to his dinner guests "I am the risen Christ," all symbolic expressions are interpretable. Broadly speaking, they are all art.

WELCOME TO THE HUMANITIES

You might think of art as relegated to the Art Department or the Louvre in Paris. But when we speak of art as any intentional human symbolic expression, we open the field to novels, films, music, dance, architecture, and theater. Still others add television shows, radio programs, Internet sites, magazine articles, billboards, posters and music videos.

Scholars who study the significance of symbolic artifacts dot your campus map, but they most likely teach in the humanities. While social science profs crowd the halls of psychology, sociology, anthropology, and communications, humanities profs usually teach in the departments of literature, languages, philosophy, fine arts (that is, music, drama, and visual arts), and communications. It's not a mistake that communication departments are listed twice. Since the 1950s, it has been common to find social scientists and humanists sharing office walls (and offices!) under the same departmental banner. As you might guess, this both/and relationship has not always been harmonious.[1]

Another word for a humanities scholar is simply "humanist." Since the rise of modernism however, the only kind of humanists and humanism some people have experienced is the *secular* type. Secular humanism stands for the idea that people, not God, are the measure of all things, and that one should appeal to human reason, values and creativity alone to understand the Taj Mahal or *Dead Man Walking*. But secular humanism is only one form of humanism. As Bruce Lockerbie notes,

...there are differences among the humanisms, of which secular humanism is only one; others to be reckoned include naturalistic humanism, biomedical humanism, ethical humanism, to name only a few. Then there's also Christian or biblical humanism.[2]

Despite its negative connotation in some Christian circles, *humanism* has noble roots and educational benefits. In fact, it was in Christian medieval universities that students were required to take *studia humanitis* (humanities studies) before preparing for professions in theology, law, and medicine. What held these courses together was their focus on the creative, cultural accomplishments of humans rather than the actions of God. But this focus was not deemed a fumbling of God's truth to us, but an exercise in discovering his general revelation.

For example, around 100 AD Justin Martyr wrote "Whatever has been uttered aright by any man in any place belongs to us Christians." Around 400 AD Augustine wrote "Every good and true Christian should understand that wherever he may find the truth, it is the Lord's." Eleven hundred and thirty years later, John Calvin urged his readers to "not forget those most excellent benefits of the divine Spirit [namely, human competence in art and science], which he distributes to whomever he wills, for the common good of mankind." Similar views were expressed by Martin Luther, John Knox and other reformers.[3]

The passion of Christian humanists today, like their medieval parents, is to understand, through the eyes of faith, the creative and cultural accomplishments of artists, musicians, television producers and even poster-makers. They begin with the assumption that our creativity is a gift from the Creator God, and though not every creative effort pleases him, creativity is intrinsically good. They also subscribe to the doctrine of common grace — the belief that God mercifully holds back the full brunt of sin's consequences so that even unbelievers may express and discover truth, beauty and moral conviction in the natural and symbolic world around them. However, the idea of common grace does not replace the need for God's Spirit to fathom spiritual wisdom (see 1 Corinthians 2:6-16).

What a Christian humanist does for a living differs across the field. A speech professor who analyzes Dr. King's speeches exercises "rhetorical criticism," and the serious Siskel-and-Ebert type who evaluates *Dead Man Walking* does "film criticism." *Criticism* is the practice of describing and evaluating a speech, book, film, or television show with a set of interpretive principles in order to grasp and appreciate its content and beauty. Other scholars do activities called "historical analysis," "cultural analysis" and "textual analysis." Still others roll up their sleeves and call themselves writers, actors, playwrights, screenwriters, orators, and artists. Labels aside, college students look for meaning and God in a host of everyday messages. Let's consider a simple example as a basis for discussing deeper assumptions that humanists hold.

Running Around in My Mailbox

I don't know how they got my name, but last summer the *Runner's World* group mailed me a "Special Preview Issue" (really a promotional flyer). In addition to the "Ten Reasons Why You Need *Runner's World*" and a tear-out, free-issue certificate, the material came complete with an 11 x 26 inch poster. The main images on the poster were a shirtless man and mid-riffed woman (in separate pictures) striding confidently across the page. Encircling the woman's image were the words *"mind…body…spirit,"* and in bold relief the primary text read, *"It's not how fast or how far you run that matters…it's what running does for you…It's how running makes you feel."* Then, in fine print, was yet another paragraph you could read while loosening up for a jog, I guess. It said

> When I run I feel alive…the beating of my heart in my ears…my lungs pulling in every breath to push me forward. Running makes me forget the world I live in and appreciate it more when I come back to it. Running is the best medicine for whatever ails you. Running makes my vision clear to all the things I can't see on a day to day basis. When I think I can't go any further, I go for a run. I plan on running into the next century, and into the next, and the next. Running promotes a healthy lifestyle. How does running make me feel? Running makes me feel great. So I run.[4]

Though not as complex as a 96-minute, heart-stopping video thriller, this runner's declaration of purpose can help us understand the assumptions humanities people bring to their work.

Assumptions Humanities People Hold

By now you've figured out that umpire #2 and #3 would feel quite at home in the humanities. Umpire #2, the subjectivist, is convinced that our world view, limited knowledge, and fallenness influences our view of reality and symbolic expressions. He calls strikes and balls as he perceives them. Umpire #3, the constructivist, takes these ideas a step further. We don't perceive reality, he says; we hammer it together in our heads with plank-like ideas, and riveting beliefs. And language serves as architect. They come to these convictions based on their assumptions about reality, art, and people like you and me.

Humanities scholars assume a subjective reality. Whereas umpire #1 and social scientists believe in an ultimate objective reality (that the world is a certain way, separate from how we know or believe or express it to be), many humanists believe that reality is personally constructed and uniquely meaningful. *Subjective* means "of or resulting from the feelings of the person thinking; not objective; personal."[5] The paragraph from the *Runner's World* poster may be an objective ink-on-paper fact, but the mental reality it creates in each of us is a personal affair. Extreme advocates of this view might go to the wall claiming that no one—absolutely no one— interprets the runner's ode identically, and they have a point. We may all identify with the runner's joy and purpose in cruising off a five-mile circuit, but I may add thoughts of my brother Brad who's an avid runner, and you might wince as you nurse a sprained ankle from yesterday's jog. Despite our mental overlap, we don't share identical meanings or mental worlds.

The moderate view though is that a well-written advertisement and even a complex cinematic thriller is open to only a limited number of readings. If you think of skydiving after reading the paragraph above, we'll understand, because, like running, skydiving is a type of sport. But if you argue that *Runner's World* really intends for us to "buy Nike products," the rest of us will likely query "ugh?" Buying Nike stuff may be an outcome of adopting a runner's lifestyle, but you can hardly get that from the example just cited.

So, whereas scientists focus on what is "out there," humanists focus on what is "in here" — things such as feelings, ideas, and meanings which they interpret from intentional symbolic expressions.

Humanities scholars assume that art depicts a world view. Or put more specifically, they assume that cultural products can be used to communicate any type of message. The message may be as apparent as "You should become a runner," or as subtle as the fantasies we spin while reading C. S. Lewis' *The Lion, the Witch, and the Wardrobe*. But whether the surface reading be runners or lion kings, artists convey their gut-level vision of life as well—their world view.

In Chapter 11 we defined a world view as *the way a group of people look at reality*. A world view "consists of basic assumptions and images that provide a more or less sensible, though not necessarily accurate, way of thinking about the world."[6] An assumption is something we hold true, but have a tough time proving. A Marxist's belief that power struggle explains most human interaction, or a feminist's view that men are responsible for the oppression of women, are faith commitments similar to our belief that God exists and is sovereign. Each group has its proof, but each world view requires its adherents to take some matters in faith. Because these commitments go deep, they eventually leak out—or gush out—in our art.

The editors of *Runner's World* would love to have me subscribe to their magazine. That's the obvious message. But deeper, there's more to the ad. What do you make of the trilogy *mind...body...spirit*? What of the repeated theme that running is not about competition but about *feeling* and *self-health*? Or what do you make of the writer's plans for "*running into the next cen-*

tury, and into the next, and the next"? First of all, the editors seem to have an appreciation for the whole person, not just the physical. (You can imagine quite a different motif in a body builder magazine.) The editors also appear to value personal autonomy and self-fulfillment. Their anonymous writer uses the word "I" ten times and "me" four times, with the goal of impressing on us that running delivers personal control and pleasure. What's missing is any reference to community with others or dependence on other runners. It's just the writer and the road. What we make (or create) from the writer's plan to run until the year 2201 is up to us. Does the writer hope to live for 205 years? Do the editors believe in reincarnation? Is someone here a Christian believer who alludes to a new body in heaven that will not wear out? To be honest, we probably won't ever decipher the original intentions of the poster-makers, but we can still pull out world view themes. What we can tell for sure is that the editors of *Runner's World* want us to adopt running as a lifestyle and buy their magazine.

Humanities scholars assume that we are active interpreters. While social scientists suggest that messages *do unto us*, a humanist believes that we *do unto the message*. Like the transformers in Chapter 10, they believe it's what we bring to a poster or TV show that makes it meaningful. Let's consider another example.

One evening my wife and I turned on the tube and caught the start of *Unsolved Mysteries*. We weren't in a particularly mindful mood, so *UM* seemed right up our alley. The first story was a combination of "lost love" and "unknown identity." A woman in her 30s had long suspected that she didn't fit in her family, and thought she might be adopted. One day she found her mother's diary and the tale was told. Her mother had met a handsome infantryman at the base near her small Texas hometown. She fell in love with him, slept with him several times, and then became despondent when she discovered she was pregnant. Despite her strong Catholic upbringing, the mother was also sleeping with her high school boyfriend. When he learned that she was pregnant, he assumed it was his child, and the two married quickly. Later they had their own children, but the first one was markedly the army private's girl. The mother hid this knowledge for twenty years, suffered from depression, and eventually died in what appeared to be a suicide car crash.

Of course the thirty-something woman is this girl, and now she wants to find her biological father. She approaches *Unsolved Mysteries*, they run the story, and in true *UM* form, the television producers bring father and daughter together for a tearful reunion.

As happy as we were for this woman and her dad, I must admit that my wife and I weren't soaking our hankies. What the show had given us was entertainment, a human interest story, and the all-important happy ending. But then came the shocker, at least for us. Robert Stack, the host of

Unsolved Mysteries, shuffled thoughtfully toward the camera in his London Fog topcoat, and summed up the case. In essence he said, "Who would imagine that *chance* and *inevitable passion* could join two lovers for a moment but separate two others for thirty-four years?" In other words, it was a lucky accident that the mother met the army guy, and unavoidable that they romp in the hay. In one summary comment, Robert Stack proved what literature and film professors assume: it's what we bring to the data that make sense of it. He cast the story as fatalistic.

You might guess that our own interpretive skills kicked in. We began to list the *choices* made by the mother and her lover. She chose to ignore her parents' wishes. She ignored her faith. Together they chose to date, chose to make love, and chose to cover their tracks. We then listed the consequences of these choices. She became pregnant. She became despondent. He lost the opportunity to raise a daughter. She probably killed herself. And their daughter felt like an alienated fifth wheel. What we brought to the facts was an interpretation quite different from Robert Stack's fatalism.

"I don't see depression or even a Big Mac. All I see is Mrs. Hugadorn hauling me off to the principal's office."

To us it was a story of poor choices. While Stack could blame the environment, we saw it as a matter of will.

John Fiske captures the difference between having messages *do unto us* as opposed to *us doing unto messages*. The first casts us as mere spectators of life, the latter as *viewers* of symbolic expressions. In regard to television, he writes, "A viewer is engaged with the screen more variously, actively, and selectively than is a spectator."[7] Obviously our mindfulness is a matter of degree, and the difference is often, again, a matter of effort.

Humanities scholars assume distinct criteria for communication theory. Do you think a lot of television programs depict romantic encounters as fatalistic? Do you think Stack or the Stroms had a better read on *Unsolved Mysteries*? How would you say television producers characterize love? While a social scientist might do a content analysis of every kiss and innuendo, humanists are likely to rely on their own observations and mental framework to argue a theory. Em Griffin articulates again the criteria that people such as John Fiske might hold as they theorize about *Unsolved Mysteries* and other intentional symbolic expressions (see Figure 13.1)

Imagine, if you will, that Robert Stack is not just a TV show host, but a theorist who makes the claim that "Depictions of love and romance on television are largely images of fatalistic encounters between people." Consider as well that my wife and I represent a position that asserts, "Depictions

1. <u>New Understanding of People</u>. A good humanistic theory helps us understand what it means to be human.

2. <u>Clarification of Values</u>. A good humanistic theory makes clear the theorist's values and examines the values of the message being studied.

3. <u>Community of Agreement</u>. A good humanistic theory gains the acceptance of a wide number of scholars because it has been scrutinized openly in the marketplace of ideas.

4. <u>Aesthetic Appeal</u>. A good humanistic theory not only makes claims about art, but is art.

5. <u>Reform of Society</u>. A good humanistic theory creates change in the culture where it is argued.

Figure 13.1.   Humanistic Standards For What Makes A Good Humanities Theory

of love and romance on television cast people as moral agents who make good and bad choices." Although both of us would have to prove our thesis with examples and the like, let's consider how these stand-alone claims measure up to the criteria outlined by Griffin.

Do we shed light on the human condition? Stack sees us in postmodern relief as social nodes in a complex web of symbolic relationships. We don't really have choice, he'd say, just the illusion of choice as we react to powerful forces in our environment. The Strom view casts TV lovers as choice-makers. We draw on our view from the Christian belief in free will, but also from the modernist idea of the autonomous self. You'll see this tension between free will and environmental determinism in a lot of prime time drama. Which interpretation wins out may depend on your theology of God's sovereignty, our freedom, and outside factors.

What values do the theorists hold dear? What values do they interpret from the show? As we noted in Chapter 9, values are those things we consider of ultimate worth. Stack's theory of fatalism values passion and fate as driving forces that draw lovers together. They are the only factors he musters to explain the situation. Stack seems to accept the idea that chance encounters and animalistic urges are as common among people as are cereal and toast for breakfast. He does, however, lament the unfortunate consequences; he hates seeing people get hurt and separated. The Strom theory hints that self-control is more valued than self-autonomy or fatalistic determinism. Given time and space, we would argue that the television industry's value for immediate gratification and personal freedom leaks out in TV characters who seek pleasure in a responsibility-free zone. These values make it difficult, if not impossible, for TV producers to depict prime-time characters who exercise self-control.

Does anyone agree with Stack? How would we nurture a community of agreement around the Strom theory? Persuading others in the scholarly community that your ideas make sense and ring true with life experience is what scholarship is largely about. If we wanted to promote our "moral agents" theory of lovers on television, we would probably begin by writing papers and presenting them at the National Communication Association convention or publishing articles in scholarly journals such as *Media, Culture and Society* or *Journal of Communication*. Even this submission process entails consensus, because journal editors and convention planners must consider your ideas valid enough before accepting them for wider distribution. Later, perhaps, we might write a book that scholars could use in their courses with students. Eventually our ideas might become second nature, even common sense, to most students. Nicholas Wolterstorff did something like this when he wrote *Art in Action: Toward a Christian Aesthetic*.[8] It was published by a respected press, and included a chapter titled, "The Artist as Responsible Servant." Although Wolterstorff is not writing about lovers on television, he hopes that other scholars will join him in affirming that we are all moral agents who make ethical choices in life and art. The more numerous his supporters, the more credible his ideas are.

Has either theorist spoken eloquently? This is an important criterion for humanities theorists because they build their ideas with words. The more eloquent and articulate their language, the greater worth and attractive their theory. Stack could have said, "Nobody would ever think that sexual fire and pure chance could lead to such a mess." That's blunt and uninviting. Rather, the best I can recall, he said, "Who would imagine that chance and the inevitable consequences of passion could join two lovers for a moment but separate two others for thirty-four years?" His choice of words and the use of a question rather than a dogmatic statement encourage us to consider the merits of his observation. Such is a good humanistic theory.

The final criterion of a good humanistic theory is that it generates change in the culture where it is argued. When Jesus told Jews in a Roman-occupied country to love their enemies, do good to those who persecute them, and even turn the other cheek, he advanced a radically different theory of love than the eye-for-an-eye payback model. For Christ, love was action, not reaction; about choice, not coinciding hormones or heated tempers. That theory of love is perhaps best expressed in 1 Corinthians 13 and cited year after year in marriage ceremonies and private friendship pacts. A good humanistic theory not only describes our experience, but prescribes future action as well. Today millions attempt to act on the Jesus model.

HUMANITIES METHODS FOR INTERPRETING TRUTH

From the assumptions just noted, you can probably see why humanities scholars are not slavishly devoted to one method of inquiry. The messages we construct from intentional human symbolic expression are too fluid to trap in one iron-clad method like the master model assumed by social scientists. Even still, if humanists are to advance their ideas, their readers need to know how theorists go about observing communicative art, whether they be episodes of *Unsolved Mysteries*, movies, or billboard slogans.

First let's make one other point clear. Since humanists desire to interpret, value, and make sense of meanings "in here," some of them spend much time arguing for the "in here" world view or paradigm (pronounced *para-dime*) which they bring to their analysis. Other times, they assume that readers can pick up on that world view along the way in a case study, and they dive into their analysis straightway. Unlike scientists who want to prove a theory, humanists put their paradigm / world view / theory to work as they make sense of messages.

The historical-critical approach. Consider the historical-critical approach. A modernist historian who believes that historical fact is objective, is likely to say that the historical method "involves reconstruction of the past in a systematic and objective manner by collecting evidence, evaluating it, verifying it, and synthesizing it to establish facts and to reach defensible conclusions."[9] Like umpire #1 in Chapter 11 who calls strikes and balls as they are, this historian would probably write a media textbook that *describes* the invention, proliferation, and impact of media technologies from the printing press to virtual reality video games *as they happened.*

Postmodernist media historians may beg to differ. They may side with E. H. Carr who wrote in this century that "The belief in a hard core of historical facts existing objectively and independently of the interpretation of the historian is a preposterous fallacy."[10] This historian's media textbook might focus on the power struggle between inventors, government, and consumers, and present case studies of how minority groups responded to new technologies and content. As Tom Dixon writes, these "social historians [seek] to discover the history of the voiceless masses. . . . . They claim that although such peoples kept no official history, they left tracks that can be detected in their cultural practices and forms. The study of these forms and practices, *cultural history*, consists mostly of studying symbolic behavior ...."[11] This kind of historian is less apt to ask *what happened*, in preference for *what people thought happened.*

Since neither historian can work in a vacuum, their starting point includes the events, facts, opinions and testimonies of people around historical events and practices. Somewhere they will sift through newspapers, books, newsreels, and eyewitness reports of media in culture. When your mass media teacher asks you to examine the impact of the media on culture from the time of the Gutenberg press to the dawn of MTV, she is asking you to use the historical-critical approach to arrive at the truth.[12]

Cultural interpretation or ethnography. Ben Stein wanted to understand television from the inside out. So he proceeded to hang out with television executives, interview actors, and soak in the subculture of Hollywood. A lot like a short-term missionary, he observed quietly, asked questions appropriately, and took notes copiously. As James Spradley would say, Stein became a "participant observer" of and with Hollywood's elite so he could see television their way.[13] Stein's analysis is now a bit dated, but his conviction in the 1980's was that television often looked squeaky clean, materialistic, and full of white-hat morality because its producers were mainly hard-working, successful individuals who enjoy material wealth. Put another way: television mirrors the life of Hollywood elite.

Anthropologist Clifford Geertz calls this the "thick description" of a culture. It entails sitting and soaking in a people's cultural ways and then describing them and their communication practice. "As a sensitive observer of the human scene, Geertz is loath to impose *his* way of thinking onto a society's construction of reality. He wants his theory of communication grounded in meanings that people within a culture share. Getting it right means seeing it from *their* point of view."[14]

Have you ever done cultural interpretation or ethnography? Our students take a stab at it when they write up their practicum reports. When they attempt to capture the significance of a cable show they've helped create through the tide and tempo of the television station, they've done a bit of ethnography. Or when they analyze the advertisements their workplace ad agency created through the lens of its creators, they exercise cultural interpretation.

Textual analysis. Broadly speaking, all humanities professors do textual analysis. That is, they attempt to interpret the dominant and the underlying meanings of a text, where "text" means any intentional symbolic expression. Literature professors wrestle with the writing of Keats, film instructors critique the films of Ingmar Bergman, and popular culture experts muse on the significance of everything from CD covers to billboard signs. This approach grew out of wedding hermeneutics (the art of biblical interpretation) and phenomenology (the study of how people experience life through their five senses). The goals of textual interpretation are to explain the text, understand deeper messages, and consider its influence on the reader.[15]

While driving through Portland, Oregon last summer our family saw a billboard off Interstate 5 that showed a woman's hand adorned with a brilliant gold and diamond ring. The ad was from a jewelry outlet—no surprise—and sported an intriguing line: "For the marriage with no planned exits." You don't have to be a high-power textual critic to explain that the dominant message of the billboard was "you should buy one of our rings." Those words don't appear on the sign, but the context of a billboard on a superhighway calls us to see it as such. There is a deeper message too—an affirmation of marriage and lifelong commitment. The effect may be buying the ring or just squeezing the hand of your mate as you cruise I-5.[16]

How Christians View Humanistic Scholarship[17]

I have already described *Christian humanism* as a worthwhile perspective. However, some believers would consider this phrase an oxymoron— a contradiction of terms. They consider the wisdom of people to be foolishness (see 1 Corinthians 3:19), and stick to the scriptures. On the other hand, there are some believers whose minds are so open to new ideas that they rarely distinguish between Christian ones and the others. They regard the best of culture as Christian, whether humanistic scholarship or a well-done novel. A third set of believers might be characterized as those who find a balance between complete rejection of humanistic scholarship and uncritical acceptance of it. If you find that this analysis sounds like the media grid from Chapter 9, you're right. But rather than see it as a re-hash, consider how believers have responded to the humanities, not just media technology and messages.

REJECT CULTURE—THE SEPARATIST, ASCETIC RESPONSE

As just noted, some Christians put a higher value on personal piety and knowledge of God's word than on learning about culture through the writing of humanists, Christian or otherwise. Rather than influence culture, they would rather live within well-defined expressions of culture they consider safe and holy.

One of the early church fathers, Jerome, came to this conviction after a nightmarish dream where he encountered God as judge. To that point Jerome had been a Christian rhetorical scholar who felt free to read the best of Cicero and other Roman speech scholars. Then one night he dreamt that he stood before God who thundered "Thou art not a Christian, but a Ciceronian. Where thy treasure is, there is thy heart also." [18] In a now famous letter, he wrote the following advice to the virgin of Eustochium: "What communion hath light with darkness? What concord hath Christ with Belial? What has Horace to do with the Psalter, Vergil with the Gospels and Cicero with the Apostle [Paul]? ...we ought not drink the cup of Christ and the cup of devils at the same time."[19] Some scholars have shown that Jerome's writings did not refer to scholarly works for fifteen years following his vision. He read only the scriptures and theological books.

In the media chapter we saw how this way of thinking translates into a life of modern day separatism. Amish groups in Pennsylvania and Iowa, and Hutterite groups in North Dakota and Manitoba live and worship communally and experience a rich existence with little or no exposure to what you'll read in Communications 111 or Introduction to Film. They take seriously, and behaviorally, Paul's instructions to Roman believers to "not conform any longer to the pattern of this world, but be transformed by the renewing of your mind" (Romans 12:2). They contend that physical separation better guarantees a mind for Christ.

This thinking is also expressed in the asceticism of believers who join religious orders within the church and vow to carefully guard their intake of cultural ideas. To some degree we might envy the lifestyle of these believers, for they avoid the barrage of 181-channel television, the blare of radio news, commercials that preach happiness through things, and TV preachers who occasionally offend. But their life must ring hollow at times as well. They seldom see a play, visit an art gallery, or receive a blessing from a well-known minister. From behind their cloistered walls, they form few opportunities to make new disciples, change the course of local politics, or alter what millions of others watch and read every day.

For most students at Christian colleges or Bible schools, the separatist, ascetic response to culture is hardly an option. Sticking our heads in the sand ignores the incarnational strategy of God in Jesus Christ. He entered the world in time and space, as a Jew in Roman-ruled Israel, to use cultural forms of communication and the heritage of Jewish law to convey his radical message. The separatist response to humanistic studies ignores that we are spiritual *and human*, and that God can reveal himself and his truth through the still small voice of even fallen unbelievers.

EMBRACE CULTURAL EXCELLENCE AS AN EXPRESSION OF GOD'S TRUTH AND GOODNESS

At the other end of the continuum are believers who do not consider Christian thought as a type but as a quality. Christ is not *against* culture, rather Christ is *of* culture in the sense of what is excellent and pure and good. These believers hold that "the Christian system is not different from culture in kind but only in quality; the best culture should be selected to conform to Christ."[20] Just what this looks like is captured well in a comment I received while laying the groundwork for this book.

In order to get a feel for whether a book like this was deemed worthwhile, I sent a one-page survey to roughly 200 scholars at Christian institutions to solicit their opinions. In addition to completing the form, several made additional comments. One scholar wrote, "A 'Christian' approach begs the question that the pursuit of academic excellence by the practitioner in the field is somehow inadequate. Isn't good scholarship Christian? I don't believe in 'spoon feeding' people just because they have a christocentric philosophy of life!"[21] I suspect that the person who wrote this positions himself in the Christ *of* culture camp. Like other believers, he believes that Christian activity and thought is consumed with the pursuit of "*whatever* is true, *whatever* is noble, *whatever* is right, *whatever* is pure, *whatever* is lovely, *whatever* is admirable" (Philippians 4:8, italics added). Anything that is excellent or praiseworthy is fair game for our thought.

ACCEPT CULTURAL FORMS AND MORAL CONTENT— THE CENTERED MAINLINE AND EVANGELICAL RESPONSE

Between the rejection position and the whatever-is-excellent position stand a good number of believers who see merit in both poles. Remember their response to media? It was the view that technology is morally neutral, but what can bless or kill you is the content. Their rule: Use the technologies freely, but avoid questionable content. Some hold the same view with regard to humanistic scholarship. As long as the truth we discover in humanistic scholarship compliments biblical truth, then the believer should feel free to read widely and consume cultural art carefully. But beware. Falsehood loves to masquerade in eloquent, fine-sounding argument.

St. Augustine was perhaps the most prominent scholar of rhetoric in all of northern Africa when he was attracted to the preaching of Ambrose. When Augustine converted to the faith, he had a decision to make, as did Jerome, about studying non-biblical books. You can see that he came to a quite different resolve when he wrote, "Now, the art of rhetoric being available for the enforcing either of truth or falsehood, who will dare to say that truth in the person of its defenders is to take its stand unarmed against falsehood?"[22] In other words, if public speaking is a neutral tool, let us use the insights of respected secular scholars so we may advance God's gospel through better speech-giving.

The same mentality applies today across the curriculum in communication departments. You're apt to read Steven Katz's *Film Directing Shot By Shot* (Michael Wise Productions, 1997) because Katz is an expert through and through. You're likely to use Judith Martin and Thomas Nakayama's *Intercultural Communication in Contexts* (Mayfield Publishing Company, 1997) because Martin and Nakayama are established scholars in this field. This is not to suggest that everything Katz, Martin and Nakayama say about communication may square with our read of scripture, but there's an assumption that truth belongs to God wherever it is found.

However, some believers in this camp hasten to add one proviso. While experts may know their field, everything about that field may not honor God. Because some humanistic theories may be wolves in sheep's clothing, it's best to be shrewd as serpents but innocent as doves (see Matthew 10:16).

CRITIQUE CULTURAL FORMS AND CULTURAL CONTENT— THE CENTERED PARADOX AND TRANSFORMER RESPONSE

Other believers in the church-of-the-center don't see things in such black-and-white terms. They might ask evangelicals or mainliners how they can determine what is of God when they hold to a sacred versus secular view of truth. Knowing the difference is not only difficult, but also makes us tiptoe through culture like soldiers fearful of landmines. Isn't God-in-us bigger than that, they might ask. One author in this camp suggests that we should be more fearful if we don't even understand the landmines. He writes, "We have more to fear from naivete with regard to error than we do from clear knowledge of error that we recognize as error."[23] That is, we should be more afraid of being culturally ignorant than fearful of understanding wrong-headed thinking if we want to be able to acknowledge it as such.

Paradox believers express the frustration with having one foot in God's kingdom and another in Los Angeles. They want to follow the Savior, but they live in the culture of *The Los Angeles Times* and jewelry store billboards. Transformer believers conclude that a foot in each kingdom is no problem as long as we remember which is influencing the other, and that God is sovereign over all. Even if humanistic scholarship and popular media depict wrong-headed ideas or a fallen world, we are better off understanding these messages so we may speak to them in our relationships with people who embrace them. Like the medical student who studies disease so she can better understand health, our study of fallen culture may actually enhance our understanding of scripture. As Leland Ryken writes in *Culture in Christian Perspective*,

> The question that has perennially engaged Christians is not whether culture requires their attention, but how does it. Christian thinking on the question has moved between the poles of total rejection and total affirmation of culture...[but] neither extreme does justice to the biblical data. To think Christianly about culture and the arts means to look at them through the "lens" of biblical doctrine.[24]

POLISHING OUR LENS

In the Western Cascades where we live, there are parks and campgrounds galore that invite us to explore nature. During one camping expedition recently our family took in the science presentation on the cosmos given in the campground amphitheater. Just weeks earlier we had our noses glued to the television to watch the Mars land rover bump its way across the Red Planet. With images of dusty rocks and starry backdrops still in our heads, we listened to the astronomer from the University of British Columbia.

What he told us surprised me. I had known that stars really don't twinkle, but that atmospheric debris defracts their light, and breaks up their signal. But what of Mars? Is it really red? You could almost hear the sigh of disappointment when the expert stargazer said "no." In the same manner that the sun appears red as it pierces the thick summer air at dusk, so too atmospheric dust warps the light Mars reflects to a pinkish hue. Up close the Red Planet is moon-like gray.

After the presentation, the astronomer invited us to an open-air parking area for a peek through a 6-foot telescope aimed at Mars. Even with the cleanest of lenses and the clearest of skies from our 5,000-foot perch in the Cascades, Mars still looked red.

I share this story to make a point about how we might conceptualize our approach to humanistic scholarship. As Ryken suggests, the issue is not whether culture requires our attention, but how we pay attention to culture. He believes that a biblically informed mind can decipher truth amidst error, beauty in the beastly, and virtue in the vile. Like the high-powered lens of the astronomer, a biblical lens brings us up close to God's truth. But like atmospheric debris, our sin and fallen ideas hinder a pristine picture. Some implications from this metaphor seem appropriate to end this chapter.

A Christian humanist knows the faith. Lens crafting is a time-consuming job, but once polished to concave or convex perfection, a lens helps us see more clearly. So too with the faith. Spiritual maturity and biblical knowledge don't form overnight. Denominational doctrines are rarely presented to us on a platter. While quick-fix advocates would like us to believe that *this tape* or *that practice* will turn us into Augustines or Grahams by next Tuesday, we know it's a long haul. Do we have more than a Sunday-school knowledge of the scriptures? Have we ever considered the history of the faith after AD 33? Can we begin to quote any of the great creeds that embody our teaching? Do we have the mind of Christ? If we shrug off the task of mastering the faith, we are going to be poorly armed for encounters with the world. Or to use our lens metaphor, we'll look to the stars only to find that our lens is smudged, scratched, or shattered altogether.

Christian humanists understand other world views. For some that means attending graduate school to discover how romanticist, structuralist, feminist, Marxist, and postmodernist ideals apply to everything from classical literature to episodes of *Unsolved Mysteries.* For others, it means not just understanding these lenses, but borrowing features from them that appear to enlighten the Christian mind. For example, for all the difficulties that postmodern thought poses to the faith, Christians can appreciate a view that decries rugged individualism and humans as the center of the universe. We may not agree with the notion that truth is a mere construction of our language group, but appreciate the view that our community contributes to a sense of purpose and meaning for us. Until we understand the world views being taught in universities that find their way into popular media and art, we will have a tough time fitting their manifestations into the larger puzzle. We may even get duped by them.

Christian humanists look for christian meaning in non-biblical texts. We've said this before in different words, but what does this look like in practice? Just how it looks may differ as you read a comparative religions textbook as opposed to viewing *Dead Man Walking,* but some concepts hold across media. You will encounter *propositional truths* such as, "People's communication is largely the product of fatalistic factors beyond their control." You may not agree, but at least the author has proposed a truth about the world that is straightforward and testable.

Value statements say less about how the world *is* and more about how it *ought to be*; not in terms of actions, but in terms of what should be valued. After watching *Dead Man Walking*, I was less sure if I favored capital punishment or life imprisonment for convicted killers. The character found guilty of murder showed genuine repentance for the atrocity, but the state still administered him a lethal injection. On the other hand, my value for selfless love increased as I viewed the Susan Sarandon character minister to the killer. Christian virtues such as love, sacrifice, joy, justice, peace, patience, reconciliation, kindness, gentleness, faithfulness, and self-control parade in glorious Technicolor across screens and in dog-eared novels if we simply look for them.

Allegorical symbols are the biblical images and meanings we bring to humanistic scholarship and popular art if we dig a little. The billboard line "For the marriage with no planned exits" shows a value for committed love. Play with it for a while and you can also imagine a bride and groom, the church and Christ, and even his hands with scars that proved he didn't exit the road to Calvary.

Finally, Christian humanists may also search for *signs of fallenness* and *rays of hope*, or what Francis Schaeffer has called, respectively, the *minor theme* and the *major theme* of our faith.[25] As you read human scholarship, you're bound to observe the minor theme that people have revolted from God, turned their backs on Christ, and face eternity removed from his presence. You will also read of believers who struggle in sin and limp around in the kingdom like the sick. Both minor strands set the stage for the major theme, namely, that God offers meaning and purpose to life. The backbone of this theme is the fact of God's existence and the knowledge that his moral character pervades all of life, including his provision of salvation in Jesus Christ. Looking only for the minor theme betrays the hope within us. Focusing entirely on the victorious major theme promotes unrealistic romanticism.

Schism in the Communication Department?

Perhaps the last two chapters have helped you come to grips with why professors in your communication department seem to be from different planets at times. Professors may share a love for how we communicate, but after that the similarities end. The tension is even felt in how we name our departments. During the 1970s you would probably study communication in the *Speech* Department from a humanities perspective. In the 1980s, when interpersonal communication became a popular area of study from a social science perspective, you would probably register for courses in the Speech *Communication* Department. But *speech communication* was redundant, because speech *is* communicative. What its inventors were trying to say was that they studied communication in various forms (for example, speech, interpersonal communication, media production, etc.) and from different starting points, humanistic *and* social scientific. The label that some have now chosen is the Department of Communication Arts and Sciences. Despite the label, smoke still tells of hot friction in some departments. Professors who hold differing perspectives require grace to see eye-to-eye.

Raymond Tucker and his associates dislike this ongoing friction, but they are optimistic about our field for three reasons. One is that both types of scholars wrestle with the question of how people create and share meaning. Figuring out that question makes method less an issue. A second is because each approach compliments the other as we try to understand complex people. Facts and statistics merge with values and world view interpretations to piece the puzzle together. And finally, there's hope because each approach produces knowledge for future generations.[26]

As believers we might add that the work of scientists and humanists contribute to wisdom. Knowledge puffs up, but wisdom is a rare jewel. Our goal should not be to master information generated from either perspective as an end in itself. Somewhere knowledge must blossom into action or it's just dead-head data. The last chapter looks at the challenge before us as communicators. Receiving and interpreting *stuff* is only half the story. Enacting and creating redemptive communication is the rest of the story.

Summary

The humanities represent the other most common approach to studying human communication in addition to the social sciences. Humanism is the study of human achievements in literature, philosophy, music, art, drama, and communication. Christian humanism is the commitment to understanding human accomplishments and the human condition through biblical faith. Christian humanists delve into the world's scholarly writings and popular culture to discover God's generally revealed truth, beauty, and moral presence.

The methods humanities scholars employ assume a less rigid model than the one used by social scientists. Their use of historical research, cultural interpretation, and textual analysis provide the basis for a rich understanding of the meanings and impact of intentional human symbolic expressions. These scholars typically see life through a grand paradigm, and make sense of art, literature, media, and human interaction through this lens. Christian scholars value the lens of biblical faith and doctrine to enhance their read on culture and typically search for propositional truths, values, and symbolism that affirm our fallenness but reveal hope through God's grace in Jesus Christ.

Worth the Talk

1. Do you agree with the assumptions that humanities scholars hold? Why or why not?
2. What methods of research have you been required to use to write essays? Research papers? Art reviews?
3. What response do you lean toward in the issue of studying the humanities? Can you figure out why you have this tendency?
4. What television show or movie have you watched recently that can be interpreted Christianly? What godly messages can you identify?

Consider the Walk

1. Interview an art instructor or a media production instructor on your campus to determine his or her perspective of God in the arts. Discover the professor's pilgrimage with regard to the humanities approach.
2. Write a position paper that describes and defends where you stand with regard to humanistic scholarship. Make an effort to include your religious convictions and biblical references to articulate your stance today.
3. Expand on number four under the "Worth the Talk" section. Write a paper that describes the propositional truths, inherent values, Christian symbolism, and other messages that the television show or movie depicts. Consider using the *minor theme* and *major theme* of the faith to explain its messages and evaluate its moral worth.

Notes

1. For a good overview of the historical development of communication departments and their divided methodology, see Em Griffin's "Talk About Communication" (Chapter 2), in *A first look at communication*, (2nd ed.), McGraw-Hill, Inc., New York, NY, 1994, pp. 19-31.
2. D. Bruce Lockerbie, *Thinking and acting like a Christian*, Multnomah, Portland, OR, 1989, p. 84.
3. These quotations of Justin Martyr, St. Augustine, and John Calvin are from Lockerbie, pp. 87 and 92.
4. *Runner's World*, Special Preview Issue, undated (mailed in 1996).
5. Webster's *New world dictionary of the American language*, Warner Books, New York, NY, 1984.
6. Michael Kearney, *World view*, Chandler & Sharp Publishers, Inc., Novato, CA, 1984, p. 41.
7. John Fiske, *Introduction to communication studies*, Methuen, London, 1982, p. 17.

8. See Nicholas Wolterstorff, *Art in action: Toward a Christian aesthetic*, William. B. Eerdmans Publishing Company, Grand Rapid, MI, 1980 as a good example of transformer's look at Christian doctrine and life as they relate to the craft and calling of artists.

9. Raymond K. Tucker, Richard L. Weaver, II, and Cynthia Berryman-Fink, *Research in speech communication*, Prentice-Hall, Inc., Englewood Cliffs, NJ, 1981, p. 68.

10. E. H. Carr, *What is history?*, Random House, New York, NY, 1961, p. 10 as quoted in Dennis McCallum (Ed.), *The Death of truth*, Bethany House Publishers, Minneapolis, MN, 1996, p. 131.

11. Tom Dixon, "Postmodern Method: History," (Chapter 8) pp. 133-134 in D. McCallum (Ed.), *The Death of Truth*, 1996, pp. 127-142.

12. See Harold Innis, *Empire and communication*, Oxford University Press, Toronto, 1950, and Harold Innis, *The bias of communication*, University of Toronto Press, for two works from one of the first scholars to address this question using this method.

13. See James P. Spradley, *Participant observation*, Holt, Rinehart & Winston, New York, 1980, for a full description of this research method.

14. Em Griffin, *A first look at communication theory* (2nd ed.), McGraw-Hill, Inc., New York, NY, 1994, p. 16.

15. See Stephen W. Littlejohn, *Theories of human communication, (5th ed.)*, Wadsworth Publishing Company, Belmont, CA, 1996, pp. 211-213.

16. See Fiske as an example of an introductory textbook which uses textual analysis as its dominant method for analyzing media and culture.

17. These three responses to humanistic scholarship are based loosely on the analysis provided by H. Richard Niebuhr in *Christ and culture*, Harper & Row, Publishers, New York, 1951.

18. This translation from Pierre DeLabriolle, *The history and literature of Christianity from Tertullian to Boethius*, New York, 1924, pp. 11-12.

19. Jerome, Epistle XXII (CSEL, LIV), translated in Gerald L. Ellspermann, *The attitude of the early Christian Latin writers toward pagan literature and learning*, Catholic University of America Patristic Studies, Vol. 82, Washington, D.C., 1949, p. 159-160.

20. David J. Hesselgrave, *Communicating Christ cross-culturally*, Zondervan Publishing House, Grand Rapids, MI, 1978, pp. 79-80. Hesselgrave is not advocating this view, but is describing the work of Niebuhr's book, *Christ and Culture*, where Niebuhr describes the "Christ of culture" position as one of five responses Christians have often taken.

21. For reason of confidentiality, I am unable to provide the author's name and educational institution. I received his note in 1994.

22. Augustine, *On Christian doctrine*, Book 4, Section 3, n.p.

23. James Sire, *The joy of reading*, Multnomah Press, Portland, OR, 1978, p. 146.

24. Leland Ryken, *Culture in Christian perspective: A door to understanding & enjoying the arts*, Multnomah Press, Portland, OR, 1986, p. 12.

25. Francis A. Schaeffer, *Art & the Bible*, InterVarsity Press, Downers Grove, IL, 1973, p. 56.

26. Tucker et al., p. 276.

CHAPTER 14

Building Temples

King Solomon sent to Tyre and brought Huram.
Huram was highly skilled and experienced in all
kinds of bronze work. He came to King Solomon
and did all the work assigned him.

1 Kings 7:13, 14b

The previous chapter ended with the resolve that receiving and interpreting *stuff* is only half the story. Enacting and creating redemptive communication is the rest of the story. What I mean is that your college or university education molds more than your mind; it also transforms your character and hones your skills. Believe me; after you graduate you will forget a sizeable portion of the theories and facts you take in today. What will remain are aspirations to engage in life fully and act on what you know.

That's why this chapter is a trumpet call to consider your education and your skills as gifts from God. Like Huran, who was sought out by Solomon because of his refined facility, you might consider your talents as similarly valued. And for those of us who feel nothing like the servant who received ten talents, this is a message of encouragement to invest our one or two talents in the kingdom just the same. All of this sounds optimistic and hopeful, but unfortunately some believers consider skills as the lesser sister of knowledge.

THE PROBLEM

One of the drama instructors on our campus joked with his students that "skit" is a four-letter word. What he meant was that the kind of skit you might see in an elementary school program or on a church platform, pales in comparison to what *drama* is intended to be. This example captures the problem for many communicators, including believing ones. We may become so accustomed to B-grade drama, film, television, speech-giving, or everyday conversation, that we lower our expectations and aim for the wall rather than the sky.

Put another way, some believers are prone to think that content is more important than delivery; that the message is more important than how you say it, write it, shoot it, or whatever. I recall how this issue arose in a church business meeting when someone asked why a previous pastor had been asked to resign. The moderator approached the microphone and answered that, among other things, people were not pleased with his quality of preaching.

In defense of the pastor, a man named Dennis stood up and said, "That's atrocious. The only grounds on which we should ever ask a pastor to resign are heresy and sexual infidelity."

I recall how the room fell silent. Had we committed a grave mistake by dismissing this man? Then a mature member stood up, a man who had been a pastor and knew the demands of the position. He said, "Brother Dennis, preaching is a lot like food preparation. We expect food placed before us to be more than simply *not* poisonous. We also expect it to look and taste good as well." Heads nodded and similar comments were offered. We thought it was okay to expect more. This was the point behind the seasoned minister's statement. We all know that in a pinch for time or under famine conditions we would settle for a plate of flattened shepherd's pie. But when we know that the chef has had time to do the job well, we cringe if the presentation is always dull. Like King Solomon, we didn't want just any kind of preacher preaching. We wanted a skilled craftsman like Huram.

In his book *The Christian, The Arts, and Truth,* Frank E. Gaebelien puts it pointedly when he laments how some believers settle for second best, but judge those who excel. He writes,

> They are the kind of people who look down upon good music as high-brow, who confuse worship with entertainment, who deplore serious drama yet are contentedly devoted to third-rate television shows, whose tastes in reading run to the piously sentimental, and who cannot distinguish a kind of religious calendar art from honest art. For them better aesthetic standards are "egghead" and spiritually suspect.[1]

Gaebelien is a believer who takes our creativity seriously. To him, creativity is good in and of itself. All creative work may not please God, but tacky work is an affront to his Creator character. Gaebelien would likely agree with Elton Trueblood, a theologian, who quipped, "Holy shoddiness is still shoddiness." Conveying God's redemptive truth to needy people is of high priority, but if we fumble the ball of delivery, we may never enjoy victory.

Way down deep there is another issue here. See if you can figure it out from these recollections. In Chapter 1 we observed that what spills from our lips begins with our heart (Matthew 12:33-34). In Chapter 2 we noted that our attitudes toward others eventually leak out in our nonverbal cues. In Chapter 3 we saw that our self-talk shapes our talk with others. I could go on, but will end with a recent observation. In Chapter 13 we observed that an artist's worldview comes out in her art. Taken together, these observations suggest that our craft is intimately linked to our character and spiritual sensitivity. Honest art and genuine skills eventually show our colors. This is not to say that the more sanctified our life the greater our talent. What it means is that we will not likely settle for performing our second best or for content that betrays our human identity in Christ.

Put more broadly, the issue is how we live our life. I like the way Francis Schaeffer summarizes his essay on art and the Bible. He writes,

> No work of art is more important than the Christian's own life, and every Christian is called upon to be an artist in this sense. He may have no gift of writing, no gift of composing or singing, but each man has the gift of creativity in terms of the way he lives his life. In this sense, the Christian's life is to be an art work. The Christian's life is to be a thing of truth and also a thing of beauty in the midst of a lost and despairing world.[2]

Schaeffer's comments extend to us in communication departments. We may have no gift for speaking, or publishing, or media production. We may get our degree still longing for talent like the lead actor in the play or the roommate filmmaker. Schaeffer's point is that life is about more than skills. It's about a life dedicated to God.

But let us return to the key point. Until we understand that God is as much concerned about our craft as our content, we will continue to propagate a false division between what we say and how we say it. We will be prone to settle for second-rate sit-coms, half-baked journalism, and Sunday-school level drama. Professional communicators begin with different assumptions and strive for a higher standard.

Allow me one more reference to my experience as a communicator; then we will look at assumptions and standards.

THE 16- AND 36-YEAR-OLD VENTRILOQUIST

Every summer during my youth, my parents took our family to the Okoboji Lakes Bible and Missionary Conference in northern Iowa. Year after year, during the baking hot weeks of early August, I attended the morning children's hour and the adult speaker sessions alongside my siblings. In the evenings, when the speakers were given 40-50 minutes, boys and girls like me welcomed our dismissal to a kids program in a nearby hall. That's where I met Wally Schoon.

Wally was a ventriloquist, and a funny one too. We could hardly wait for the singing to end so we could hear Wally and Leroy duke it out with verbal jabs and hilarious slapstick. I was so hooked on the duo that I attended the kids program for two years past the 12-years-and-under cutoff. Eventually I bought the book *You Can be a Ventriloquist*, and read every word.

From age fourteen to sixteen I fooled around with this odd art. I bought a cheap dummy and had an old one given to me. During the summer you might have found me on my front steps with Arthur or Charlie in hand and six neighbor children huddled around. Other times you might have seen me perform for twenty kids at Jackson First Baptist Church. Those venues changed when I entered my junior year in high school and became a member of an 18-member Youth for Christ singing group. For the next two years we would perform some sixty concerts, and at most of them I would perform with my new professional dummy, Archie.

I will never forget my first major public performance with that group. The break in our program meant it was time for me to give my 5-minute gig. I had written it myself with some guidelines from printed materials, and I had practiced it enough to get through it all right in private. The crowd numbered only fifty or so, but these were adults, not children. In addition, my friends were listening in the wings for my bang-up debut.

I delivered the first few lines well, with Archie getting the best of me. My voices rang strong and clear with the aid of the sound system. I'd set up the joke. Archie polished it off. I'd ask a question. Archie had a nutty answer. It seemed to go like clockwork.

But then tragedy struck. I figured out later that my routine was not much more than a string of jokes held together by a thinly glossed theme, and remembering which joke couplet came next was not easy. I forgot a line. And then another. Try as I may, I could not get back on to the string of jokes I had planned. Sweating profusely and very nervous, I ad-libbed a few corny jokes, wrapped it up, and ended my debut at the two-minute mark. My friends told me it went well, but I could see through their praise. I felt awful.

Twenty years later, and some 200 performances under my belt, I was asked by my academic dean to perform during our college's chapel time. I knew that our modest gym would be packed with 600 students and 100 faculty and staff. I didn't want to let them down.

Two weeks before the performance I put pen to paper and wrote a 3-minute dialogue. I considered the theme the academic dean had requested, thought of audience members who might be gracious targets of jokes, and began to memorize the script. My family listened patiently as I practiced the lines out loud with Archie on my knee. By the tenth run through my three-year-old was beating me to the punch line! This time I had prepared a 3-minute gig and had taken about five hours to write it and practice it. What a difference compared to my high school experience! I was ready, I thought, to face 700 mindful, expectant faces.

What transpired was what I consider my best-ever ventriloquial perfor-mance. I did not forget a single concept or joke, and managed a 90% suc-cess rate on the exact words I had practiced aloud in my living room. I read my audience and played to their laughter with timely pauses and a couple of ad-libbed lines. My professional colleagues seemed pleased too, despite the innocent jabs lobbed their way.

My experience as a ventriloquist illustrates that time and effort can dig us out of the ditch of mediocrity and onto the hills of high standards. It also serves to highlight the values and assumptions that professional commu-nicators hold. Let's turn to them now.

Assumptions Professional Communicators Hold

By professional I don't necessarily mean *paid for one's services*, but it's not a bad standard. When professional speakers charge $500-1000 for a speech or when video editors require $50 per hour to transform your raw footage into a finished product, you know they can justify these fees, in part, by their competence. In a very real sense, you get what you pay for. But pro-fessional can also mean *the highest standard in the field*. We can aim for these without charging a dime, and we begin with some foundational assump-tions.

PEOPLE CAN IMPROVE THEIR SKILL LEVEL

This is so basic it almost goes without saying. When I was sixteen, I could write dialogue, speak without moving my lips, and develop a per-sonality for my dummy. What I lacked were memory skills and the ability to put it all together under the stress of public performance. After twenty years of practice those skills have become refined, and I know that repeti-tion sharpens my memory.

Fortunately many college administrators understand that practice makes perfect, and that practice begins with opportunity. That is why they re-quire you to take English, art, and communications to earn your degree. Some students dread these courses for whatever reason. I can think of at least two.

One reason is that they believe our God-given skills are locked into a certain level, and no amount of practice improves them. Very clearly, we are instructed that "there are different kinds of gifts" (1 Corinthians 12:4) given to us according to the grace given us (Romans 12:6). To those endowed with the ability to teach, Paul says teach! To others with the gift of encouragement, he says encourage! What we have to guard against is the notion that a lack of gifts means that there's no room for improvement in those deficient areas. Paul also says, "Since you are eager to have spiritual gifts, try to excel in gifts that build up the church (1 Corinthians 14:12). He says this in the context of believers who struggle over the gift of tongues. He says tongues are fine, but if no one can understand you, "you will just be speaking into the air" (verse 9). His call that we *try to excel* in gifts that build up the church tells me we've got a choice, and that our talents, however weak, can be improved.

The other reason some people may shrug off any effort to improve their skills is because they think communication is a natural skill. They liken it to breathing and eating. Obviously these individuals don't equate acting skills or video editing skills on par with munching down a Big Mac. But they may think that interpersonal skills, such as listening, showing empathy, using confirming messages, and the like are too insignificant for our attention. Students in counseling psychology will beg to differ. They are required to take courses and internships with the express goal of improving *helping skills*.

MASTERING SKILLS TAKES HARD WORK

In our pop-a-tab-and-quench-your-thirst-quickly environment, the idea of working hard for less tangible gains sounds burdensome. That burden lightens, though, when we realize that the sports stars, musicians, actors and speakers we emulate achieved their fame through hard work. Remember my philosophy colleague who debated the politician? He invested 120 hours in research before approaching the rostrum for his thirty-minute speech and rebuttal. Again, we may not have this kind of time on our hands during the blur of a college semester, but somewhere the likes of Paul Chamberlain will rise to the occasion and the rest of us will be watching from padded chairs.

About a year ago when I began looking for a publisher for this book, I checked out a volume titled *Publish, Don't Perish*. The author smashed a few myths about people who get published. They were a great encouragement to me. His research showed that

1. Published people work hard
2. Are not necessarily brilliant
3. Do not enjoy the rigors of writing
4. Write regularly (e.g., 30 minutes a day) to promote creativity

5. Are not overly self-critical, especially on first drafts
6. Get bright ideas away from their desks
7. Have their own style[3]

Items 1-4 convinced me I wasn't alone in my trudge up writer's mountain. It seems other writers feel overworked, overwhelmed, rarely enamored with the task, and wishing they could toss their PC's out the window for a day. But they stick with it.

Plato knew the role of the professional communicator well. And he knew that after dusting the books for truth, there was still the challenge of mastering delivery. He wrote, "Several years of silent inquiry are needful for a man to learn the truth, but fourteen in order to learn how to make it known to his fellowmen."[4] We might be able to ace the material, but mastering the craft requires equal if not more attention.

LEARNING SKILLS CHANGES OUR REALITY

Specifically, learning skills makes us think differently about ourselves and our potential. Only a few masterful artists are geniuses. Most of us are plodders. I didn't rival Wally and Leroy in those early years, much less Edgar Bergen and Charlie McCarthy. But with time came the opportunity to stretch my wings beyond the singing group concert settings. I did a Mother-Daughter banquet here, and a high school talent show competition there. Eventually I believed that with the right preparation I could perform most anywhere.

Maybe you've known for some time that you enjoy producing videos, giving talks, or writing articles. With time and practice, you will see your ability as a blessing for others. I encourage you to let that happen. Let the fact that the God who was faithful to you as you were faithful to Him in using your five talents, free you to respond to his call to invest ten talents more. Maybe this means taking on that teaching position you didn't think you could handle, or writing for the school paper with others who at first intimidated you.

There's a cycle of learning, experience, confidence, and more learning that kicks in when you test your skills through an act of faith. For example, you may take a course such as *Writing for Publication*, but never get published in that brief semester's time. But you wrote five solid articles for your professor, and you received good feedback on what you produced. If you take the next step, and submit these articles to magazine editors, one acceptance can boost confidence. That confidence motivates you to learn more about writing (or at least to do more of it), which in turn gives you more experience and more articles you can mail out. Your view of yourself, your writing, and your goals change with time. The same pattern holds for speaking and media production.

TEACHERS OF SKILLS ENVISION AN IDEAL REALITY

I doubt if you know the name Nadia Comaneci (pronounced *ko-ma-neecha*). In 1976 she was the first Olympic gymnast ever to be awarded a "10." Critics scoffed at the idea that any performance could be perfect. But Nadia seemed to meet the grade, at least in the eyes of one judge. (After the first 10, other judges followed suit on later routines.)

Speech teachers and media profs are like judges, and they envision an ideal performance. They evaluate your work by industry standards set down in textbooks and massaged by previous student performances. A responsible instructor will articulate those criteria and use them to offer you feedback. "Good organization, passable evidence, weak delivery" may earn you a C. But don't be miffed if you get a tough marker. Usually he or she is only thinking of your good. Some professors use soft standards for student performance, believing that a critical appraisal will harm a person's esteem. Or perhaps they are soft because the student has made a noble effort. Neither of these reasons, nor the inflated marks you receive, do justice to you as student. Inflated grades can deceive you into believing you are up to par, only to discover that you are sub-par when you enter the workforce. Inflated grades also do little for our names as Christians in the field. They

"So the minister turns into a Zorphian and begins attacking his own people until All Star Theo corners him at Destiny Diner where they duel with laser swords before a crowd of admiring seminary students who chant 'Theo! Theo!' What do you think?"

are partially responsible for poor preaching, biased "Christian" journalism, and B-grade films. If God's ideal is perfection, our ideal should at least be a high human standard.

PERFORMANCE CAN CREATE KNOWLEDGE

When a colleague read that I believe performance produces knowledge, he cried foul. His epistemology (that is, his theory of how we come to know) regarded knowledge as the outcome of humanistic or social scientific inquiry. After amassing knowledge these ways, we then apply it in our performance, he suggested.

Maybe I don't understand his position fully, but I beg to differ with his response. It seems to me that we learn all kinds of things through our experience, communication truths included.

A classic definition of knowledge is "justified, true belief,"[5] and it seems to fit my thinking. I may believe that "practice makes perfect," and this claim may even be true. But until it has been *justified* through evidence or personal experience, it's just an idea I take on faith. When I was a sixteen-year-old ventriloquist, I *believed* that "practice makes perfect," but after umpteen gigs since then I now *know* that "practice makes perfect."

I believe this applies to spiritual knowledge as well. That is, once we act in faith, we often convert what we believe into what we know for sure, about God and ourselves. The account of Jesus healing the official's son in John 4 is a case in point. The official travels fifteen miles, from Capernaum to Cana, where Jesus is. The man begs Jesus to come to Capernaum and heal his son. Jesus rebuffs him, claiming, in effect, that this man is asking for a sign or wonder so he may know that Jesus is as great as everyone has claimed him to be. The man does not go away. He begs again, "Sir, come down before my child dies" to which Jesus then responds "You may go. Your son will live."

At this point the man has a decision to make. As Jim Sire writes, "What a dilemma! If he continues to beg, he puts his faith in Jesus in jeopardy; if he returns to Capernaum without Jesus, he runs the risk of losing his son."[6] What does he do?

As we know, the man sets out for home without Jesus. On his way he meets his servant who brings the news that his boy is alive and well. When the father asks at what time the boy got better, he realized it was exactly when Jesus said, "Your son will live." The result? "So he and all his household believed [that Jesus was the Christ]." Why did he put faith in Jesus? Because in the case of his son, he *knew* Jesus could be trusted. But his knowledge that Jesus' words were trustworthy came only after he acted in obedience and started home in earnest.

How do we *know* God can be trusted? How do we *know* God will supply our needs? How do we *know* if we are cut out for public relations, journalism, television production, or Web site management? We know after we have given God a chance by acting out in faith.

This is why we should not underestimate the value communication skills have for instructing us. This is one reason why my department has recently begun a practica (or internship) program. My colleagues and I believed—and now know—that students learn as much on the job at radio stations and public relations firms as they do with their noses in books. But they have to take the risk through a step of faith.

Let me share a personal example about my wife. Shelaine is one of the most interpersonally competent people I know. She uses tact and candor to encourage and advise needy friends. One day she felt the prompting of God to acquaint herself with a woman who had been recently separated from her husband. For six months Shelaine faithfully kept in touch, not quite sure why God had led her to this woman. Only recently has one reason become clear: This woman has a strong sense that God wants her to go to college, and my wife, as a college graduate (and whose husband teaches at the local Christian college), has been a most capable advisor. Shelaine knows she has the gift of helping, and she knows that God commands us to help others, but only by obeying God and applying her gifts does she know God's grace and truth in meeting people's needs. I think that's the pattern here. Knowledge of God increases following acts done in faith.

WHERE DO WE GO FROM HERE?

I'd like to say "nowhere but up," but that sounds schmaltzy. I think we should be optimistic about God's work in our lives and our using talents for him, but we also need sober judgment about our aptitudes and what we can handle.

Of one thing I'm pretty sure. Skills are to theory as works are to faith. That is, we don't rely on works to gain our salvation, but allow works to flow from a redeemed and renewed heart. Similarly, skills are not performed out of duty, but flow from our knowledge *and* heart for God. The more we know our craft and seek to glorify God, the greater our return for talents invested for Christ and his kingdom. How can we make that happen?

Consider your communication skills gifts from God. We have all heard of the splendor that was Rome's. We sometimes forget about the splendor of the Israelites as they followed God's plan to build the tabernacle, or the monumental task this required. Exodus 31 describes God's personal call and imbuing of skills to a craftsman named Bezalel, his assistant Oholiab, and all the workers.

Then the LORD said to Moses, "see, I have chosen Bezalel son of Uri, the son of Hur of the tribe of Judah, and I have filled him with the Spirit of God, with skill, ability and knowledge in all kinds of crafts — to make artistic designs for work in gold, silver and bronze, to cut and set stones, to work in wood, and to engage in all kinds of craftsmanship. I have given skill to all the craftsmen to make everything I have commanded you: the Tent of Meeting, the ark of the Testimony with the atonement cover on it, and all the other furnishings of the tent — the table and its articles, the pure gold lampstand and all its accessories, the altar of incense, the altar of burnt offering and all its utensils, the basin with its stand — and also the woven garments... They are to make them just as I commanded you. (Exodus 31:1-5, 6b-10a, 11b)

What an enviable position! First God says he has filled Bezalel with his Spirit, plus the skill, ability and knowledge of all kinds of crafts, and then he hands Moses the blueprints for the whole project. Bezalel could have squandered his talents, but we know that he rose to the challenge. Recognizing that God doles out gifts is tough for some of us to swallow. After all, *we* put in the hours, and *we* know we're talented. That's an easy perspective to adopt with mega-gifted athletes selling us shoes and soft drinks based on their accomplishments. God must smile and gently whisper, "But don't forget who made you just a notch below the angels."

A lot has to do with attitude. You've probably heard the story of the three workers laying bricks to build one of Europe's finest cathedrals. The rector wanted to encourage them, so struck up conversation with each one by asking "Hello. What are you doing?" The first man, disgruntled and dirty replied, "What does it look like? I'm layin' bricks." The second, a more pleasant and respectful individual, replied "I'm constructing a foundation for a flying buttress." The third man, a devout and godly parishioner of that local church, beamed and announced, "I'm creating a masterpiece to the glory of God!" It seems the last worker had the mind of Bezalel. He knew his craft was a gift from God.

Offer your skills as living sacrifices. Paul encouraged the believers in Rome to offer their bodies as living sacrifices, holy and pleasing to God. He saw this as an act of worship. So too should be the offering of our skills.

The image of Abraham and Isaac comes to mind. Abraham, old in years, but blessed by God with Isaac despite Sarah's infertility, winds his way up a mountain in the region of Moriah. Isaac sees the wood and the fire for the burnt offering, but no lamb. He asks his father, "Where is the lamb?" to which Abraham responds, "God himself will provide the lamb for the burnt offering, my son" (see Genesis 22:6-14). Later, when the lamb still doesn't show, Abraham binds his son and lays him on the altar, atop the wood.

What sadness and fear must have shook his bones. God demanded a sacrifice, and he evidently wanted Isaac! Abraham raised his knife to kill his son, and an angel of God cried out "Abraham, Abraham, do not lay a hand on the boy. Now I know that you fear God because you have not withheld from me your son, your only son" (from verses 11-12).

God's testing of Abraham led to a gruesome image, but one from which we can learn. God would normally require a lamb, a perfect lamb. But God tested Abraham with Isaac, his only son. For Abraham, losing Isaac meant losing God's promised blessing. Abraham could just as well have been the one on the altar. Isaac's death would have been the end of him. Such devotion is rare, and we know God credited Abraham's faith for righteousness.

Any commitment on our part to give God our talents seems to pale in comparison to Abraham's offering of Isaac, but we can at least start there. I believe that giving him our talents simply means making them available for his ends. Are there ways we can advance his kingdom through the talents he's given us? It also means giving him our best. God didn't want any lamb, he required a perfect one. We may not be perfect in skills or in heart, but Christ justifies us before God. It also means we can perform most any vocation to God's glory. Whether that entails making films, devising PR materials, or witnessing to an immigrant, God's grace makes all things new.

CONSIDER YOUR COMMUNICATION CREATIVITY A "MUST DO" THING

Frank Gaebelein calls this the aesthetic imperative. God's command is simple: *be creative.* For communicators this means breaking the mold of computer-template business letters, formulaic sit-com script-writing, and cookie cutter speech schemes. And it means taking some calculated risks, especially with regard to your career choice.

Remember the drama student I mentioned in Chapter 10 who dove into filmmaking? He's taking a risk. While most students listened politely to the film prof, took notes, and showed competence on the exams, Grant took filmmaking to heart. I hear that he keeps crazy hours, lives on a shoestring budget, and prays to God that his films will fly. He has answered the aesthetic imperative.

I wish there were more Grants, but I don't see many. For over forty years now Christian colleges and universities have been graduating students from media programs at the estimated rate of fifty per year.[7] Often these programs are funded by philanthropic believers who assume that Christians can make a difference in television, film, and radio. Our impact in radio is significant; it's been tougher going in Hollywood. Perhaps most graduates have opted to work for Christian organizations that create Christian material for primarily Christian audiences. This is not all bad; those in the fold need to be affirmed and fed. What is alarming is the well worn statistic that a mere 200 persons or so living in the Los Angeles area are responsible for 80% of prime time television,[8] and the number of Christians in that group is probably fewer than ten. One positive development is the Los Angeles Film Studies Center, sponsored by the Coalition of Christian Colleges and Universities, which has seen a good percent of its grads move into Hollywood-based positions. Even still, the number of people who are committed to the aesthetic imperative for God's glory in major market TV and film is small.

Summary

Jesus tells the story of the master who entrusted his property to three men before taking a long trip. The employee who received five talents "went at once and put his money to work" and made five more talents. The servant who received two talents did the same and made another two talents. But the third man "dug a hole in the ground and hid his master's money" (see Matt. 25:14-28).

You probably know how the story ends. The master praises the first two for being faithful with what they had been given. The master calls the third man a "lazy, wicked servant" because he failed to even bank the money to make interest. The master entrusted the first two with more responsibility; the master stripped the third of his one talent and kicked him out of the house.

The last servant was not a bad guy. He did not squander or misplace what was given him. What he failed to do was to put his talent to use so it would bear more fruit. The parallel to investing our communication knowledge and skills is a fitting end to this chapter and book. Will we use words worthily and nonverbals mindfully? Will we find our identity anchored in Christ and seek to edify others? Will our dialogue with friends and family members be full of grace and nudge them closer to God? Will our public talks and intercultural interaction reflect incarnational love and responsible ethics? Will we exercise critical and godly thinking as we consume and produce media messages? Will we make wise choices in what we view and read? Will we pursue truth, wisdom, and discipline as if they were rare jewels? Will we employ the humanities and the human sciences to understand people so we may meet their deepest longing? God enabling, it is up to us whether or not we practice redeeming talk and actions with others to the glory of God.

Worth the Talk

1. What particular communication behaviors or skills do you do well? Do you consider your ability to speak, write, edit, create, or whatever as a gift from God? What would it take in your life to show that this ability is of God?
2. What do you think about the view that Dennis holds? He believed that it is far more important to value the content of communication (what is said) than the manner or quality of delivering that content (how it is said). What validity is there in this view that truth is more important than style or performance?

Consider the Walk

1. Compare the quality of two types of videos. One should be produced by a Christian organization and one by a non-Christian organization, and they should be chosen from the same type (e.g., children's animation, health and fitness, money management, marital issues, etc.). Use a standard set of production criteria from one of your textbooks and compare how each video rates. Explain why one video does a better job of using the video medium, and suggest recommendations for improving each of them.
2. Compare the quality of two major motion pictures using the same framework as suggested in question one. Be sure you use criteria from a textbook on film aesthetics.
3. Make a list of the communication skills you know God has given you. Be more generous than critical here. Take this list to your campus career center and ask the people there to direct you to material about communication jobs. Compare your skills with the skills listed for these jobs. Do some dreaming and praying about where God might want you after graduation.

NOTES

1. Frank E. Gaebelein, *The Christian, the arts, and truth: Regaining the vision of greatness*, edited by D. Bruce Lockerbie, Multnomah Press, Portland, OR, 1985, pp. 50-51.
2. Francis A. Schaeffer, *Art & the Bible*, InterVarsity Press, Downers Grove, IL, 1973, p. 63.
3. Joseph Moxley, *Publish, don't perish: The scholar's guide to academic writing and publishing*. Greenword Press, Westport, CT, 1992, p. 3-14.
4. Plato, *Phaedurs*, translated by H. N. Fowler, in Thomas W. Benson and Michael H. Prosser, *Readings in classical rhetoric*, Indiana University Press, Bloomington, IN, 1972, pp. 22-42.

5. See, for example, David L. Wolfe, *Epistemology: The justification of belief*, InterVarsity Press, Downers Grove, IL, 1982.
6. This quotation and use of this story to make this point about knowledge following from obedience comes from James Sire, *Discipleship of the mind*, InterVarsity Press, Downers Grove, IL, 1990, pp. 98-100.
7. Estimated from statistical data in Garland C. Elmore, (compiler and editor), *The communication disciplines in higher education: A guide to academic programs in the United States and Canada*, Association for Communication Administration, Murray, KY, 1990.
8. Todd Gitlin, *Inside Prime Time*, Pantheon Books, New York, NY, 1985.

Subject and Name Index

Scriptural Index

(Page numbers in bold italics.)